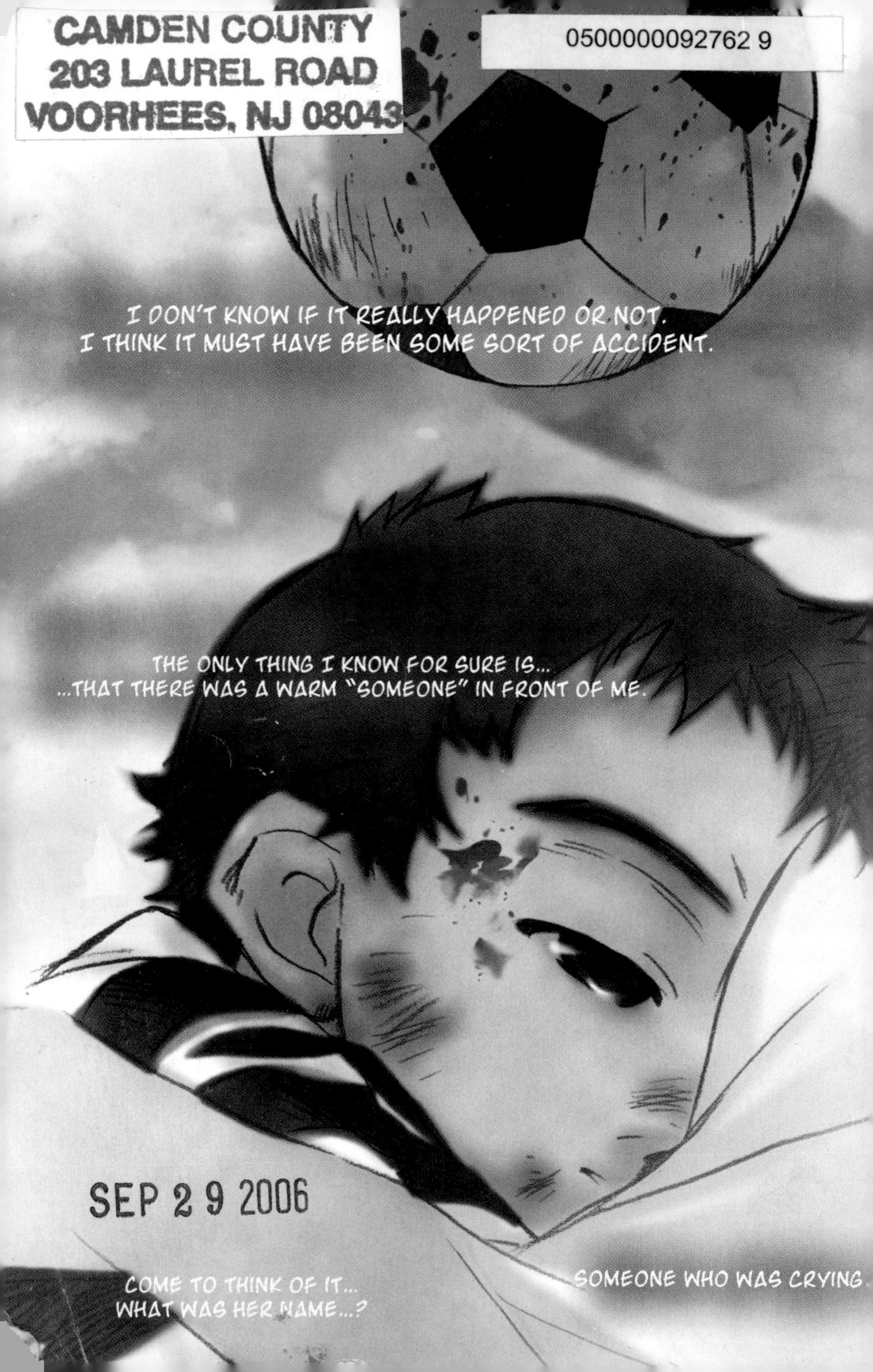
I DON'T KNOW IF IT REALLY HAPPENED OR NOT.
I THINK IT MUST HAVE BEEN SOME SORT OF ACCIDENT.
THE ONLY THING I KNOW FOR SURE IS...
...THAT THERE WAS A WARM "SOMEONE" IN FRONT OF ME.
SOMEONE WHO WAS CRYING.
COME TO THINK OF IT...
WHAT WAS HER NAME...?

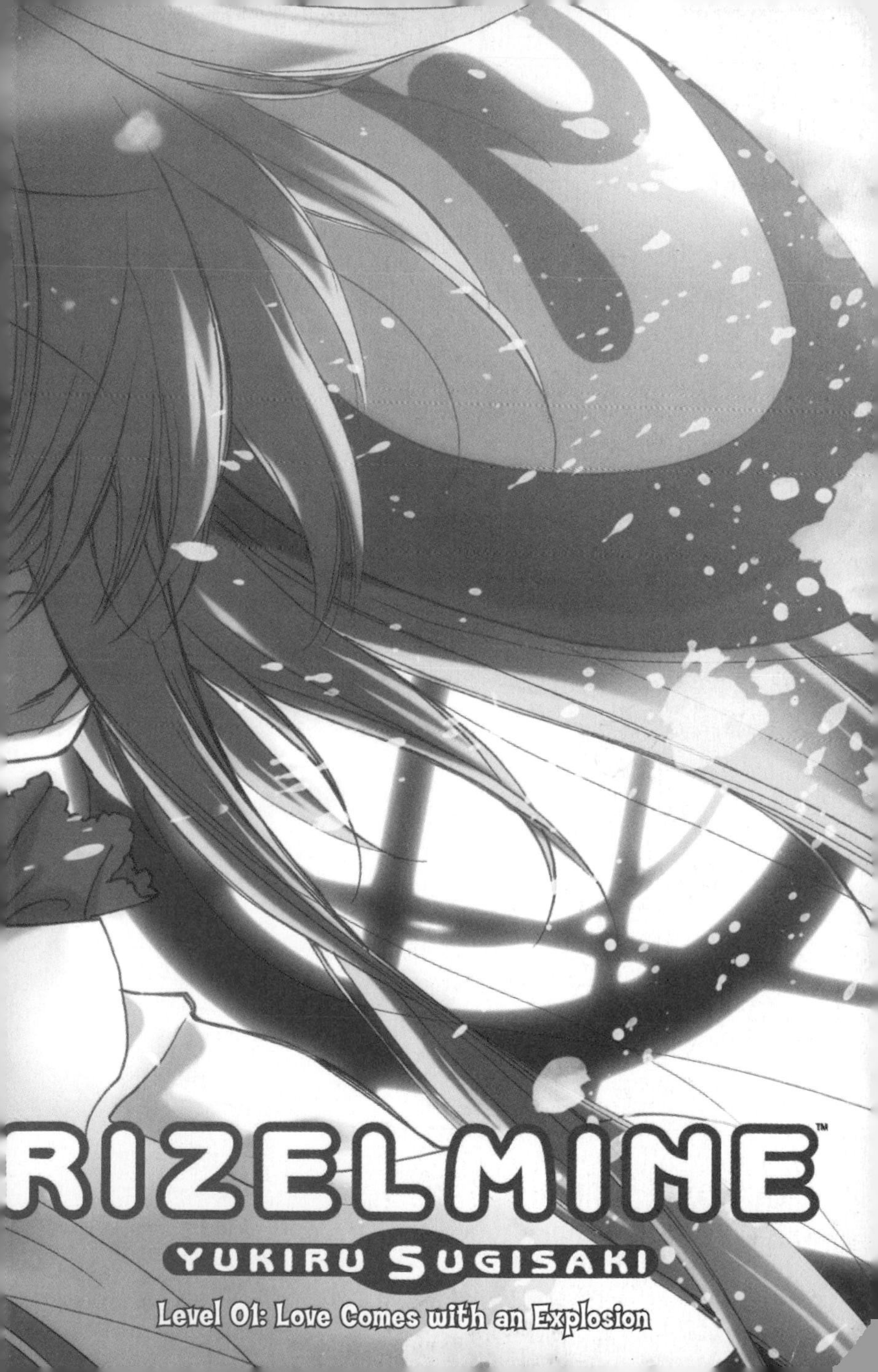
RIZELMINE™
YUKIRU SUGISAKI
Level 01: Love Comes with an Explosion

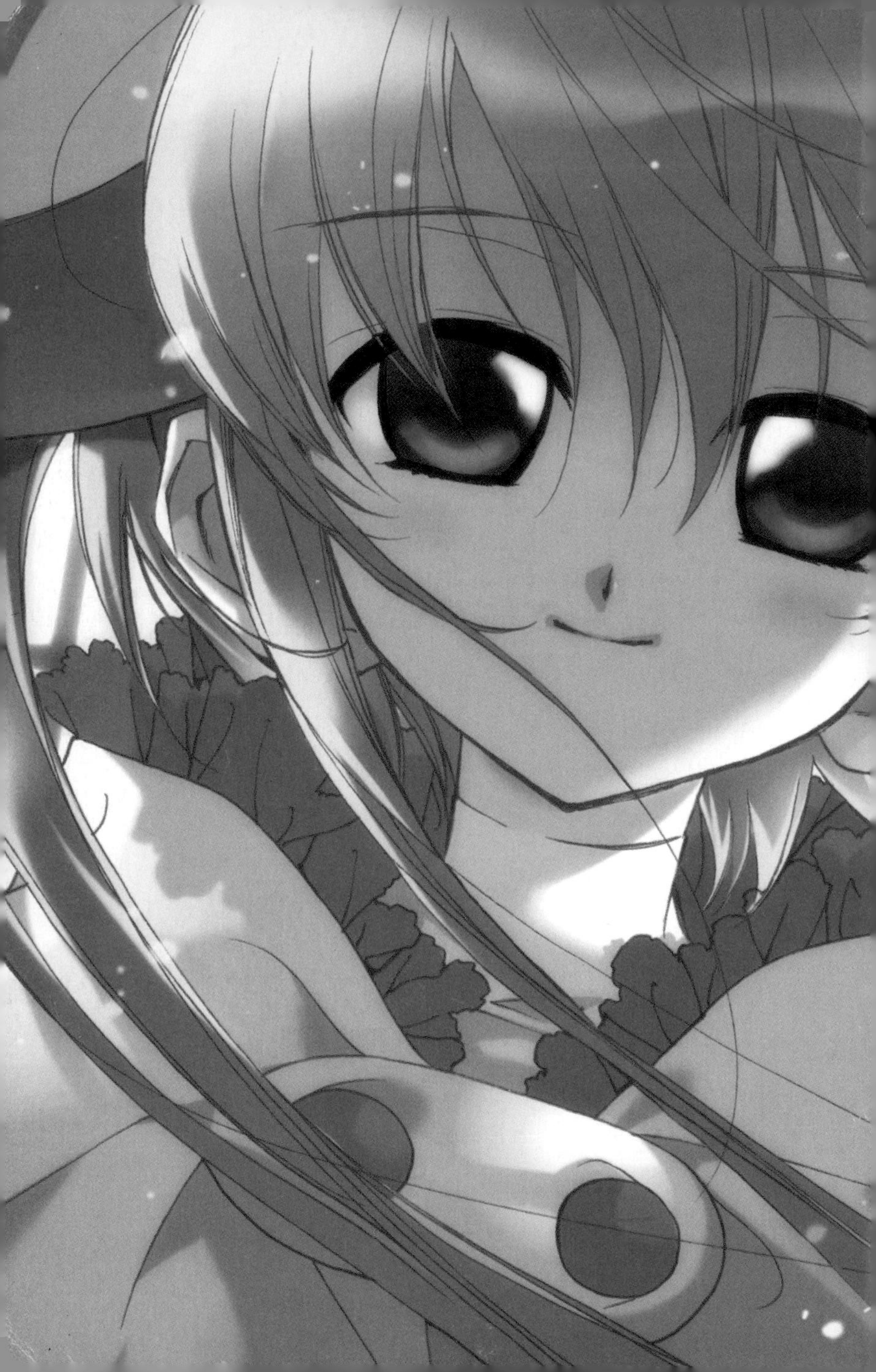

RIZELMINE™

YUKIRU SUGISAKI

Contents

RIZELMINE

YUKIRU SUGISAKI

HAMBURG // LONDON // LOS ANGELES // TOKYO

Rizelmine
created by Yukiru Sugisaki

Translation - Alethea Nibley & Athena Nibley
Copy Editor - Peter Ahlstrom
Retouch and Lettering - Bowen Park
Production Artist - James Lee
Cover Design - Thea Willis

Editor - Lillian Diaz-Przybyl
Digital Imaging Manager - Chris Buford
Production Managers - Jennifer Miller and Mutsumi Miyazaki
Managing Editor - Jill Freshney
VP of Production - Ron Klamert
Publisher and E.I.C. - Mike Kiley
President and C.O.O. - John Parker
C.E.O. - Stuart Levy

A  Manga

TOKYOPOP Inc.
5900 Wilshire Blvd. Suite 2000
Los Angeles, CA 90036

E-mail: info@TOKYOPOP.com
Come visit us online at www.TOKYOPOP.com

ISBN: 1-59532-901-3

First TOKYOPOP printing: August 2005
10 9 8 7 6 5 4 3 2 1
Printed in Canada

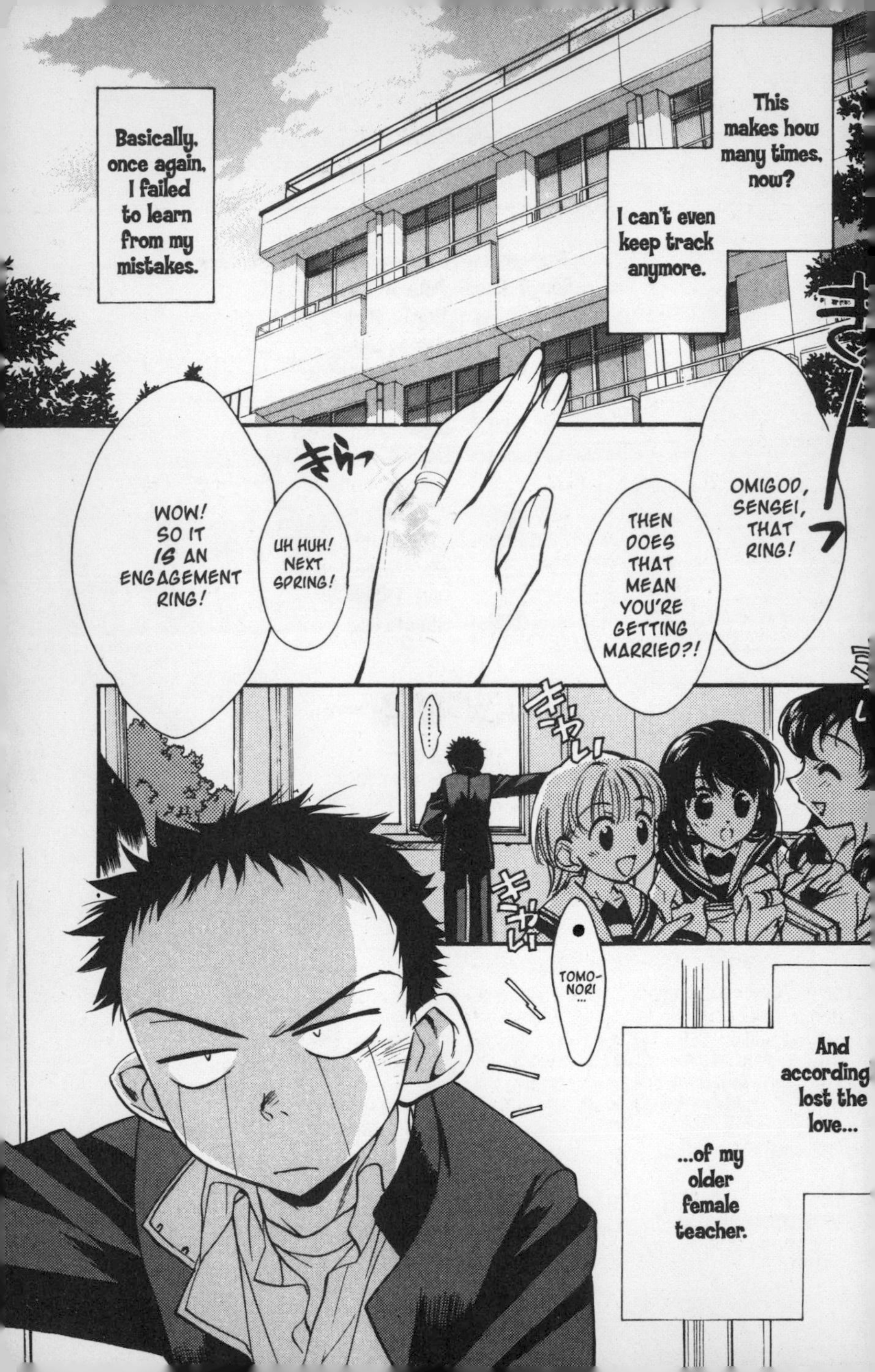
This makes how many times, now?
I can't even keep track anymore.
Basically, once again, I failed to learn from my mistakes.
OMIGOD, SENSEI, THAT RING!
THEN DOES THAT MEAN YOU'RE GETTING MARRIED?!
きらっ
UH HUH! NEXT SPRING!
WOW! SO IT IS AN ENGAGEMENT RING!
......
TOMONORI...
And according lost the love...
...of my older female teacher.

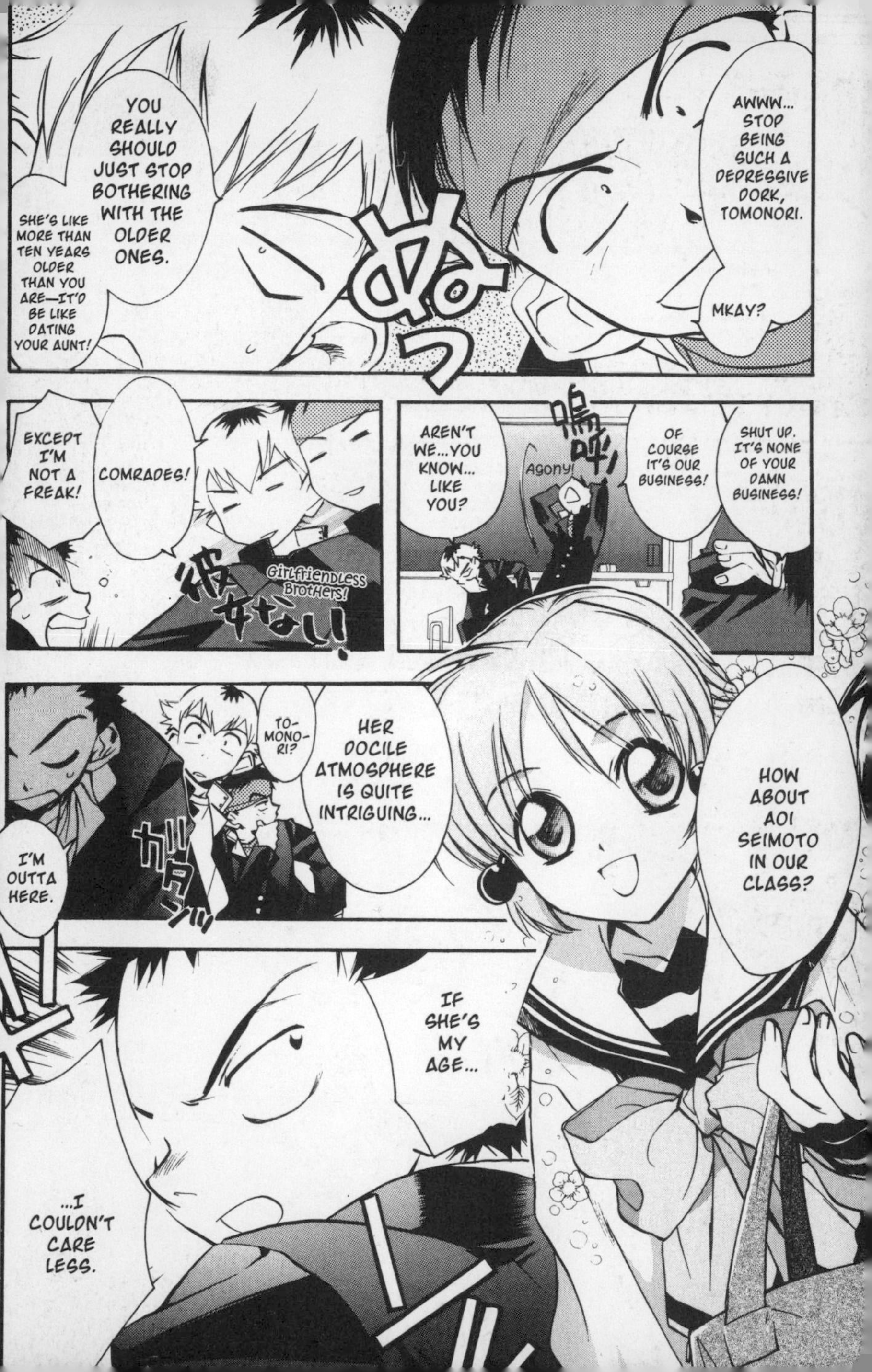
AWWW... STOP BEING SUCH A DEPRESSIVE DORK, TOMONORI.
MKAY?
ぬっ
YOU REALLY SHOULD JUST STOP BOTHERING WITH THE OLDER ONES.
SHE'S LIKE MORE THAN TEN YEARS OLDER THAN YOU ARE—IT'D BE LIKE DATING YOUR AUNT!
SHUT UP. IT'S NONE OF YOUR DAMN BUSINESS!
OF COURSE IT'S OUR BUSINESS!
嗚呼!
Agony!
AREN'T WE...YOU KNOW... LIKE YOU?
COMRADES!
EXCEPT I'M NOT A FREAK!
彼女なし!
Girlfriendless Brothers!
HOW ABOUT AOI SEIMOTO IN OUR CLASS?
HER DOCILE ATMOSPHERE IS QUITE INTRIGUING...
TO-MONO-RI?
I'M OUTTA HERE.
IF SHE'S MY AGE...
...I COULDN'T CARE LESS.

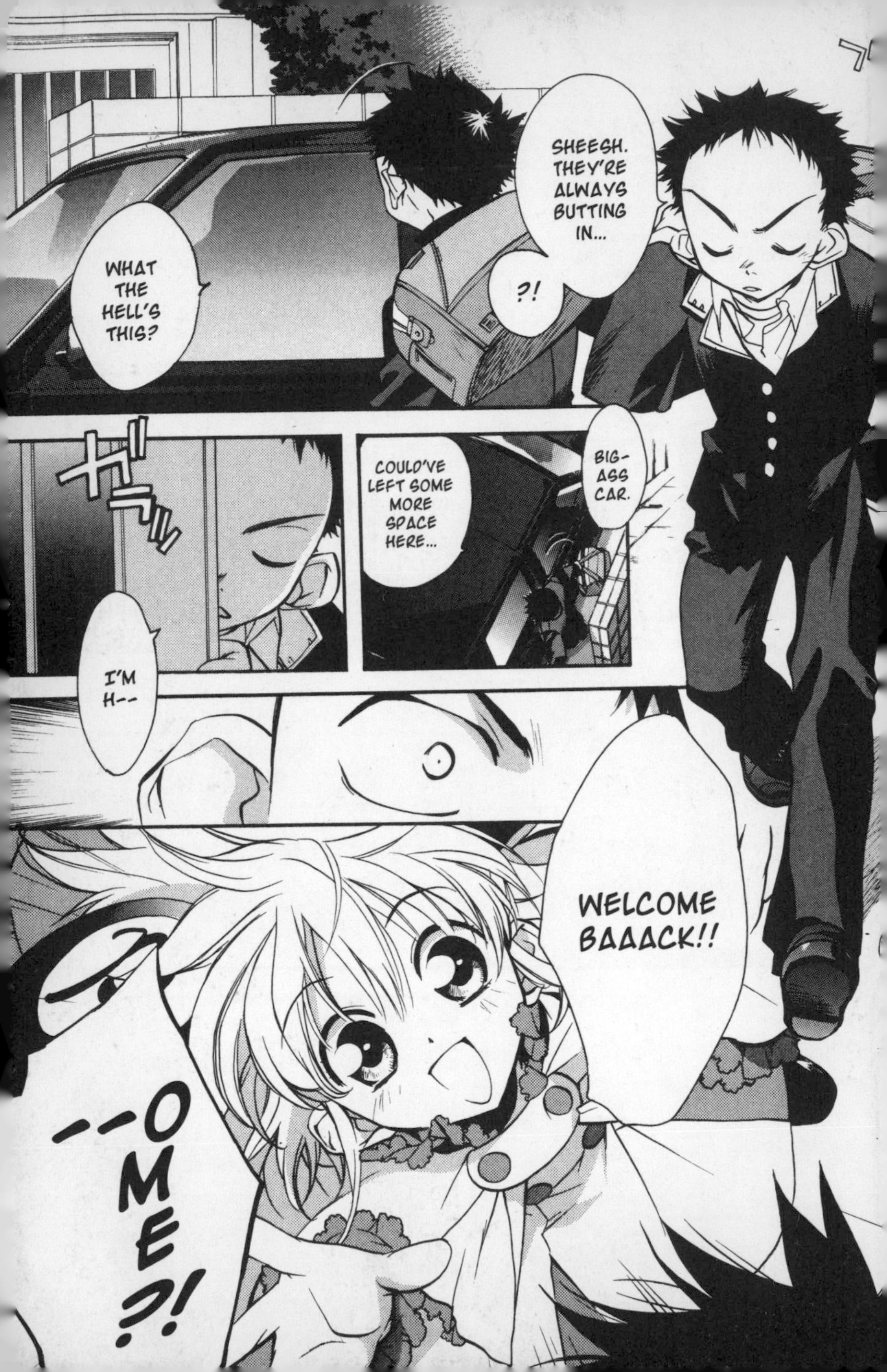
SHEESH. THEY'RE ALWAYS BUTTING IN...
?!
WHAT THE HELL'S THIS?
BIG-ASS CAR.
COULD'VE LEFT SOME MORE SPACE HERE...
I'M H--
WELCOME BAAACK!!
--OME?!

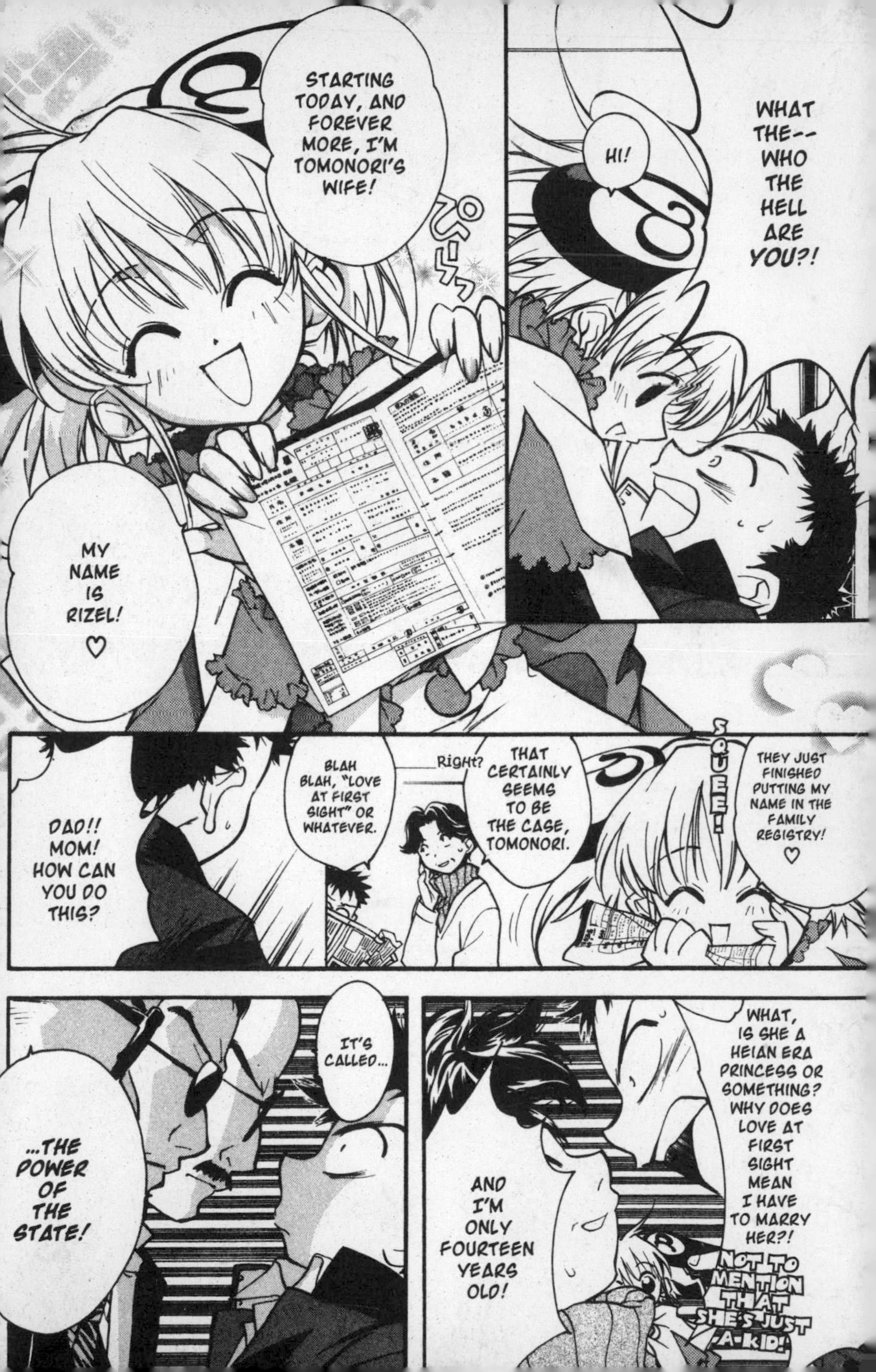
HI!
WHAT THE-- WHO THE HELL ARE YOU?!
STARTING TODAY, AND FOREVER MORE, I'M TOMONORI'S WIFE!
MY NAME IS RIZEL! ♡
SQUEE!
THEY JUST FINISHED PUTTING MY NAME IN THE FAMILY REGISTRY! ♡
THAT CERTAINLY SEEMS TO BE THE CASE, TOMONORI.
Right?
BLAH BLAH, "LOVE AT FIRST SIGHT" OR WHATEVER.
DAD!! MOM! HOW CAN YOU DO THIS?
WHAT, IS SHE A HEIAN ERA PRINCESS OR SOMETHING? WHY DOES LOVE AT FIRST SIGHT MEAN I HAVE TO MARRY HER?!
NOT TO MENTION THAT SHE'S JUST A KID!
AND I'M ONLY FOURTEEN YEARS OLD!
IT'S CALLED...
...THE POWER OF THE STATE!

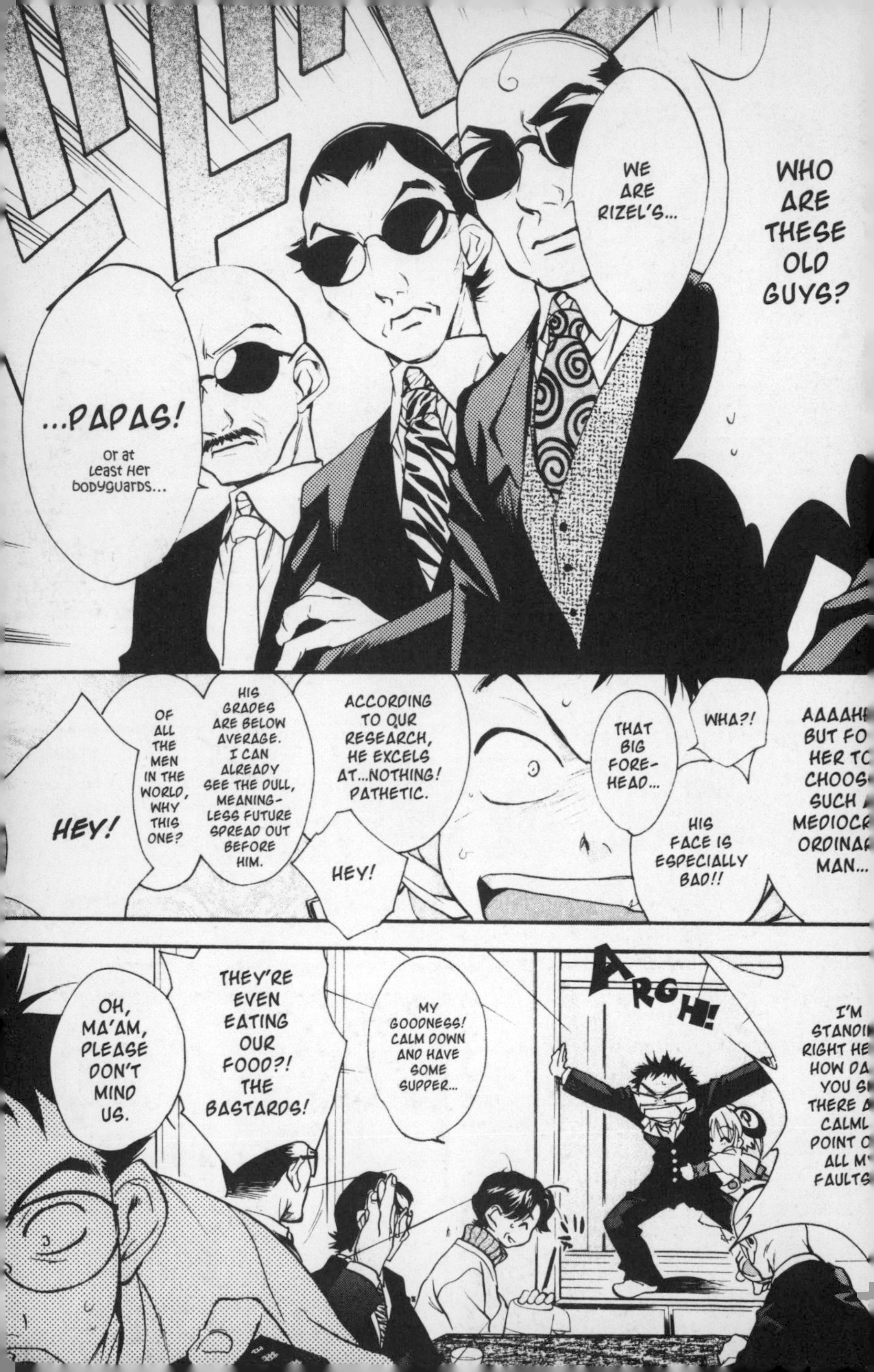
WHO ARE THESE OLD GUYS?
WE ARE RIZEL'S...
...PAPAS!
Or at least her bodyguards...
AAAAHH BUT FO HER TO CHOOS SUCH A MEDIOCR ORDINAR MAN...
WHA?!
THAT BIG FORE-HEAD...
HIS FACE IS ESPECIALLY BAD!!
ACCORDING TO OUR RESEARCH, HE EXCELS AT...NOTHING! PATHETIC.
HEY!
HIS GRADES ARE BELOW AVERAGE. I CAN ALREADY SEE THE DULL, MEANING-LESS FUTURE SPREAD OUT BEFORE HIM.
OF ALL THE MEN IN THE WORLD, WHY THIS ONE?
HEY!
I'M STANDI RIGHT HE HOW DA YOU S THERE A CALML POINT O ALL M FAULTS
ARGH!
MY GOODNESS! CALM DOWN AND HAVE SOME SUPPER...
THEY'RE EVEN EATING OUR FOOD?! THE BASTARDS!
OH, MA'AM, PLEASE DON'T MIND US.

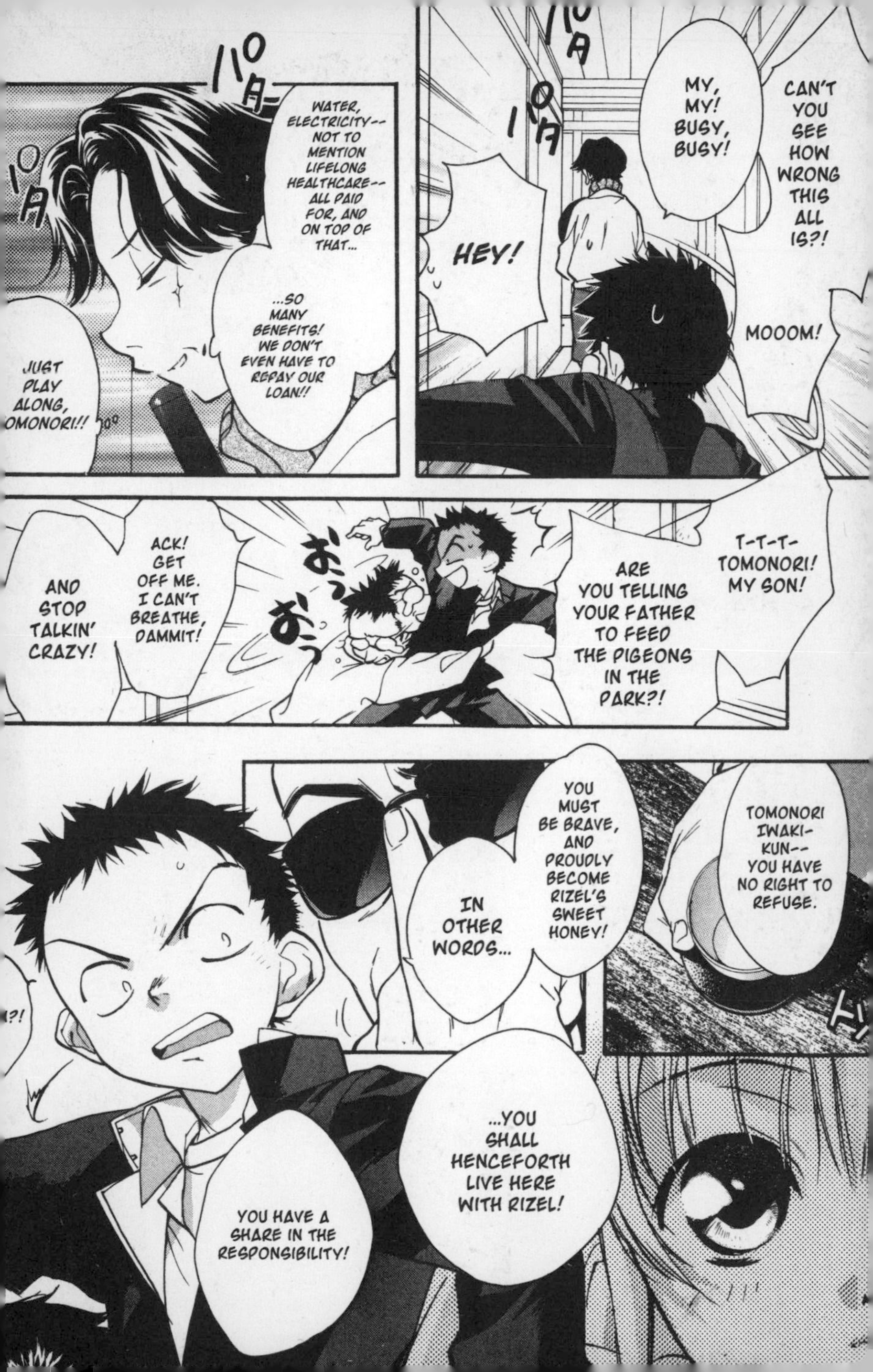
CAN'T YOU SEE HOW WRONG THIS ALL IS?!
MY, MY! BUSY, BUSY!
HEY!
MOOOM!
WATER, ELECTRICITY-- NOT TO MENTION LIFELONG HEALTHCARE-- ALL PAID FOR, AND ON TOP OF THAT...
...SO MANY BENEFITS! WE DON'T EVEN HAVE TO REPAY OUR LOAN!!
JUST PLAY ALONG, OMONORI!!
T-T-T-TOMONORI! MY SON!
ARE YOU TELLING YOUR FATHER TO FEED THE PIGEONS IN THE PARK?!
おぅ おぅ
ACK! GET OFF ME. I CAN'T BREATHE, DAMMIT!
AND STOP TALKIN' CRAZY!
TOMONORI IWAKI-KUN-- YOU HAVE NO RIGHT TO REFUSE.
YOU MUST BE BRAVE, AND PROUDLY BECOME RIZEL'S SWEET HONEY!
IN OTHER WORDS...
...YOU SHALL HENCEFORTH LIVE HERE WITH RIZEL!
YOU HAVE A SHARE IN THE RESPONSIBILITY!
?!

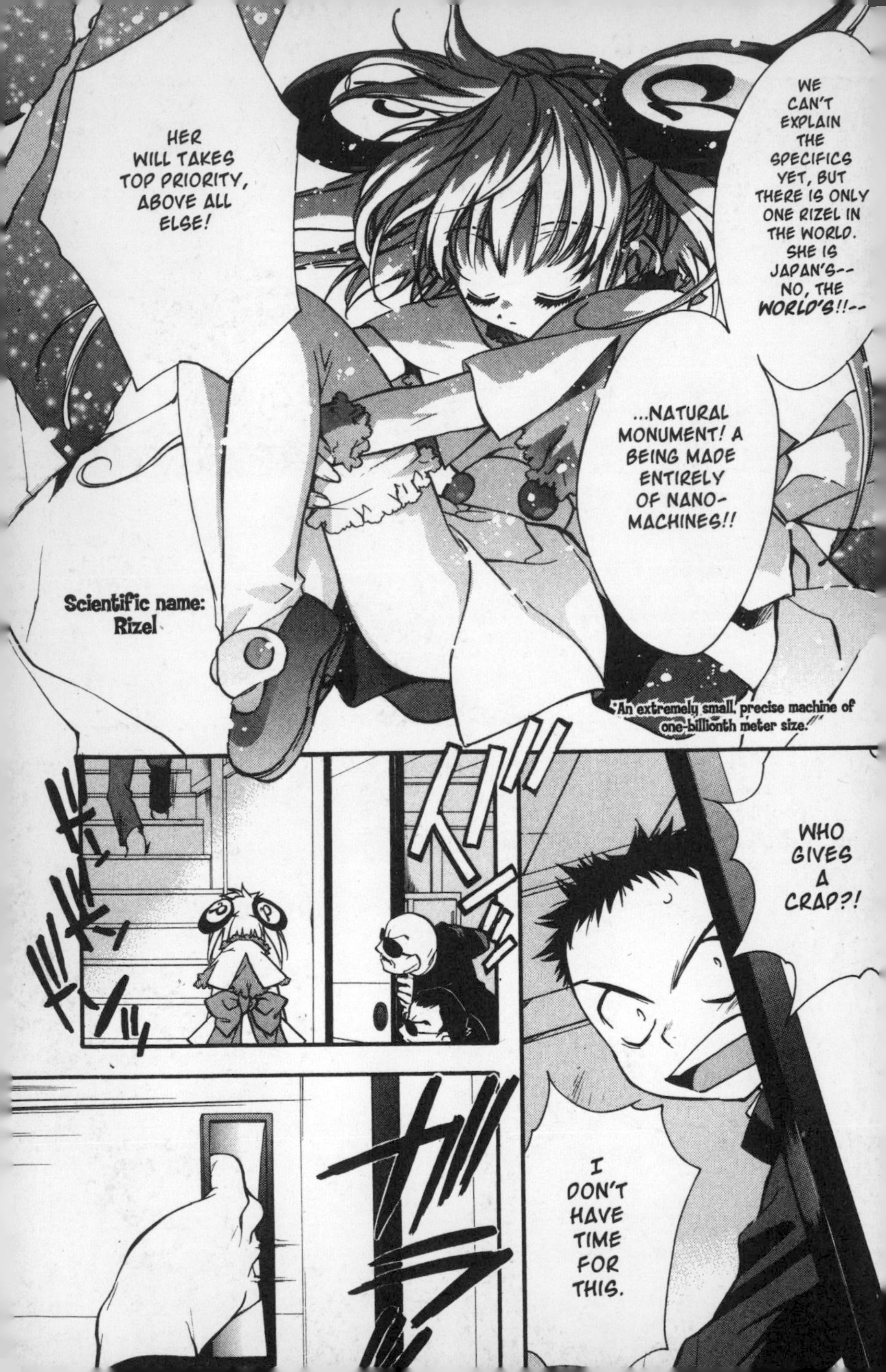
WE CAN'T EXPLAIN THE SPECIFICS YET, BUT THERE IS ONLY ONE RIZEL IN THE WORLD. SHE IS JAPAN'S--NO, THE WORLD'S!!--
HER WILL TAKES TOP PRIORITY, ABOVE ALL ELSE!
...NATURAL MONUMENT! A BEING MADE ENTIRELY OF NANO-MACHINES!!
Scientific name: Rizel
*An extremely small, precise machine of one-billionth meter size.
WHO GIVES A CRAP?!
I DON'T HAVE TIME FOR THIS.

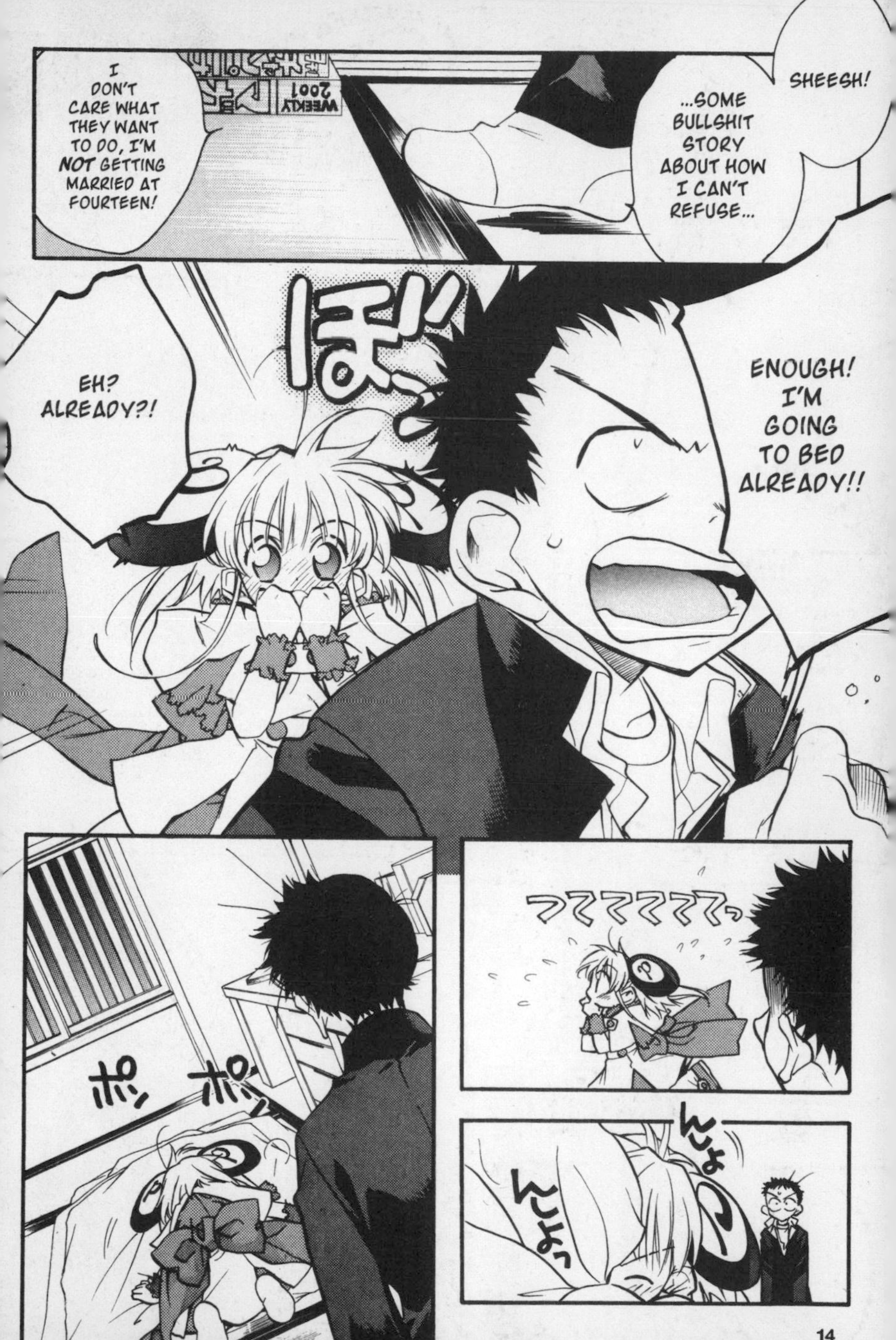
SHEESH!
...SOME BULLSHIT STORY ABOUT HOW I CAN'T REFUSE...
I DON'T CARE WHAT THEY WANT TO DO, I'M ***NOT*** GETTING MARRIED AT FOURTEEN!
ENOUGH! I'M GOING TO BED ALREADY!!
ぼっ
EH? ALREADY?!
てててててっ
んしょ
んしょっ
ポン ポン

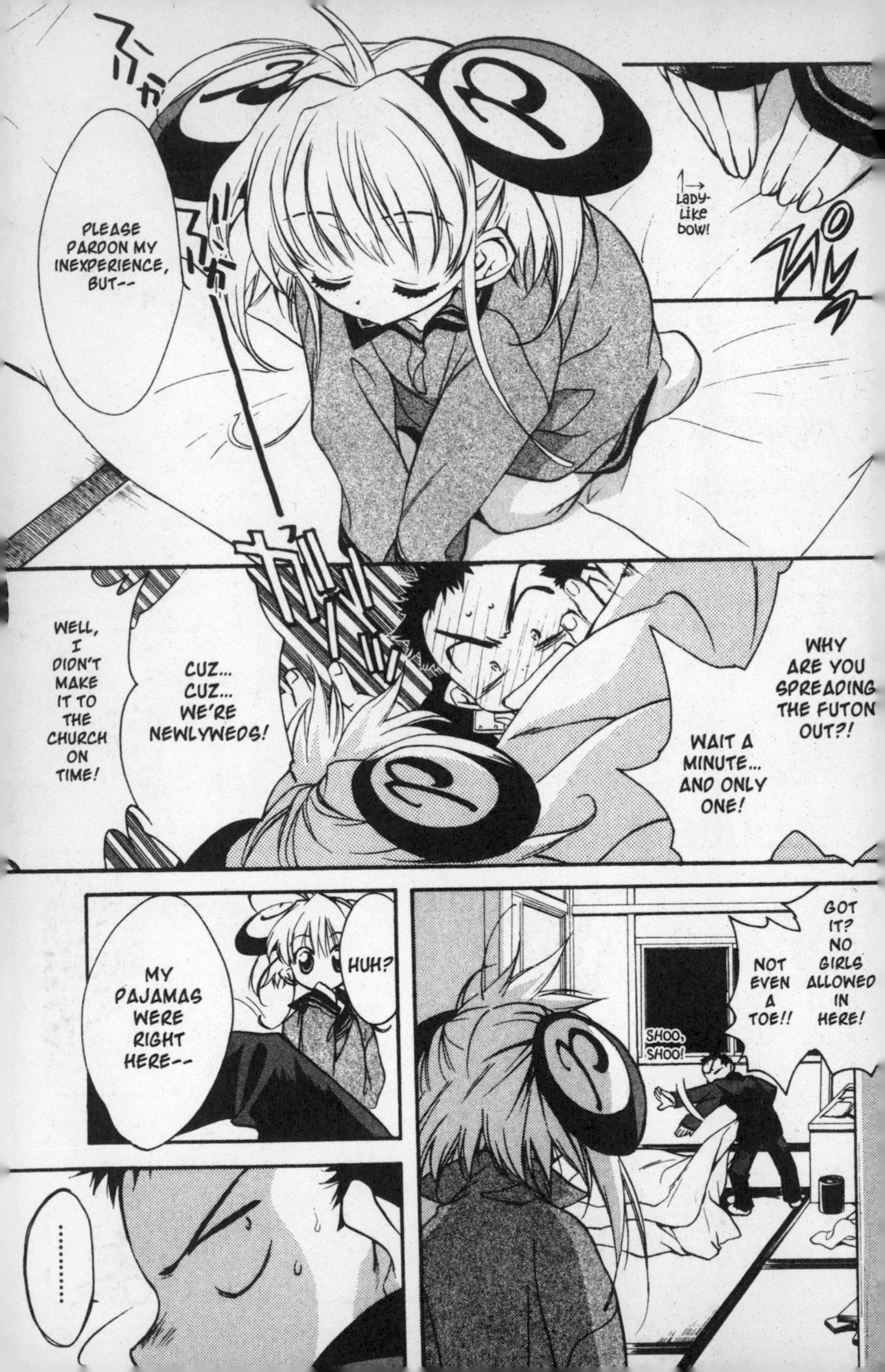
Lady-like bow!
Please pardon my inexperience, but--
Why are you spreading the futon out?!
Wait a minute... and only one!
Cuz... cuz... we're newlyweds!
Well, I didn't make it to the church on time!
Got it? No girls allowed in here!
Not even a toe!!
Shoo, shoo!
Huh?
My pajamas were right here--
....

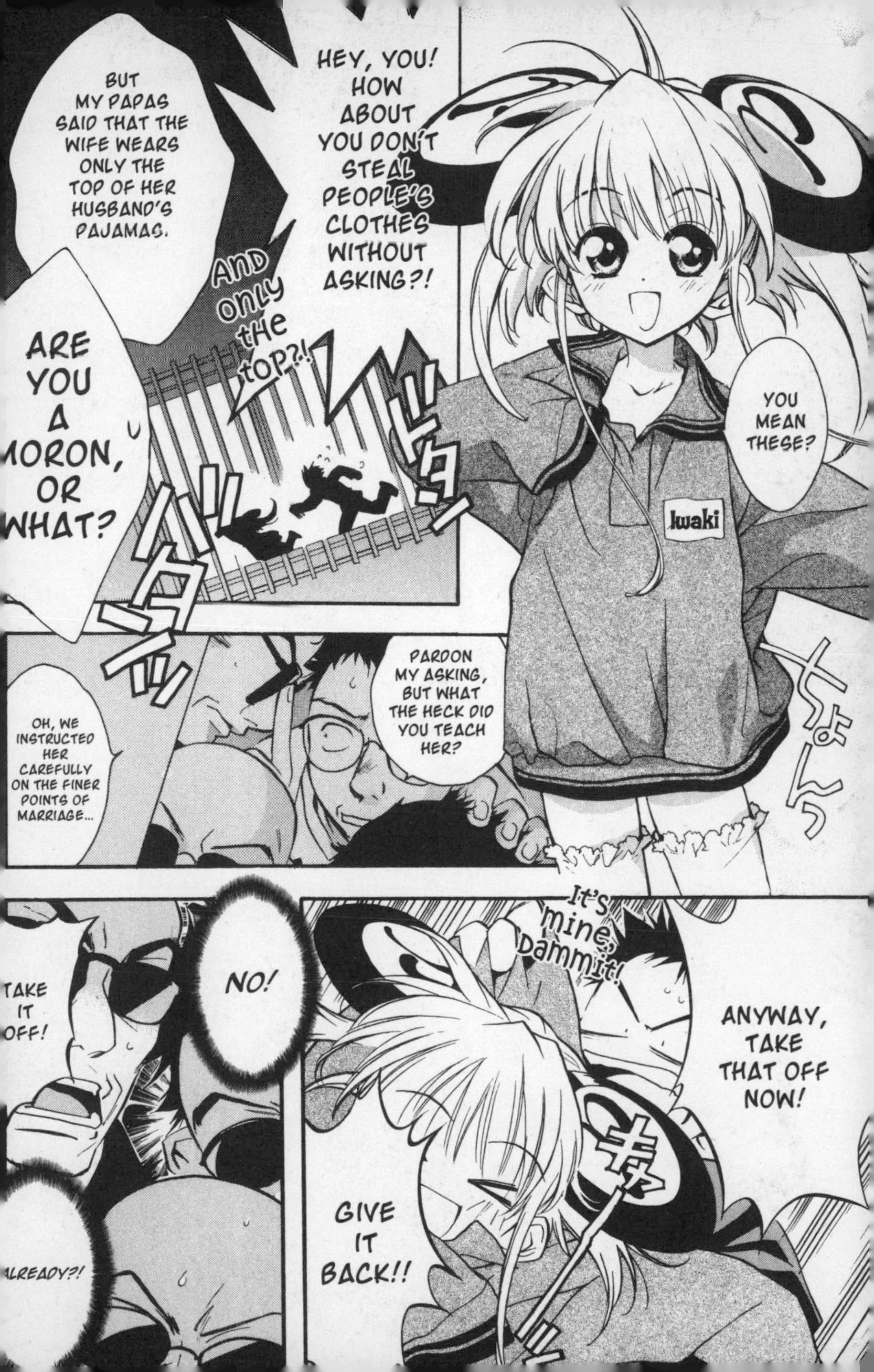

YOU MEAN THESE?
HEY, YOU! HOW ABOUT YOU DON'T STEAL PEOPLE'S CLOTHES WITHOUT ASKING?!
BUT MY PAPAS SAID THAT THE WIFE WEARS ONLY THE TOP OF HER HUSBAND'S PAJAMAS.
And only the top?!
ARE YOU A MORON, OR WHAT?
PARDON MY ASKING, BUT WHAT THE HECK DID YOU TEACH HER?
OH, WE INSTRUCTED HER CAREFULLY ON THE FINER POINTS OF MARRIAGE...
ANYWAY, TAKE THAT OFF NOW!
It's mine, Dammit!
GIVE IT BACK!!
NO!
TAKE IT OFF!
ALREADY?!

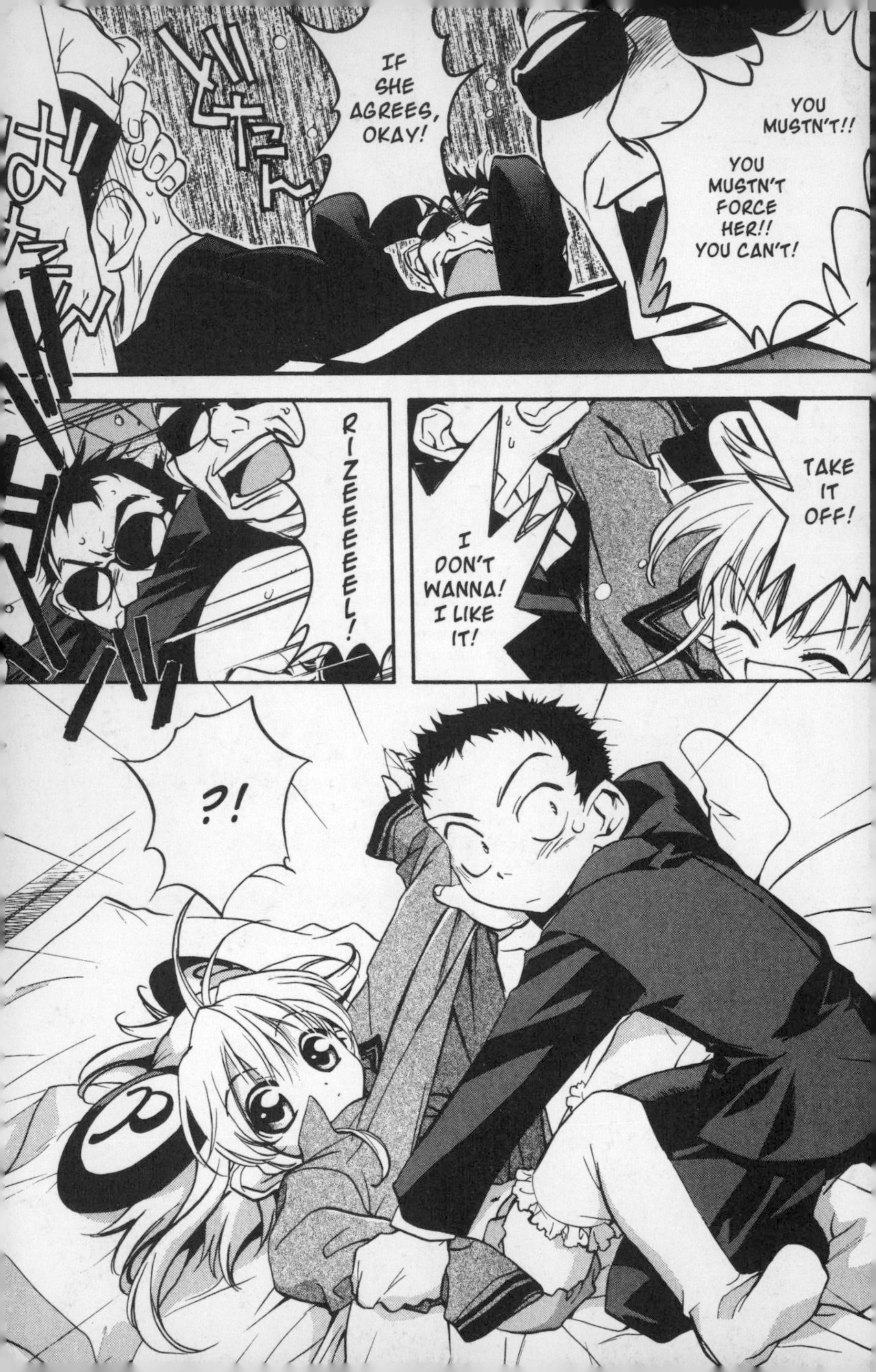
YOU MUSTN'T!!
YOU MUSTN'T FORCE HER!! YOU CAN'T!
IF SHE AGREES, OKAY!
TAKE IT OFF!
I DON'T WANNA! I LIKE IT!
RIZEEEEEEL!
?!

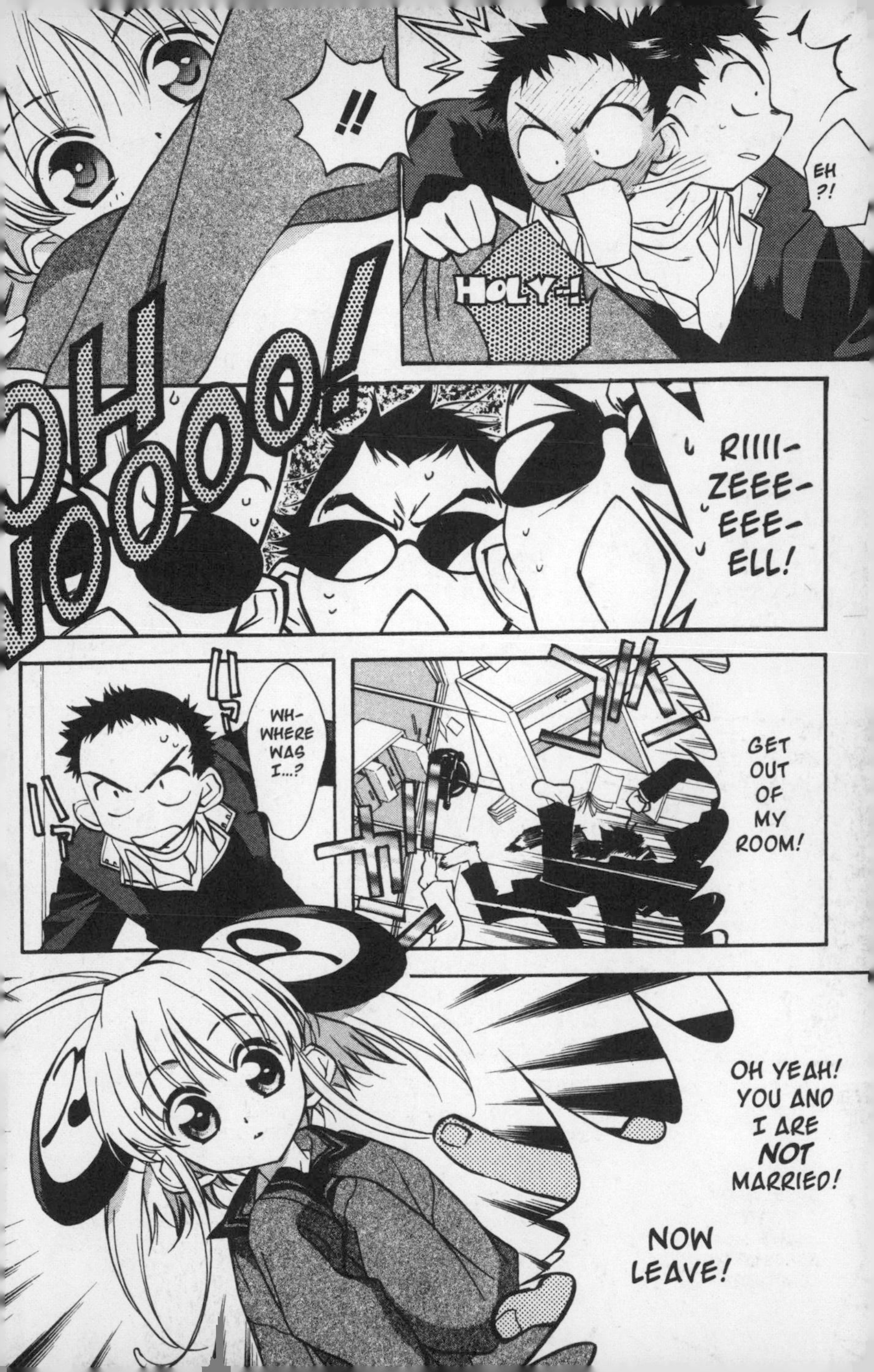
EH ?!
!!
HOLY-!
RIIII-ZEEE-EEE-ELL!
OH NOOOOO!
GET OUT OF MY ROOM!
WH- WHERE WAS I...?
OH YEAH! YOU AND I ARE NOT MARRIED!
NOW LEAVE!

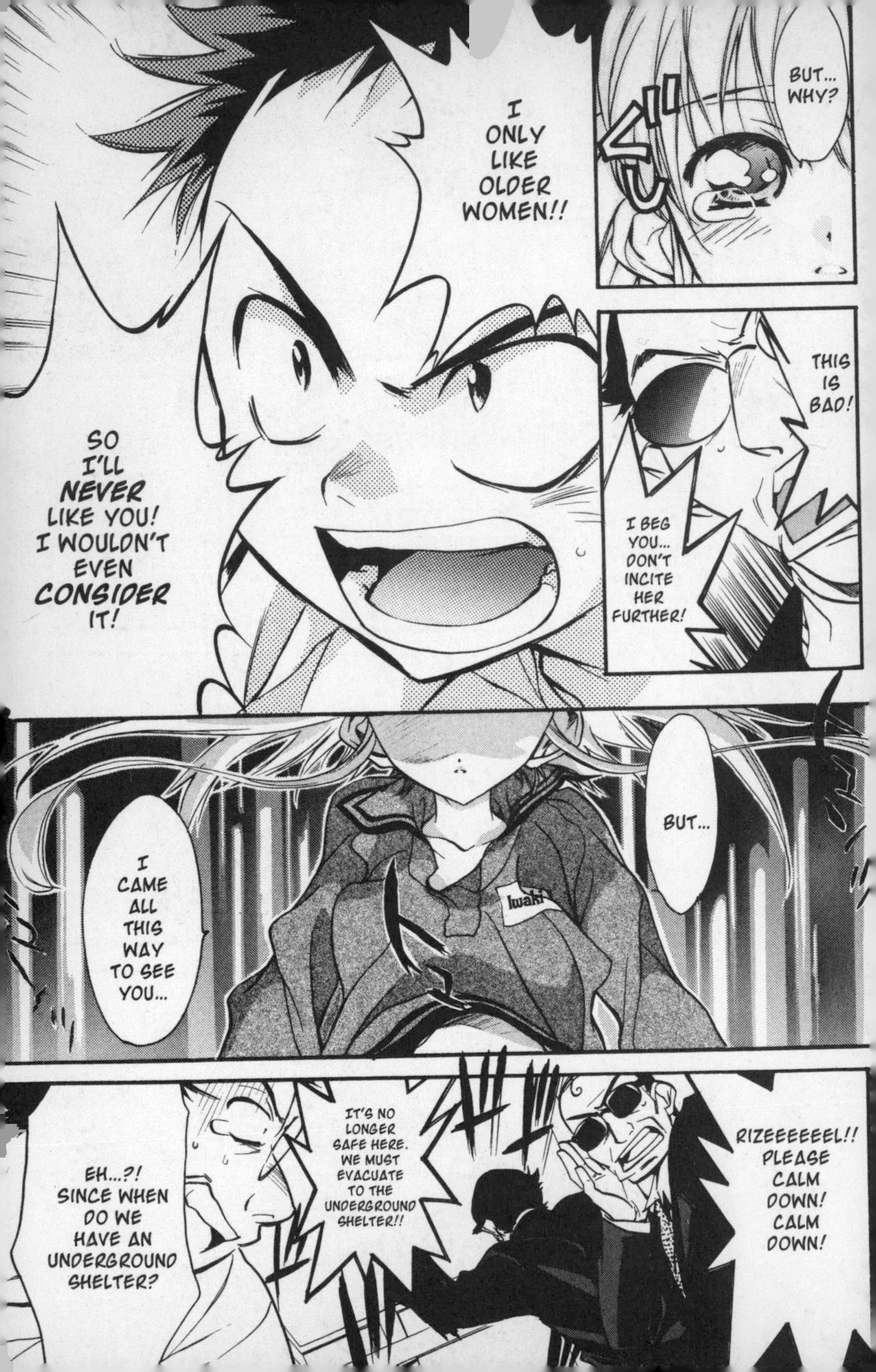
BUT... WHY?
THIS IS BAD!
I BEG YOU... DON'T INCITE HER FURTHER!
I ONLY LIKE OLDER WOMEN!!
SO I'LL ***NEVER*** LIKE YOU! I WOULDN'T EVEN ***CONSIDER*** IT!
BUT...
Iwaki
I CAME ALL THIS WAY TO SEE YOU...
RIZEEEEEEL!! PLEASE CALM DOWN! CALM DOWN!
IT'S NO LONGER SAFE HERE. WE MUST EVACUATE TO THE UNDERGROUND SHELTER!!
EH...?! SINCE WHEN DO WE HAVE AN UNDERGROUND SHELTER?

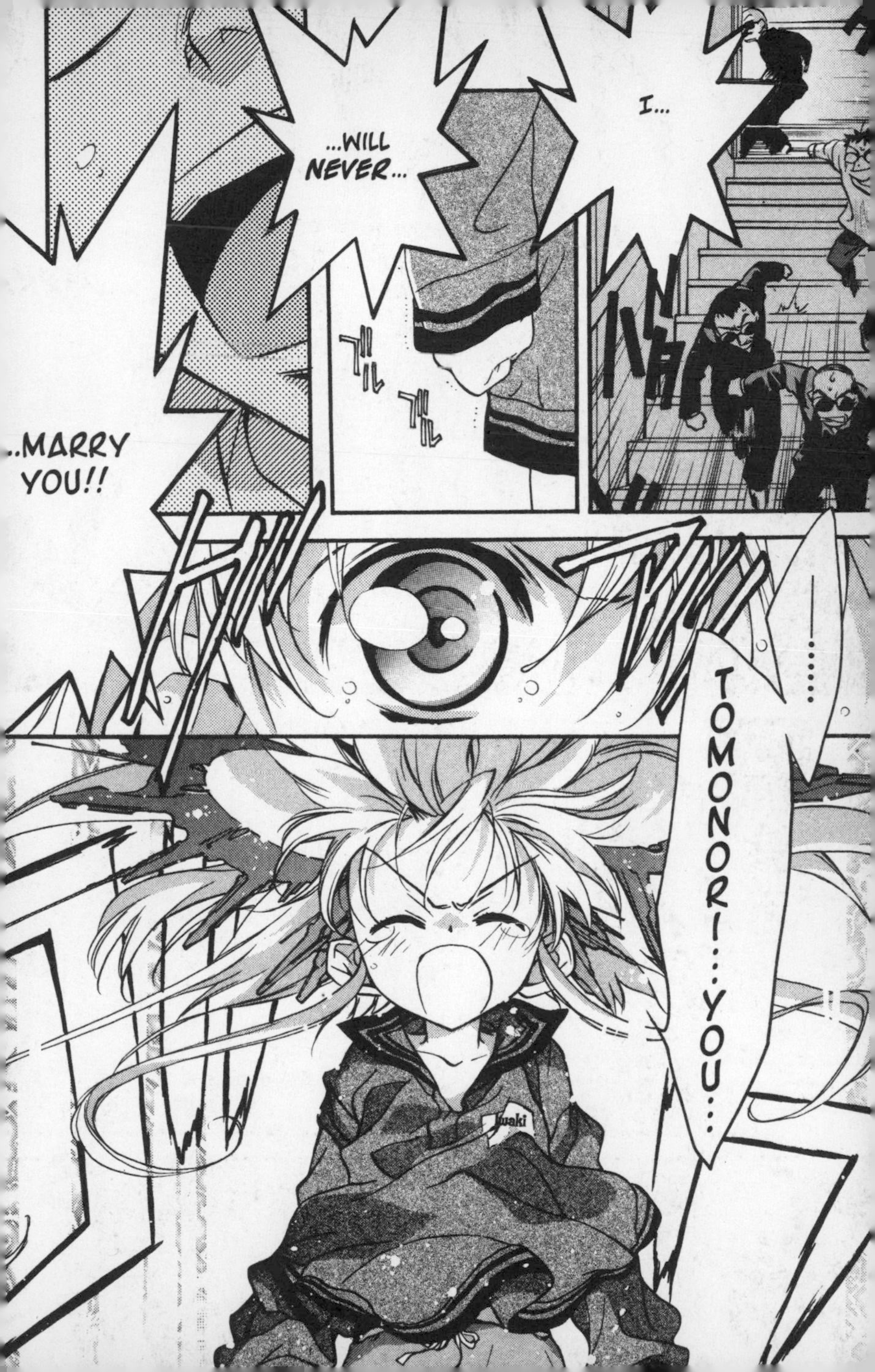
I...
...WILL NEVER...
..MARRY YOU!!
ブル ブル
......
TOMONORI...YOU...

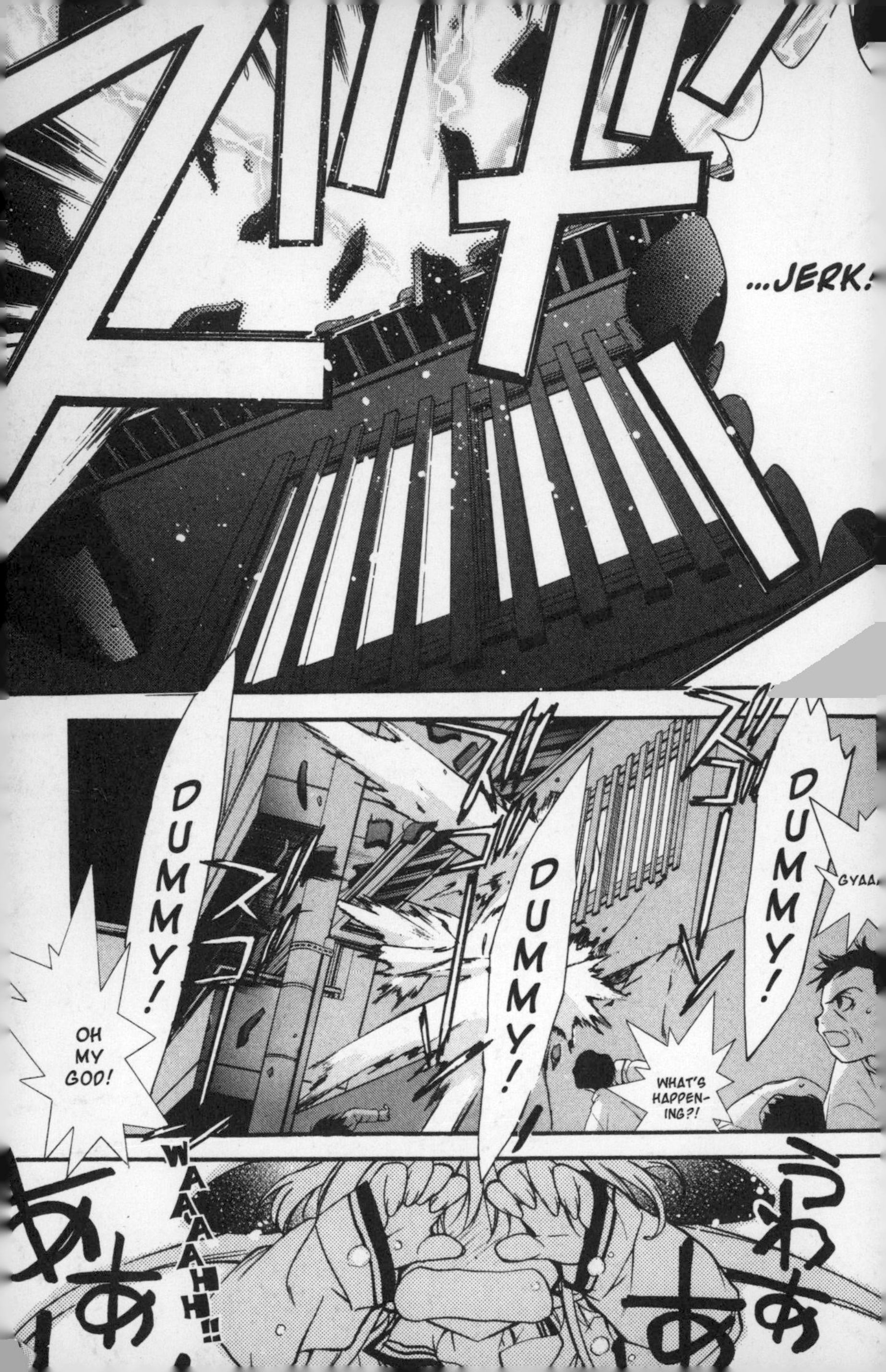
...JERK
DUMMY!
GYAA
WHAT'S HAPPENING?!
DUMMY!
DUMMY!
OH MY GOD!
WAAAAHH!!

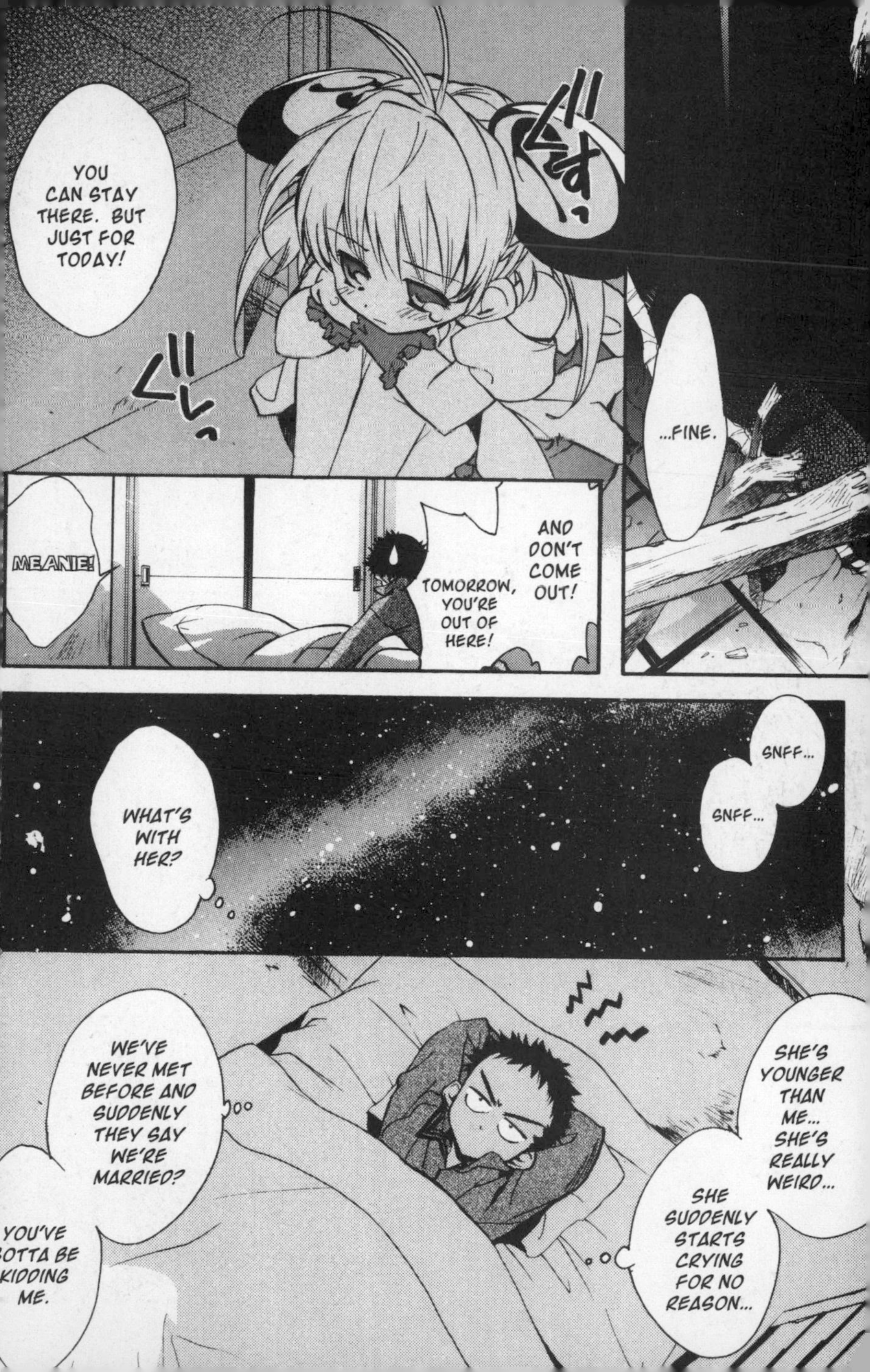
...FINE.
YOU CAN STAY THERE. BUT JUST FOR TODAY!
ぐすっ
ぐしっ
AND DON'T COME OUT!
TOMORROW, YOU'RE OUT OF HERE!
MEANIE!
SNFF...
SNFF...
WHAT'S WITH HER?
SHE'S YOUNGER THAN ME... SHE'S REALLY WEIRD...
SHE SUDDENLY STARTS CRYING FOR NO REASON...
WE'VE NEVER MET BEFORE AND SUDDENLY THEY SAY WE'RE MARRIED?
YOU'VE GOTTA BE KIDDING ME.

...NAME...

COME TO THINK OF IT, HER...

WHAT WAS IT AGAIN?

~HMMM? ゴロッ

A LITTLE BRAT LIKE THAT... A LITTLE BRAT LIKE THAT~

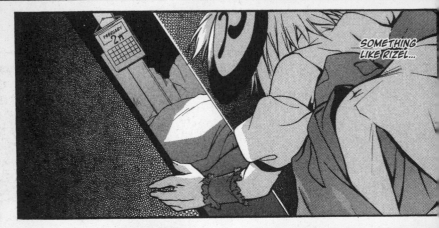

SOMETHING LIKE RIZEL...

FEBRUARY 2月

X-1

SNOOOOORE かぁ

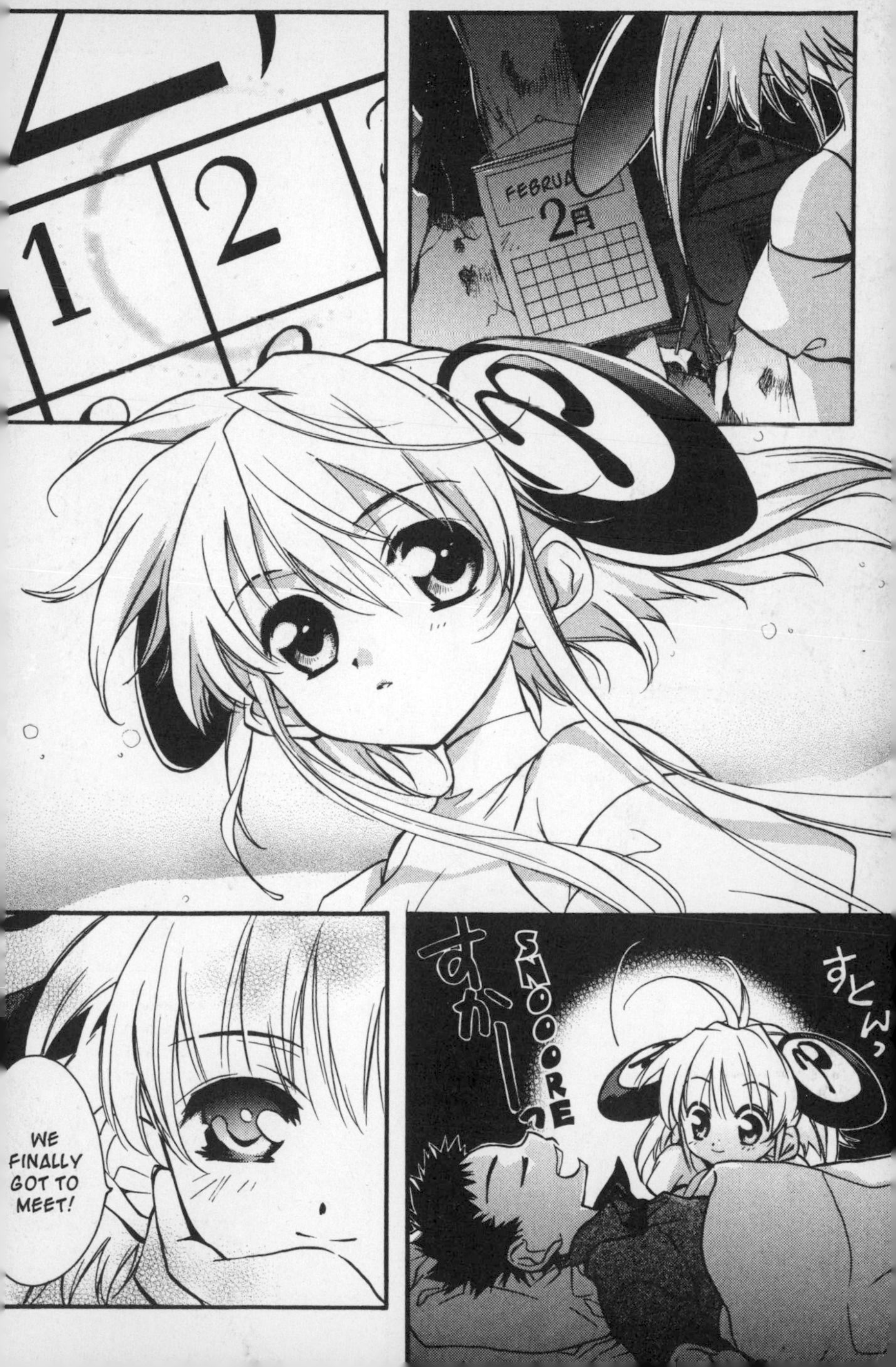
FEBRUA
2月
すとんっ
すかーっ
SNOOORE
WE FINALLY GOT TO MEET!

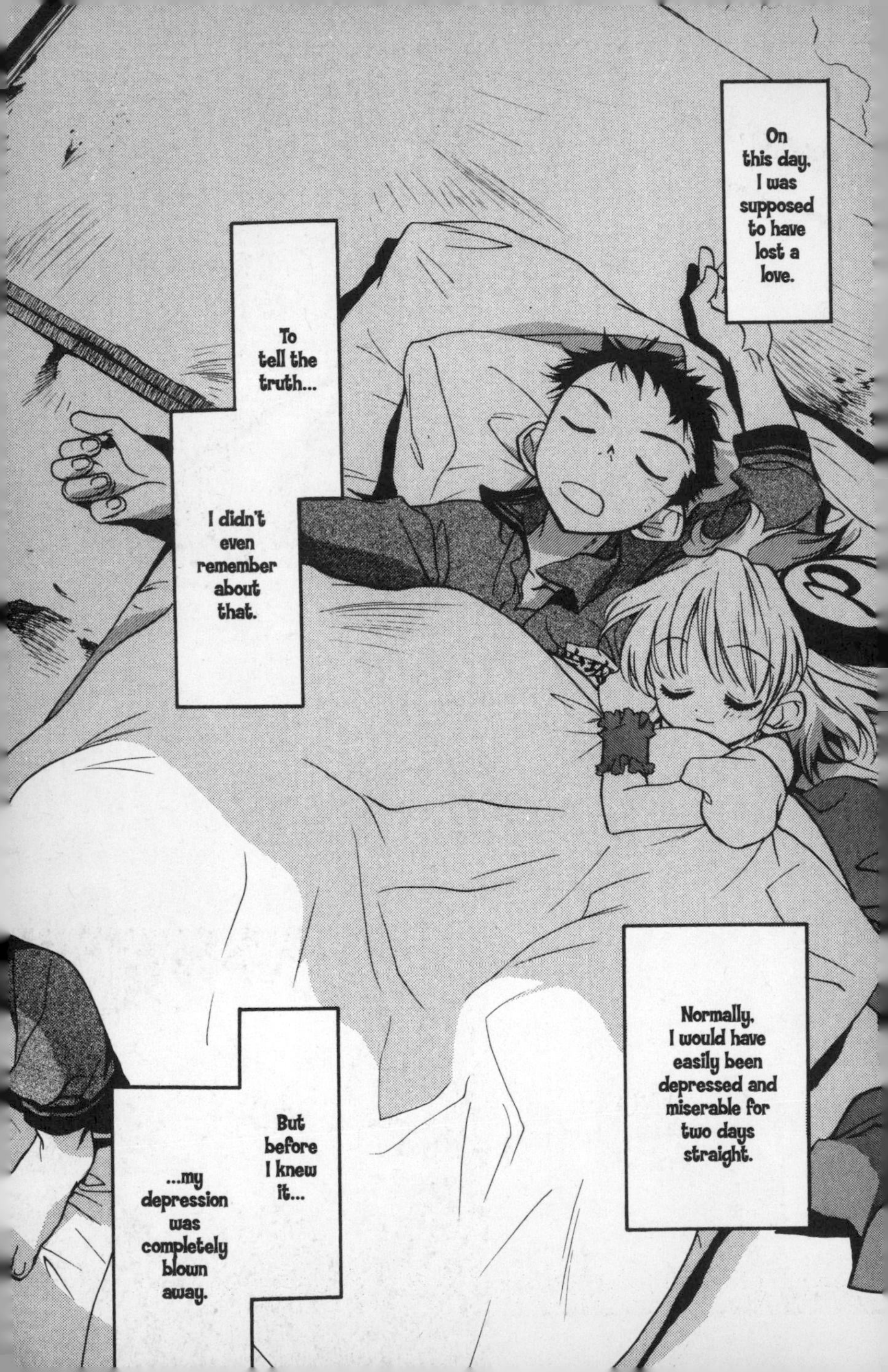
On this day, I was supposed to have lost a love.
To tell the truth...
I didn't even remember about that.
Normally, I would have easily been depressed and miserable for two days straight.
But before I knew it...
...my depression was completely blown away.

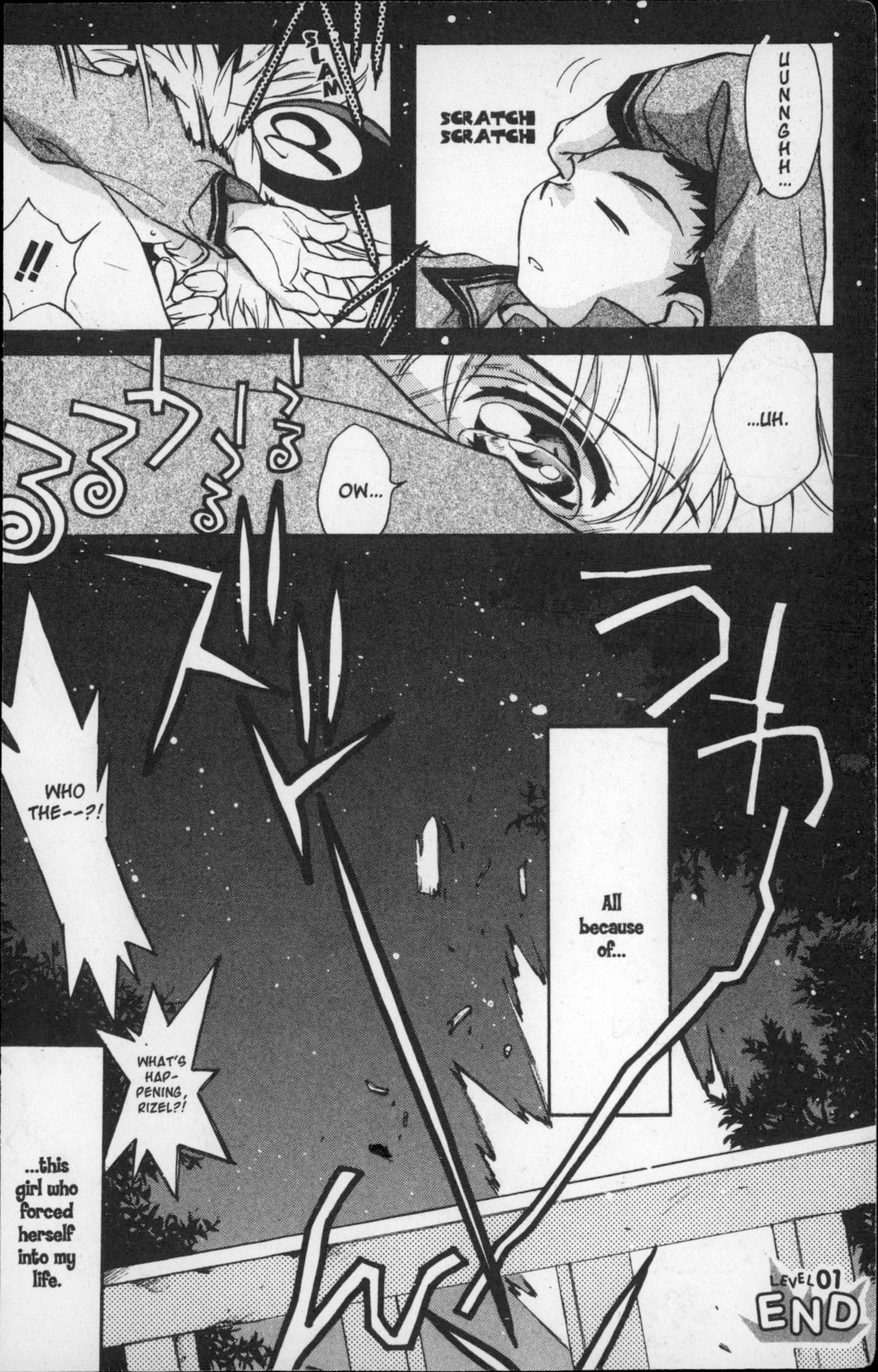
UUNNGHH...
SCRATCH SCRATCH
SLAM
!!
...UH.
OW...
All because of...
WHO THE--?!
WHAT'S HAP-PENING, RIZEL?!
...this girl who forced herself into my life.
LEVEL 01 END

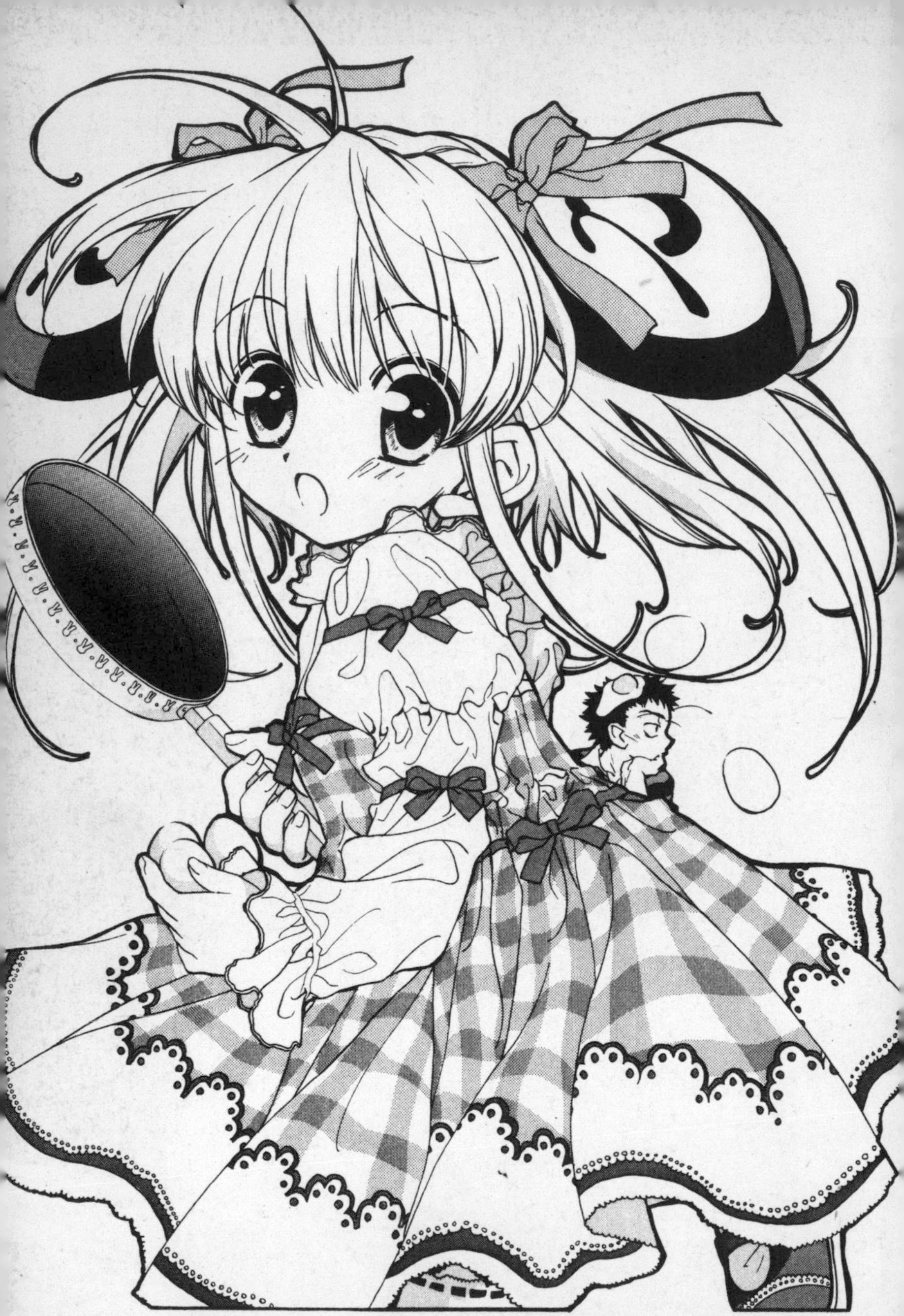

LEVEL 02 Love Comes with a Lunchbox

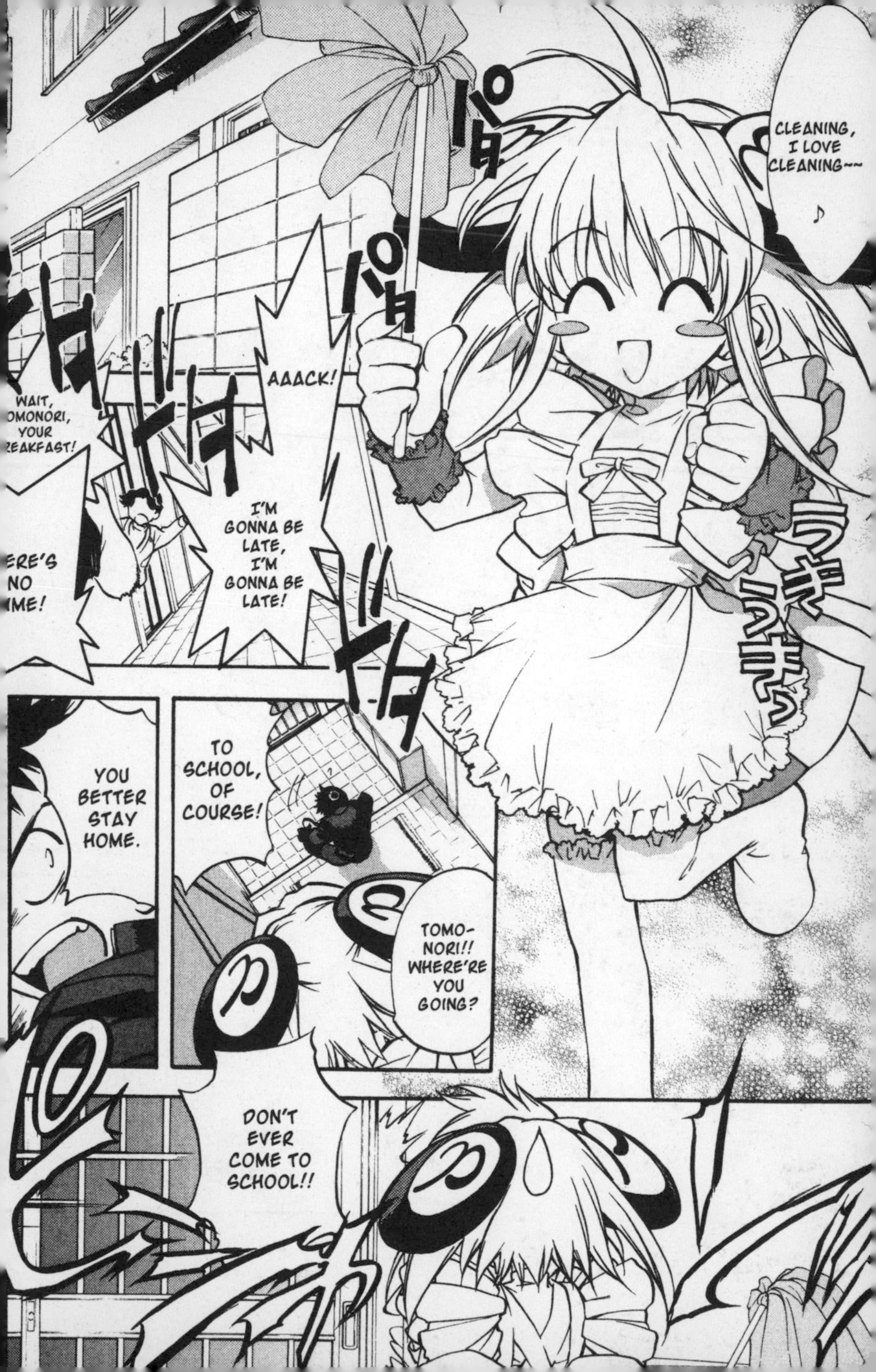

CLEANING, I LOVE CLEANING~~ ♪
パタ
パタ
うきうきっ
AAACK!
I'M GONNA BE LATE, I'M GONNA BE LATE!
WAIT, OMONORI, YOUR REAKFAST!
ERE'S NO IME!
TOMO-NORI!! WHERE'RE YOU GOING?
TO SCHOOL, OF COURSE!
YOU BETTER STAY HOME.
DON'T EVER COME TO SCHOOL!!

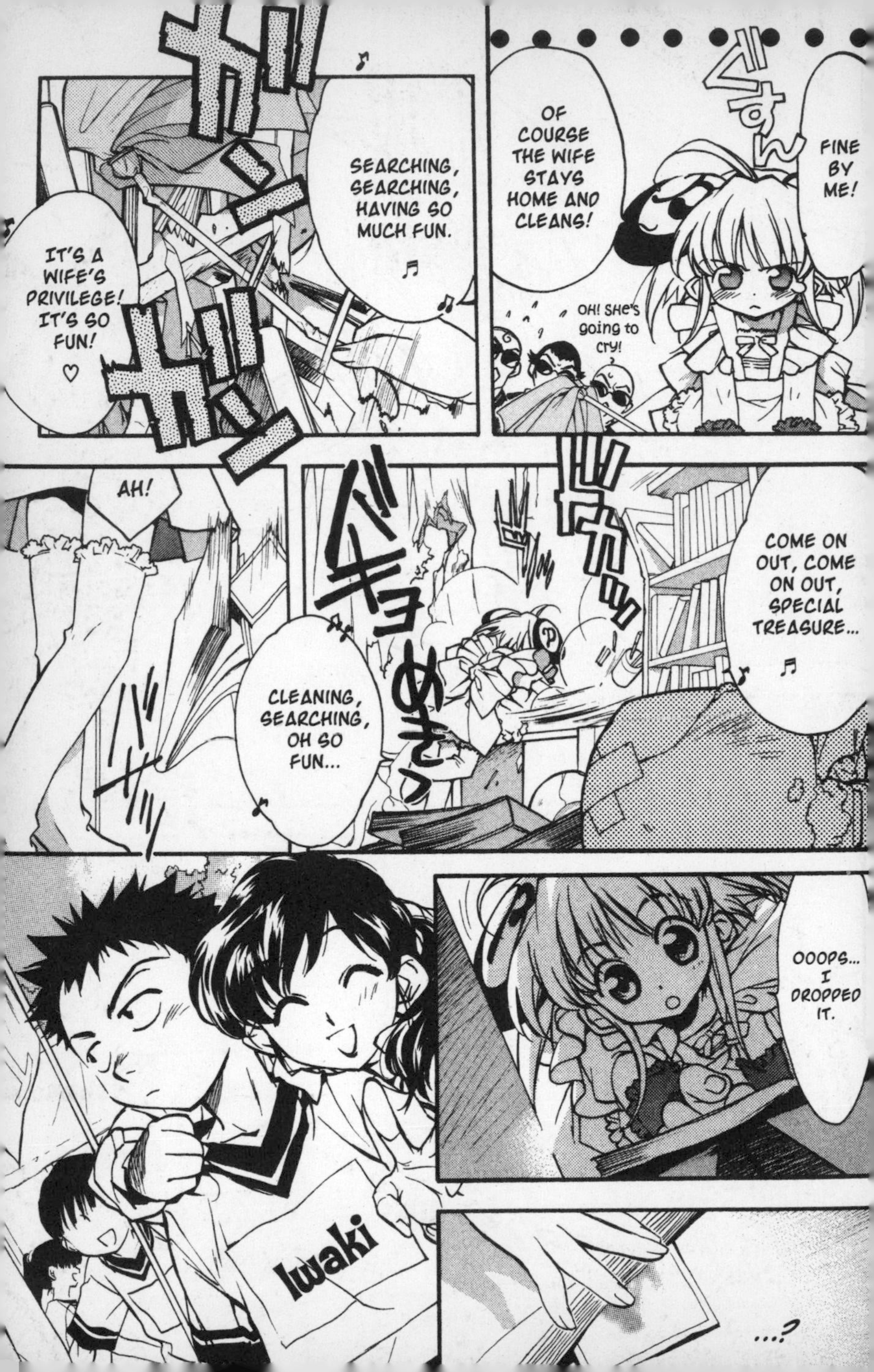
FINE BY ME!
OF COURSE THE WIFE STAYS HOME AND CLEANS!
OH! SHE'S going to cry!
SEARCHING, SEARCHING, HAVING SO MUCH FUN. ♪
IT'S A WIFE'S PRIVILEGE! IT'S SO FUN! ♡
COME ON OUT, COME ON OUT, SPECIAL TREASURE... ♪
CLEANING, SEARCHING, OH SO FUN...
AH!
OOOPS... I DROPPED IT.
...?
Iwaki

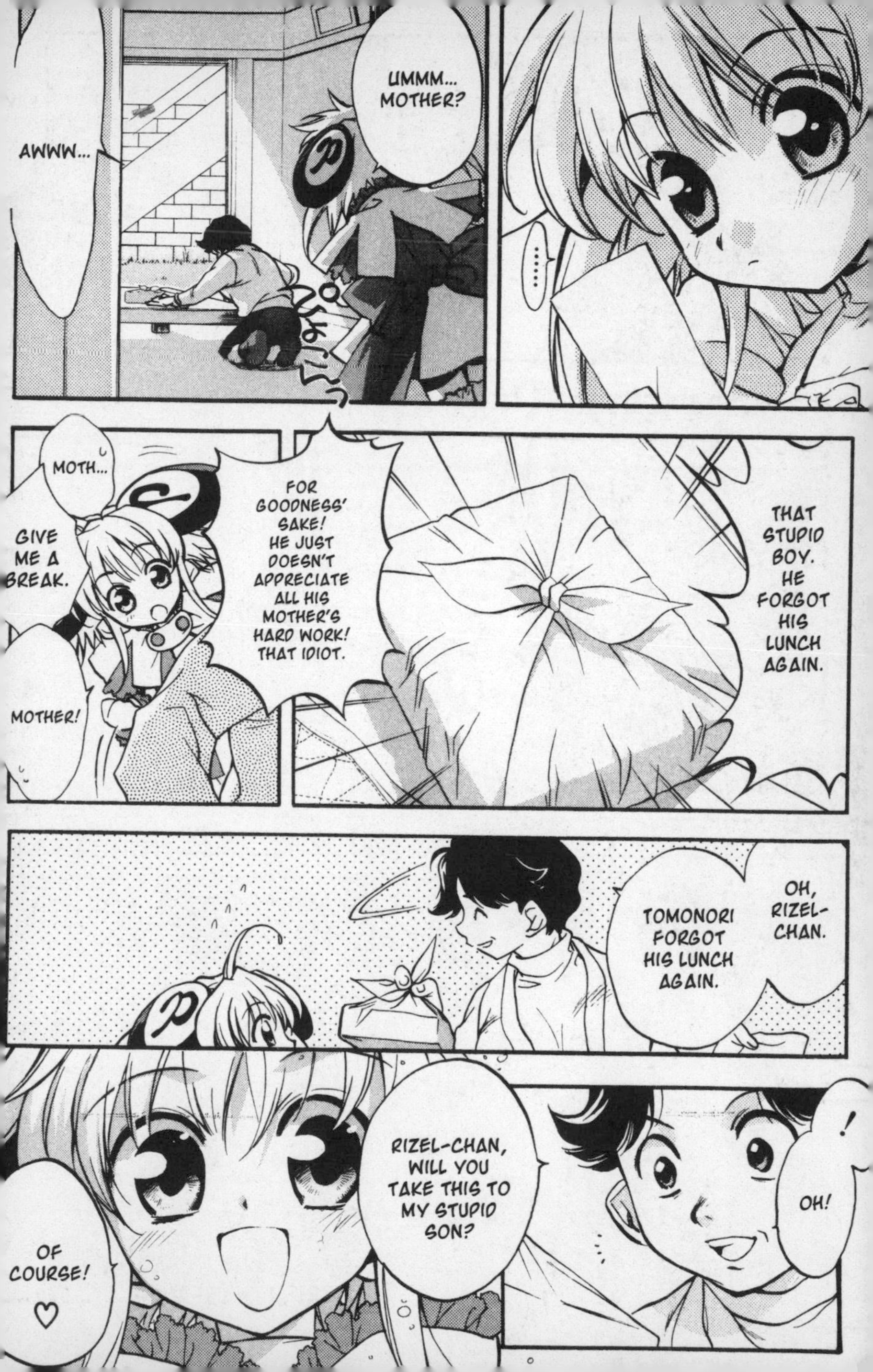
......
UMMM... MOTHER?
AWWW...
THAT STUPID BOY. HE FORGOT HIS LUNCH AGAIN.
FOR GOODNESS' SAKE! HE JUST DOESN'T APPRECIATE ALL HIS MOTHER'S HARD WORK! THAT IDIOT.
MOTH...
GIVE ME A BREAK.
MOTHER!
OH, RIZEL-CHAN.
TOMONORI FORGOT HIS LUNCH AGAIN.
!
OH!
RIZEL-CHAN, WILL YOU TAKE THIS TO MY STUPID SON?
OF COURSE! ♡

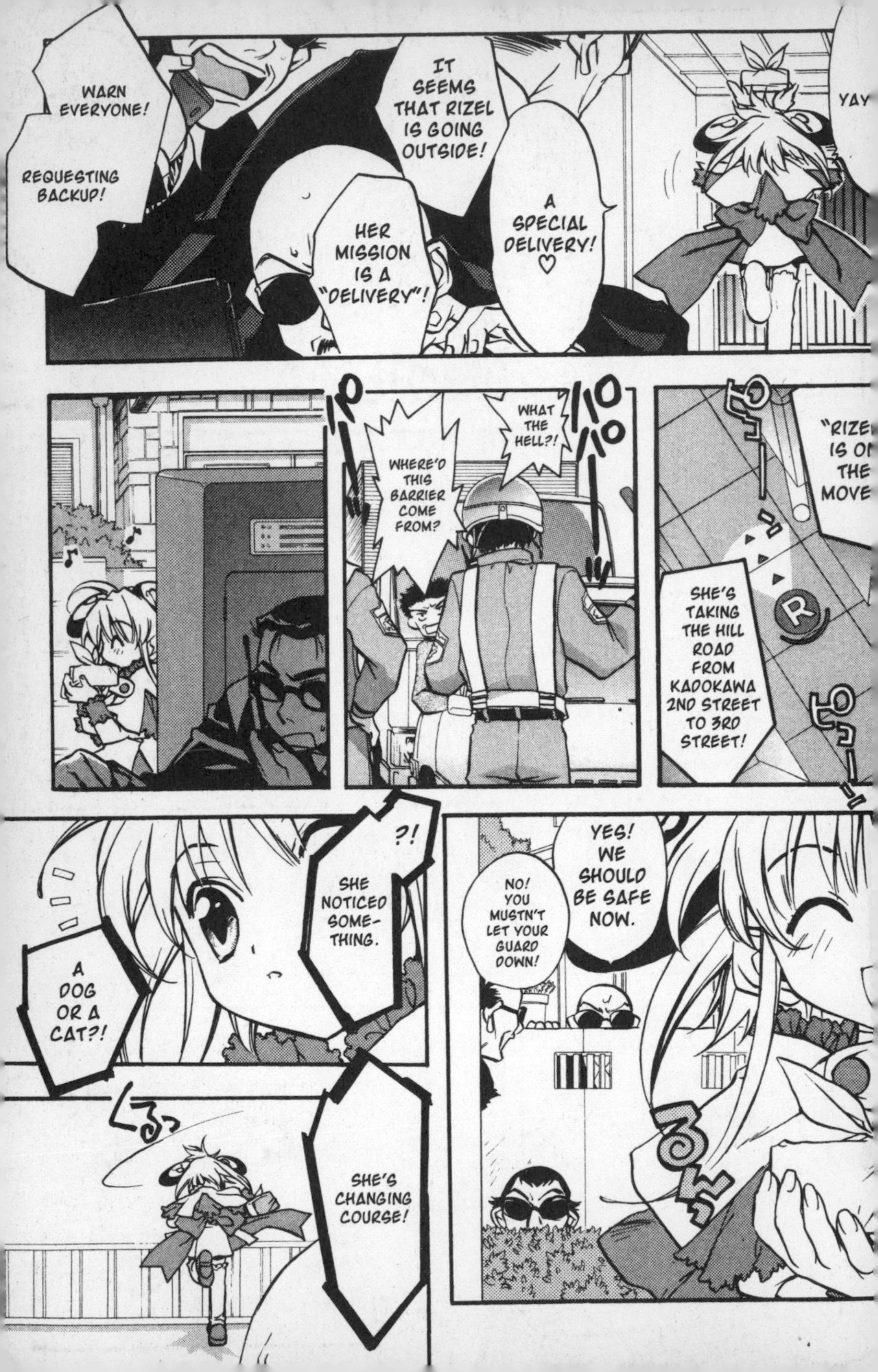
YAY
A SPECIAL DELIVERY! ♡
IT SEEMS THAT RIZEL IS GOING OUTSIDE!
HER MISSION IS A "DELIVERY"!
WARN EVERYONE!
REQUESTING BACKUP!
"RIZE IS ON THE MOVE
SHE'S TAKING THE HILL ROAD FROM KADOKAWA 2ND STREET TO 3RD STREET!
WHAT THE HELL?!
WHERE'D THIS BARRIER COME FROM?
YES! WE SHOULD BE SAFE NOW.
NO! YOU MUSTN'T LET YOUR GUARD DOWN!
?!
SHE NOTICED SOME-THING.
A DOG OR A CAT?!
SHE'S CHANGING COURSE!

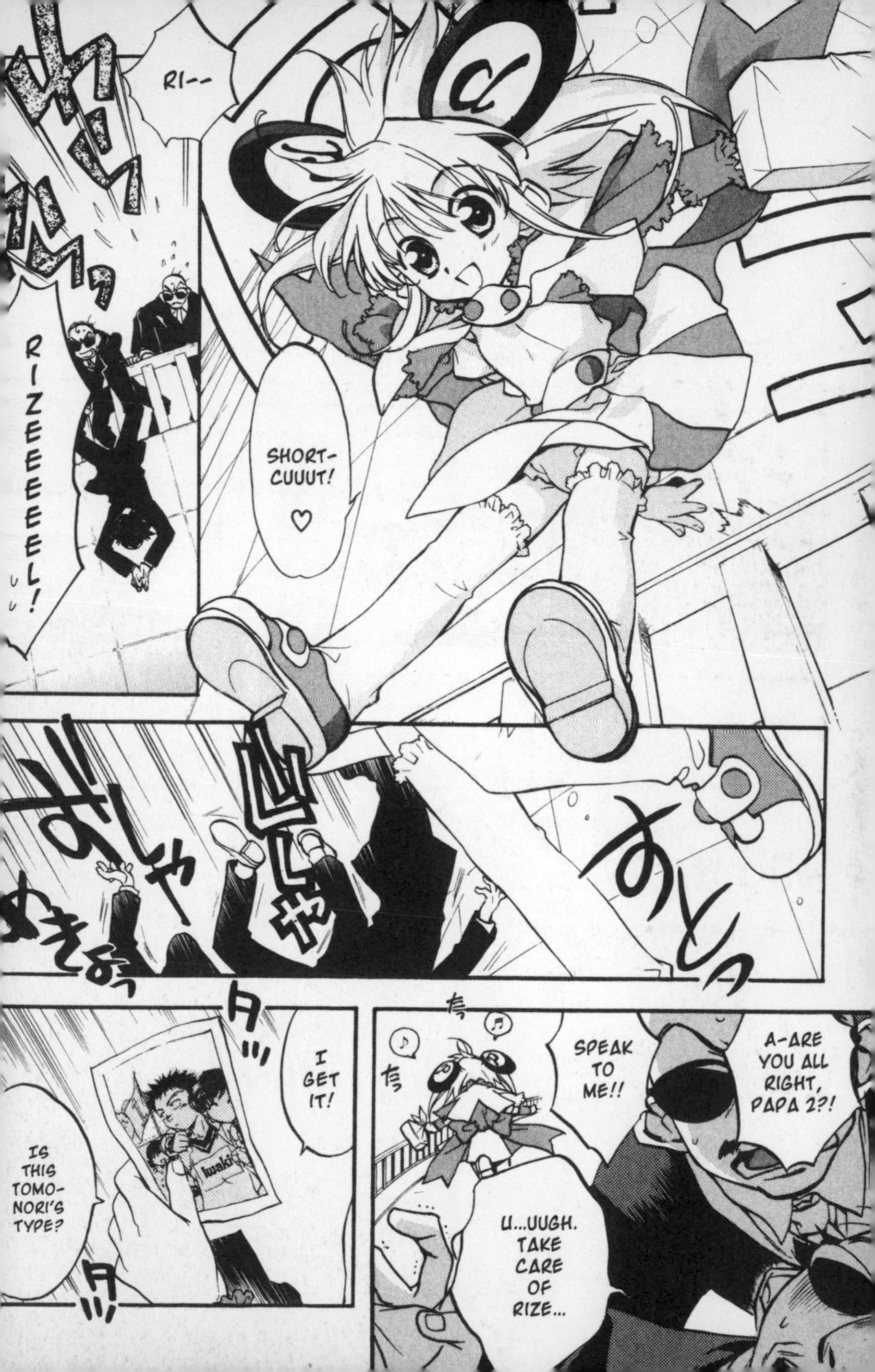
SHORT-CUUUT! ♡
RI--
RIZEEEEEEEL!
すとっ
A-ARE YOU ALL RIGHT, PAPA 2?!
SPEAK TO ME!!
U...UUGH. TAKE CARE OF RIZE...
I GET IT!
Iwaki
IS THIS TOMONORI'S TYPE?

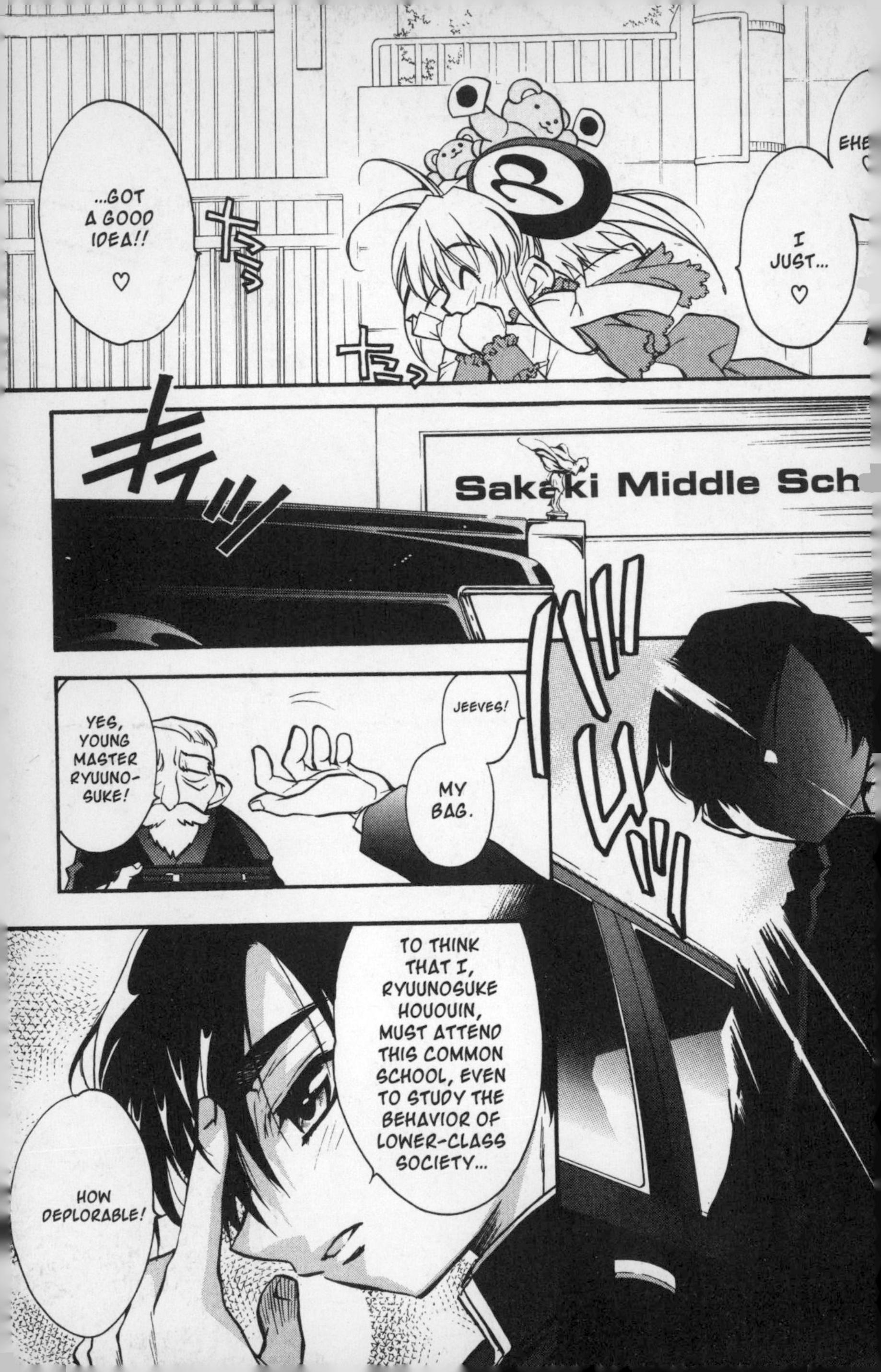
EHE
I JUST... ♡
...GOT A GOOD IDEA!! ♡
Sakaki Middle Sch
JEEVES!
MY BAG.
YES, YOUNG MASTER RYUUNOSUKE!
TO THINK THAT I, RYUUNOSUKE HOUOUIN, MUST ATTEND THIS COMMON SCHOOL, EVEN TO STUDY THE BEHAVIOR OF LOWER-CLASS SOCIETY...
HOW DEPLORABLE!

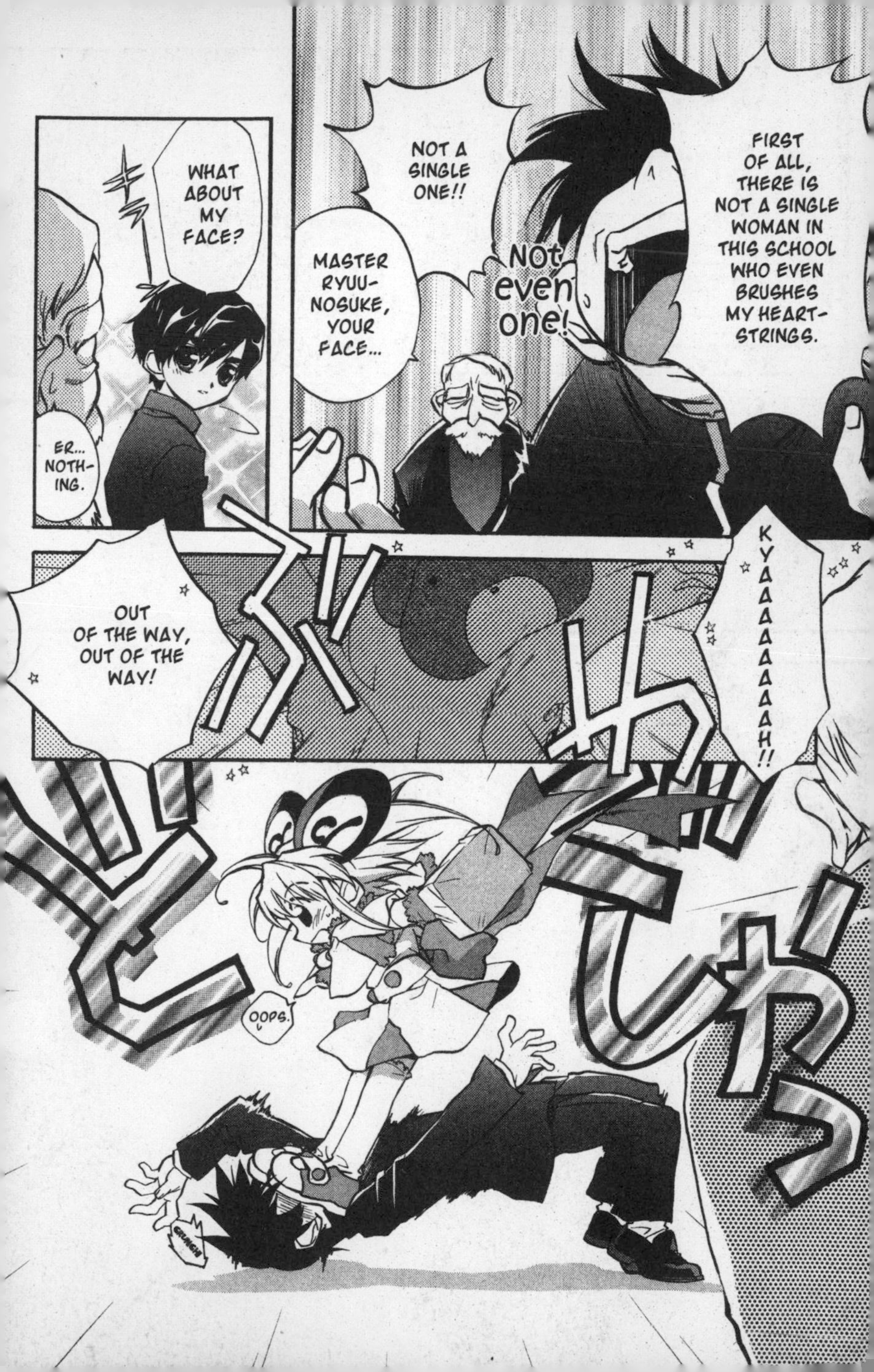
FIRST OF ALL, THERE IS NOT A SINGLE WOMAN IN THIS SCHOOL WHO EVEN BRUSHES MY HEART-STRINGS.
NOT A SINGLE ONE!!
Not even one!
MASTER RYUUNOSUKE, YOUR FACE...
WHAT ABOUT MY FACE?
ER... NOTHING.
KYAAAAAAAAAAH!!
OUT OF THE WAY, OUT OF THE WAY!
OOPS.
CRUNCH

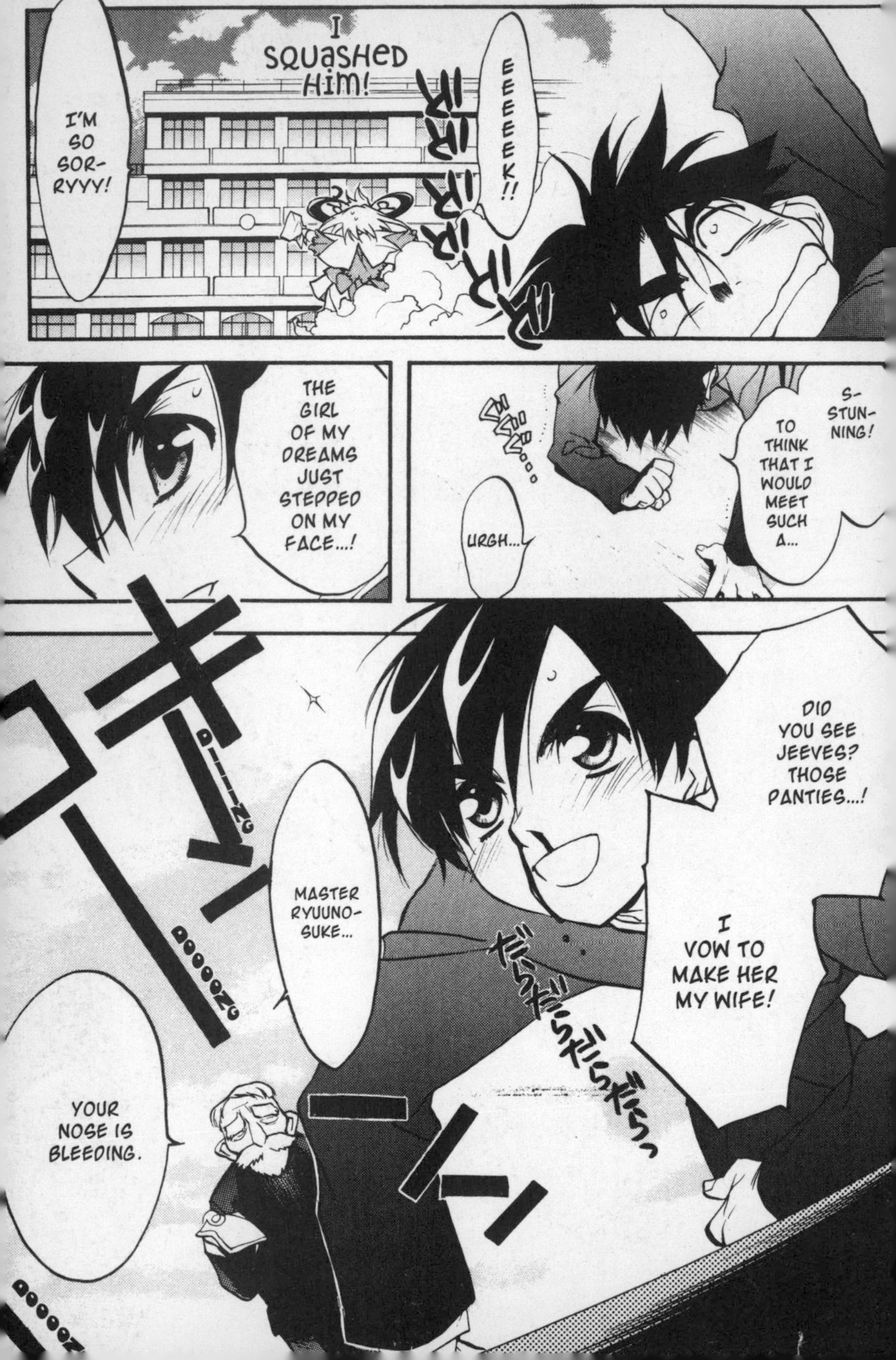
EEEEEK!!
I SQUASHED HIM!
I'M SO SORRYYY!
S-STUNNING!
TO THINK THAT I WOULD MEET SUCH A...
URGH...
THE GIRL OF MY DREAMS JUST STEPPED ON MY FACE...!
DID YOU SEE JEEVES? THOSE PANTIES...!
I VOW TO MAKE HER MY WIFE!
だらだらだらだらっ
MASTER RYUUNOSUKE...
DIIIING
DOOOONG
YOUR NOSE IS BLEEDING.

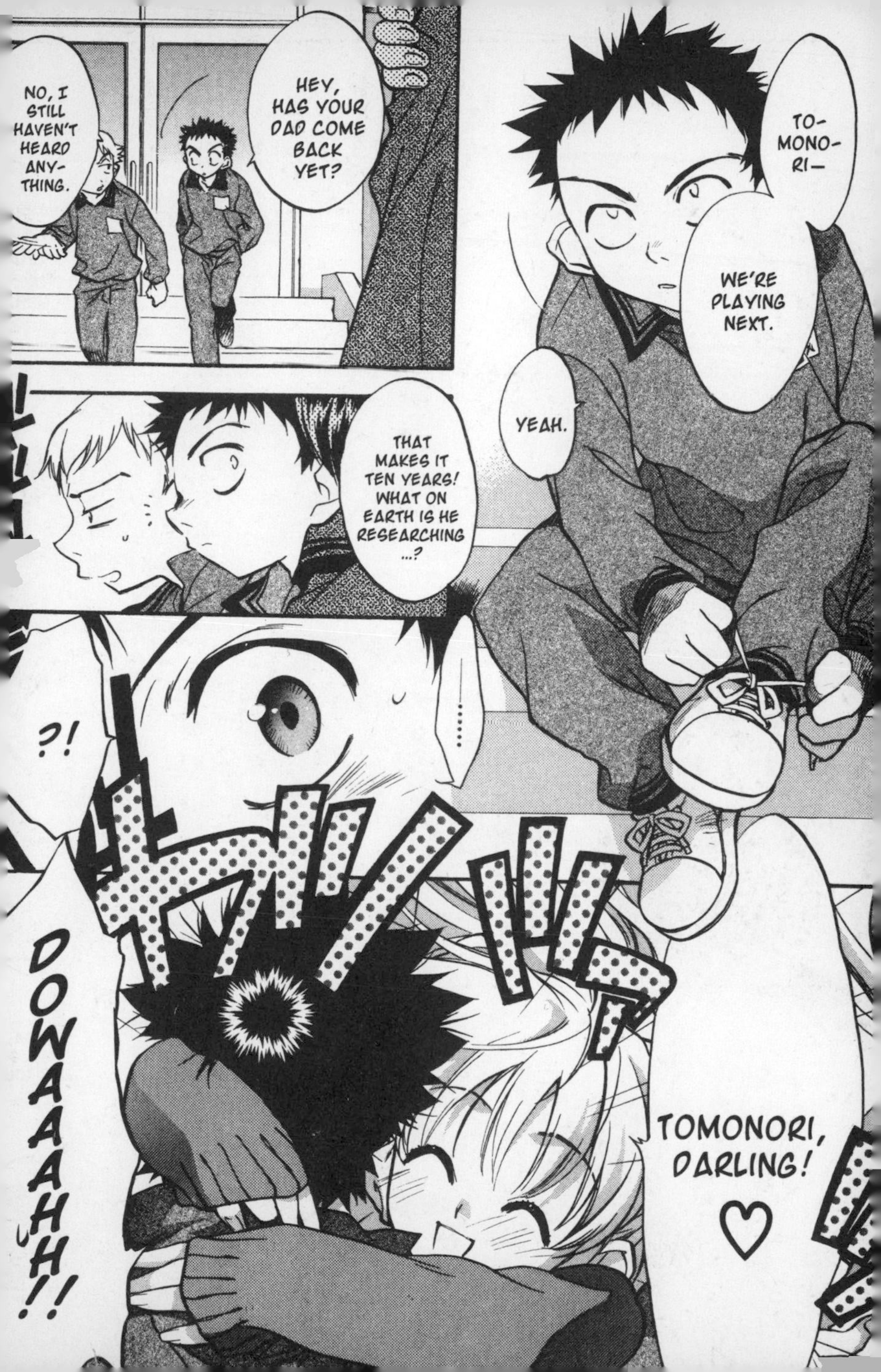
TO-MONO-RI—
WE'RE PLAYING NEXT.
YEAH.
HEY, HAS YOUR DAD COME BACK YET?
NO, I STILL HAVEN'T HEARD ANY-THING.
THAT MAKES IT TEN YEARS! WHAT ON EARTH IS HE RESEARCHING ...?
TOMONORI, DARLING! ♥
......
?!
DOWAAAAAHH!!

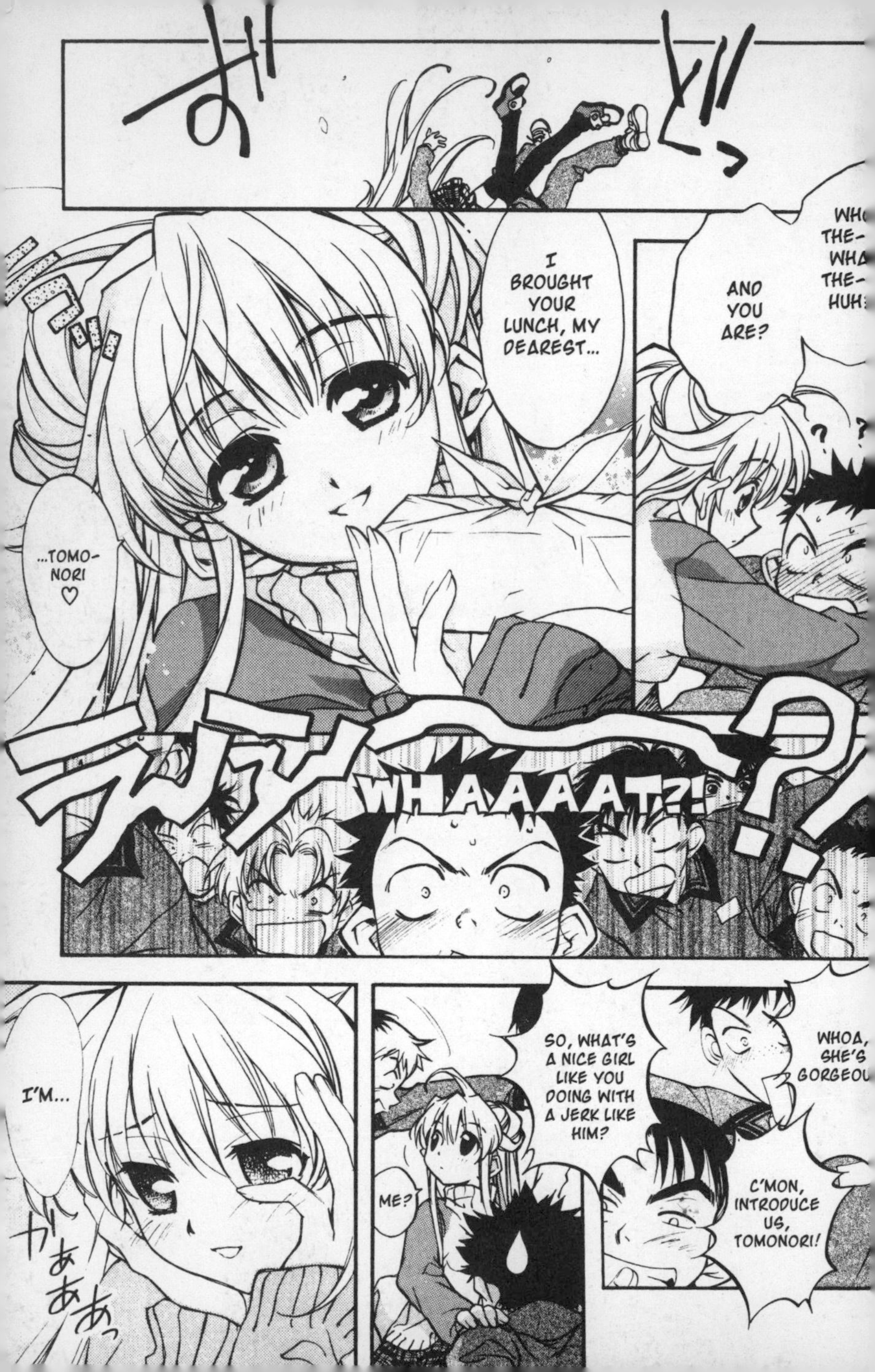
WH
THE-
WHA
THE-
HUH
AND YOU ARE?
I BROUGHT YOUR LUNCH, MY DEAREST...
...TOMO-NORI ♡
WHAAAAAT?!
WHOA, SHE'S GORGEOU
SO, WHAT'S A NICE GIRL LIKE YOU DOING WITH A JERK LIKE HIM?
C'MON, INTRODUCE US, TOMONORI!
ME?
I'M...

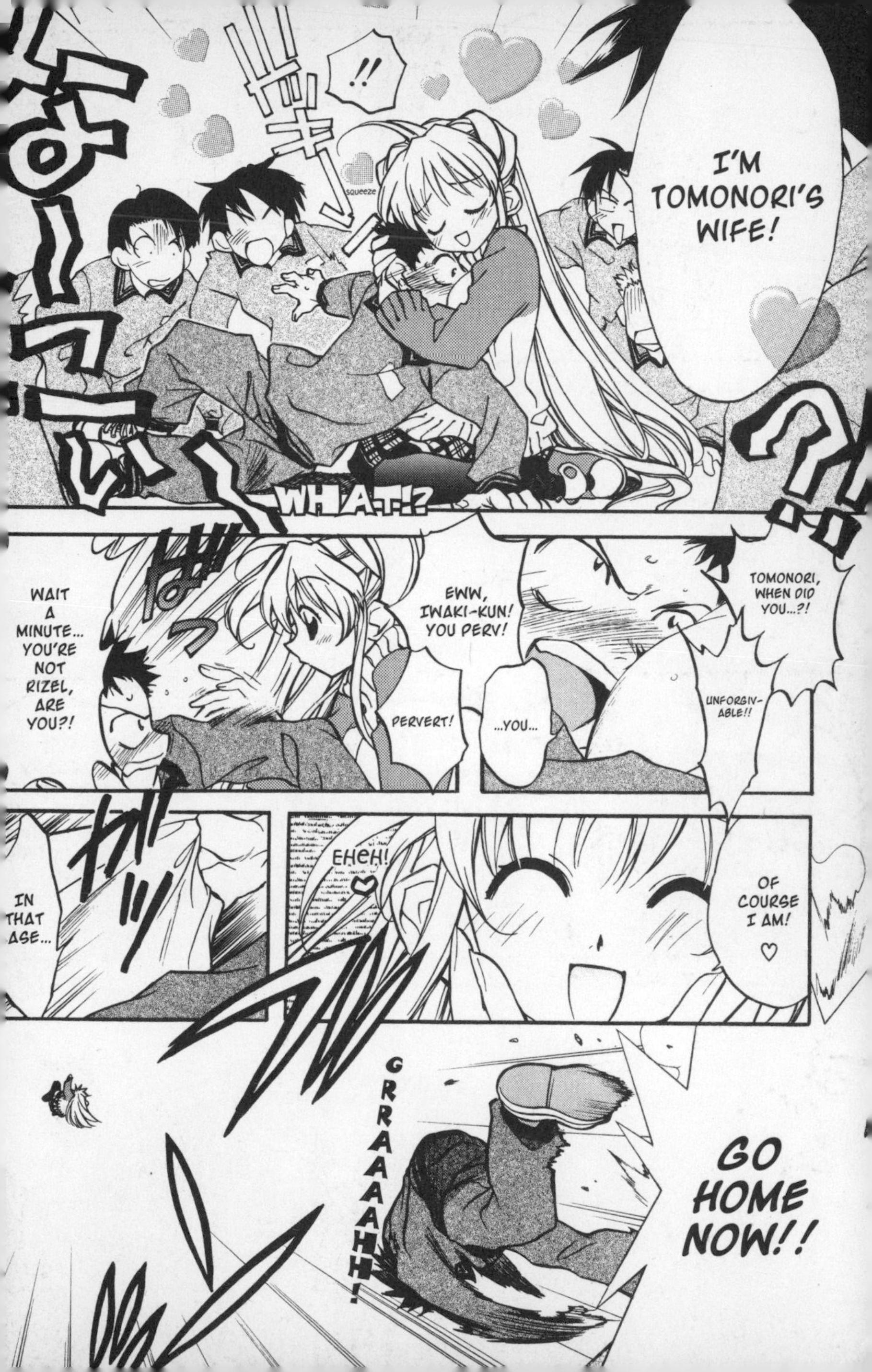
I'M TOMONORI'S WIFE!
!!
squeeze
WHAT!?
TOMONORI, WHEN DID YOU...?!
UNFORGIV-ABLE!!
...YOU...
EWW, IWAKI-KUN! YOU PERV!
PERVERT!
WAIT A MINUTE... YOU'RE NOT RIZEL, ARE YOU?!
OF COURSE I AM! ♡
EHEH! ♡
IN THAT ASE...
GO HOME NOW!!
GRRAAAAAHH!

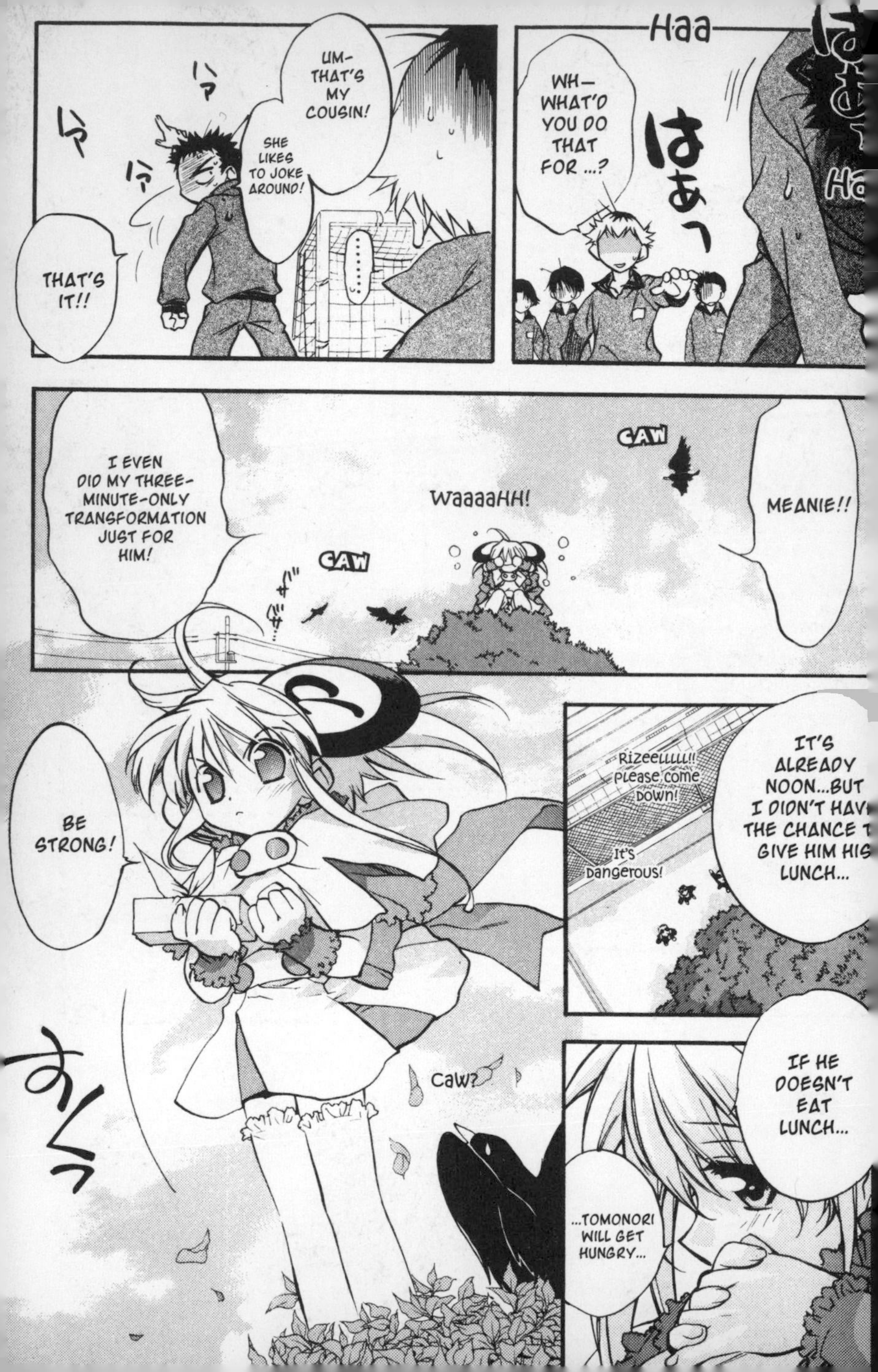

Haa
はあっ
Haa
WH— WHAT'D YOU DO THAT FOR ...?
UM— THAT'S MY COUSIN!
SHE LIKES TO JOKE AROUND!
......
THAT'S IT!!
MEANIE!!
CAW
WaaaaHH!
CAW
I EVEN DID MY THREE-MINUTE-ONLY TRANSFORMATION JUST FOR HIM!
IT'S ALREADY NOON...BUT I DIDN'T HAV THE CHANCE T GIVE HIM HIS LUNCH...
Rizeellllll!! Please come down!
It's dangerous!
IF HE DOESN'T EAT LUNCH...
...TOMONORI WILL GET HUNGRY...
BE STRONG!
Caw?

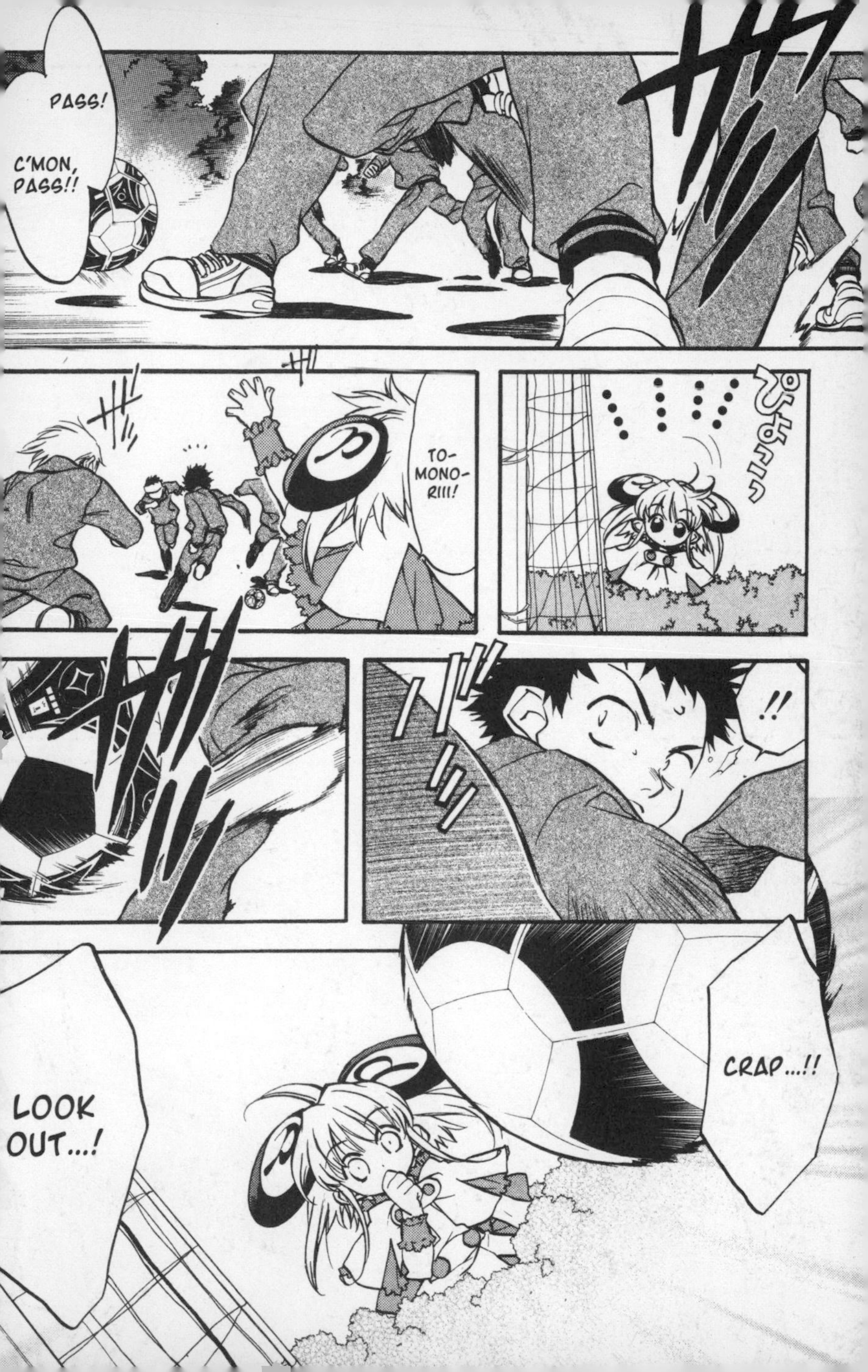
PASS!
C'MON, PASS!!
TO-MONO-RIIII!
!!
CRAP...!!
LOOK OUT...!

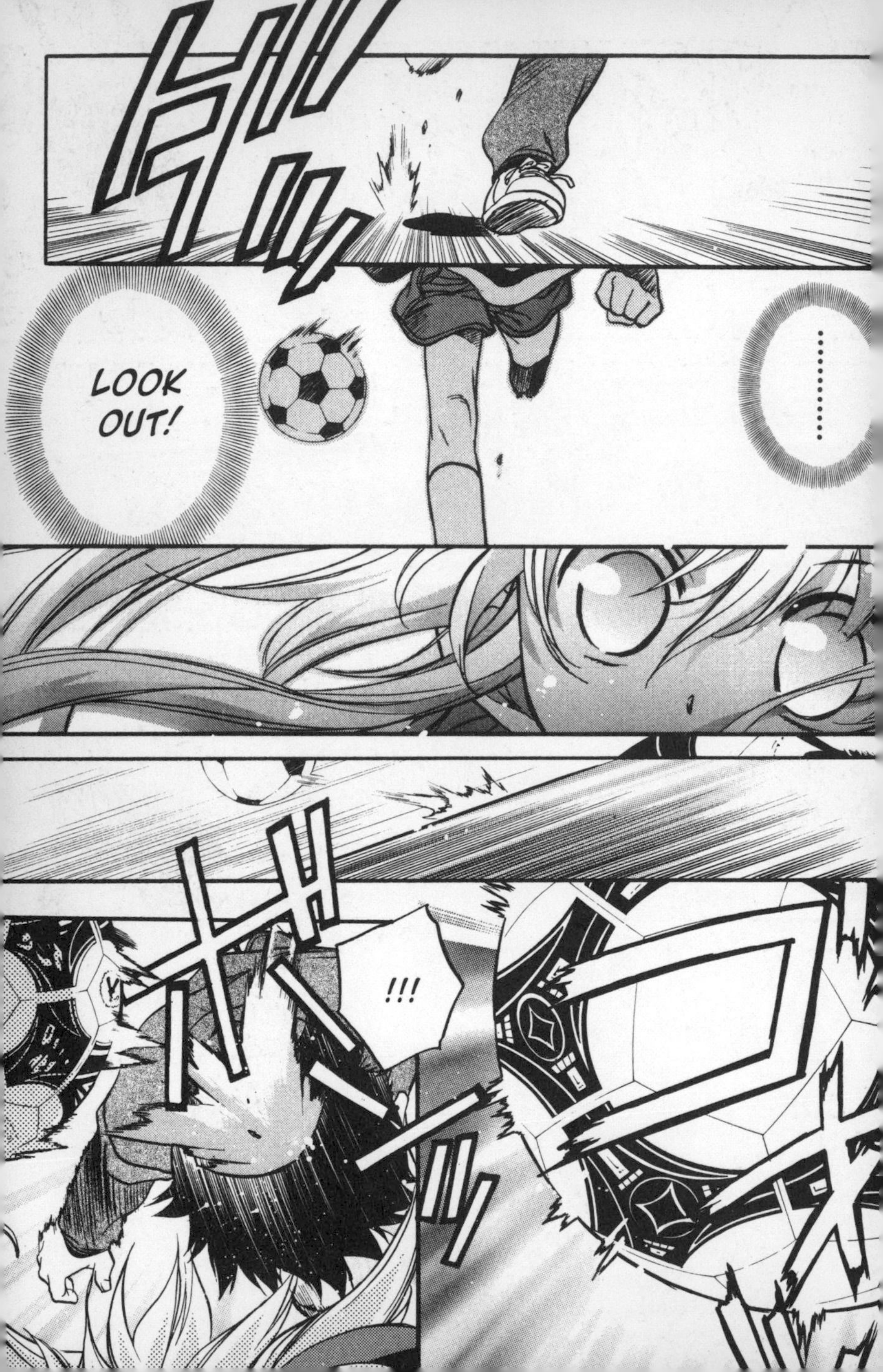

......
LOOK OUT!
!!!

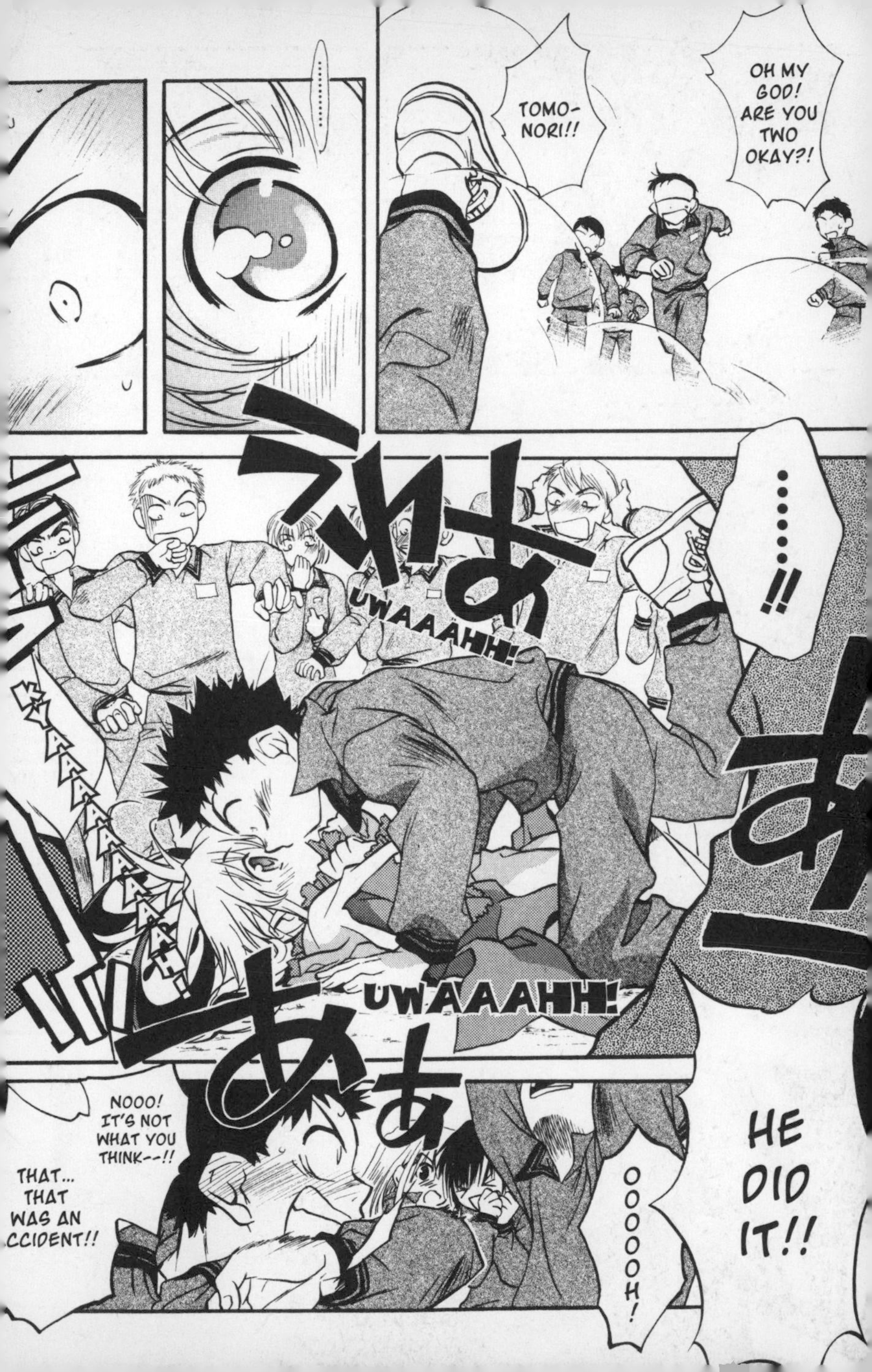

OH MY GOD! ARE YOU TWO OKAY?!
TOMO-NORI!!
......
......!!
うわあ
UWAAAAHH!
KYAAAAAAAAAAAH!
UWAAAAHH!
HE DID IT!!
OOOOOOH!
NOOO! IT'S NOT WHAT YOU THINK--!!
THAT... THAT WAS AN CCIDENT!!

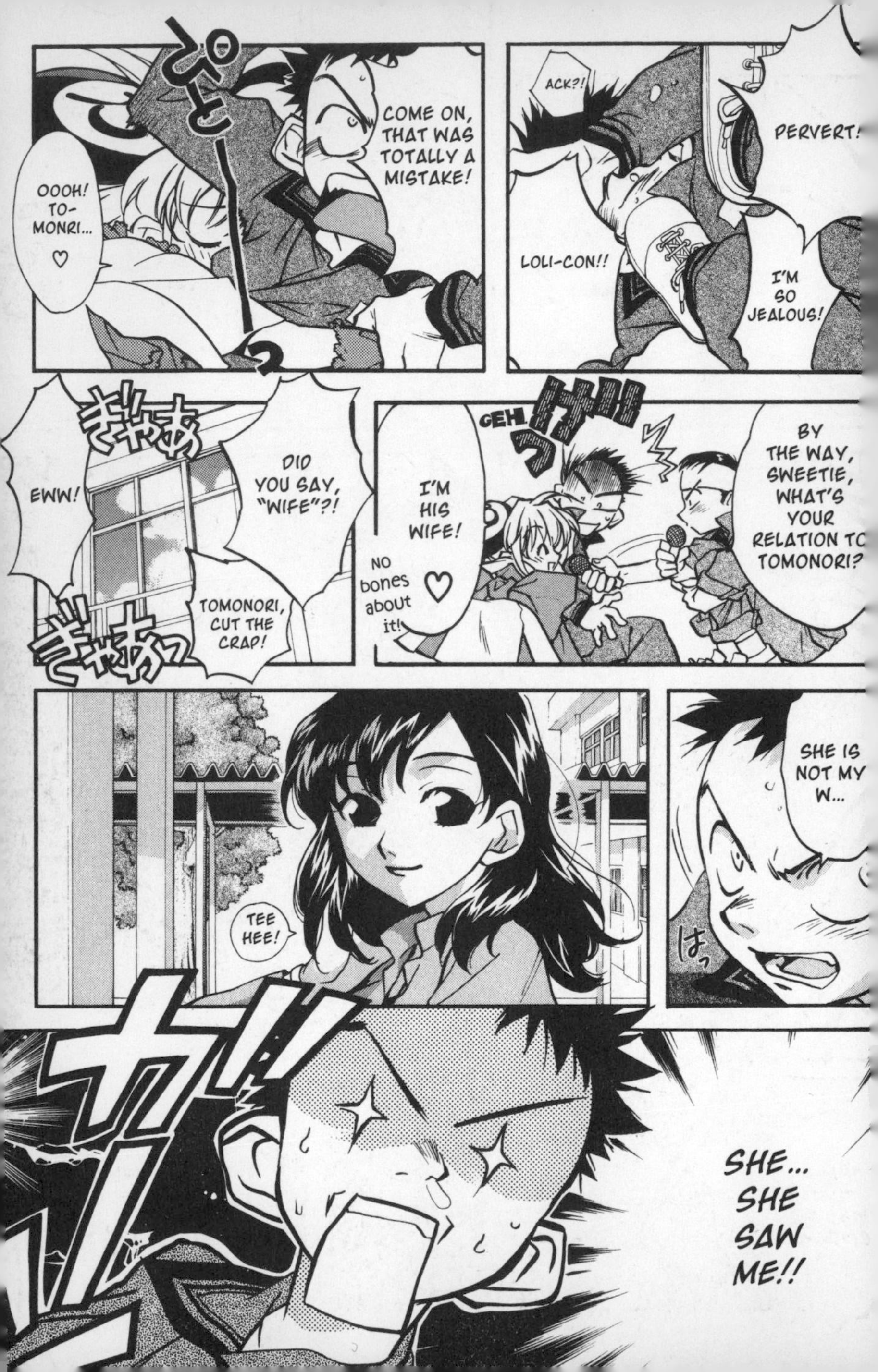
PERVERT!
ACK?!
I'M SO JEALOUS!
LOLI-CON!!
ぴとっ
COME ON, THAT WAS TOTALLY A MISTAKE!
OOOH! TO-MONRI... ♡
BY THE WAY, SWEETIE, WHAT'S YOUR RELATION TO TOMONORI?
GEH
げっ
I'M HIS WIFE!
No bones about it! ♡
DID YOU SAY, "WIFE"?!
きゃあ
EWW!
TOMONORI, CUT THE CRAP!
ぎゃあっ
SHE IS NOT MY W...
はっ
TEE HEE!
SHE... SHE SAW ME!!

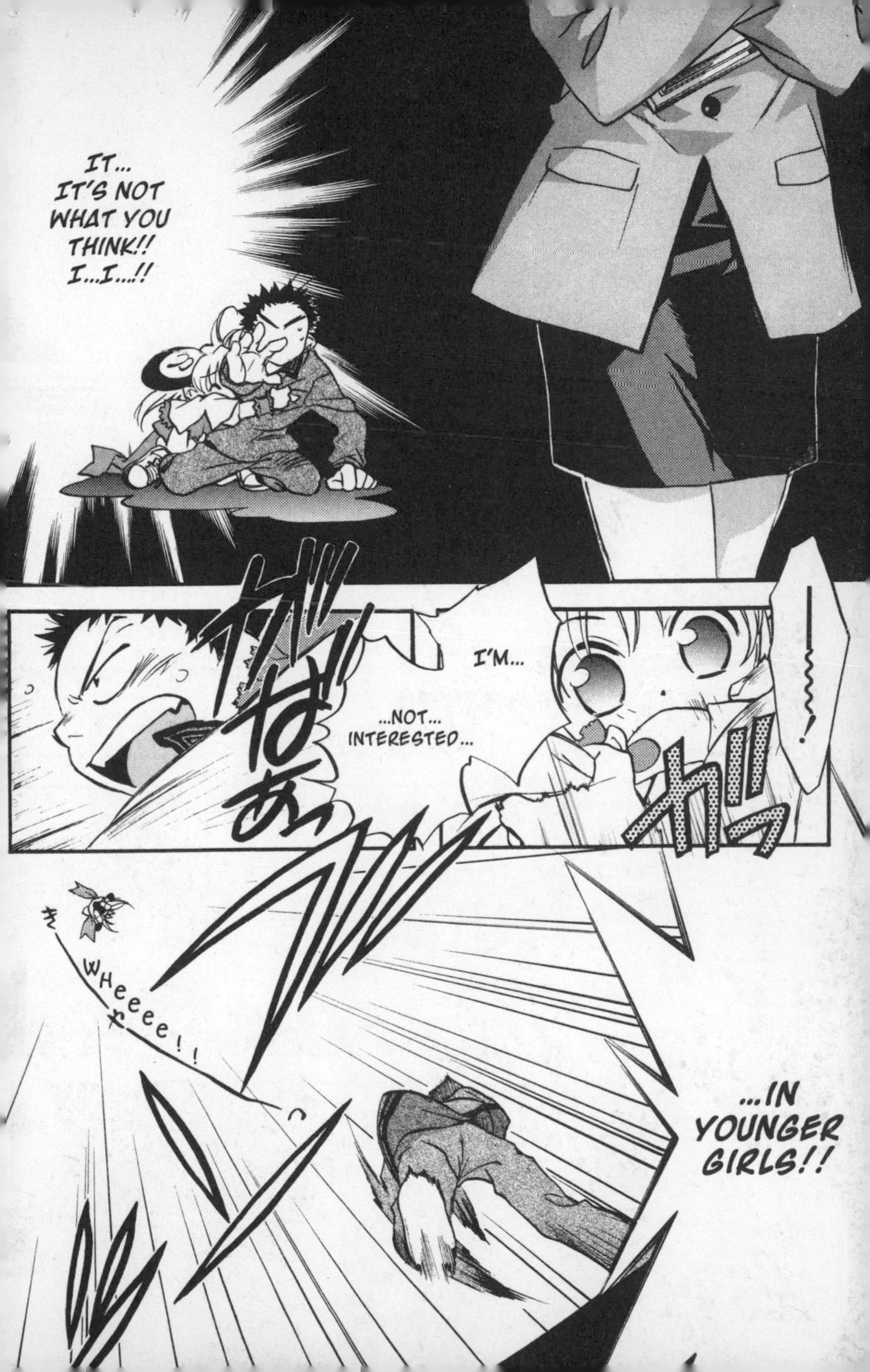
IT...
IT'S NOT
WHAT YOU
THINK!!
I...I...!!
...!
I'M...
...NOT...
INTERESTED...
...IN
YOUNGER
GIRLS!!
WHeeee!!

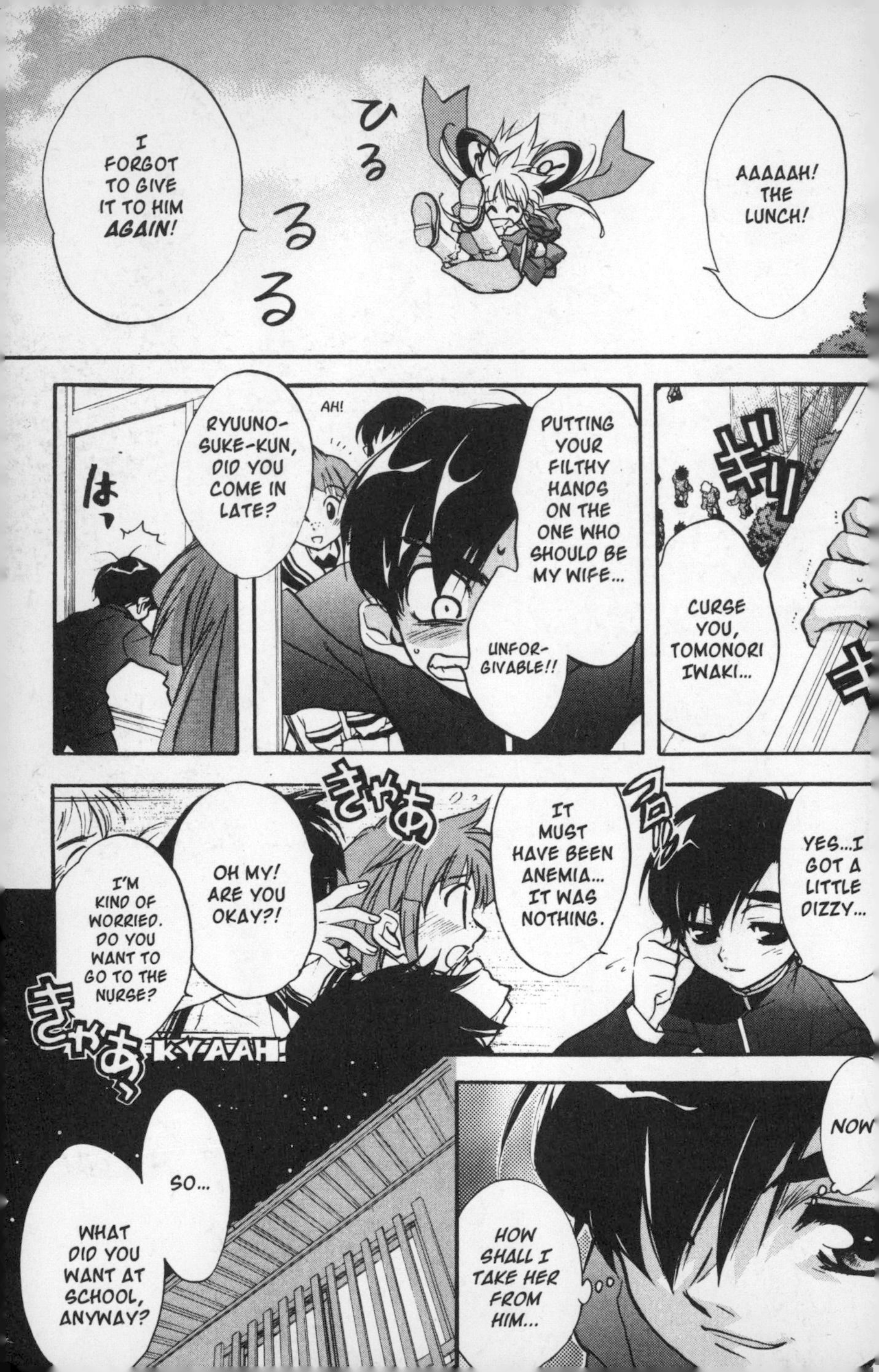
AAAAAH! THE LUNCH!
ひるるる
I FORGOT TO GIVE IT TO HIM AGAIN!
ギリ
CURSE YOU, TOMONORI IWAKI...
PUTTING YOUR FILTHY HANDS ON THE ONE WHO SHOULD BE MY WIFE...
UNFORGIVABLE!!
AH!
RYUUNOSUKE-KUN, DID YOU COME IN LATE?
は
YES...I GOT A LITTLE DIZZY...
IT MUST HAVE BEEN ANEMIA... IT WAS NOTHING.
きゃあ
OH MY! ARE YOU OKAY?!
I'M KIND OF WORRIED. DO YOU WANT TO GO TO THE NURSE?
きゃあ
KYAAH!
NOW
HOW SHALL I TAKE HER FROM HIM...
SO...
WHAT DID YOU WANT AT SCHOOL, ANYWAY?

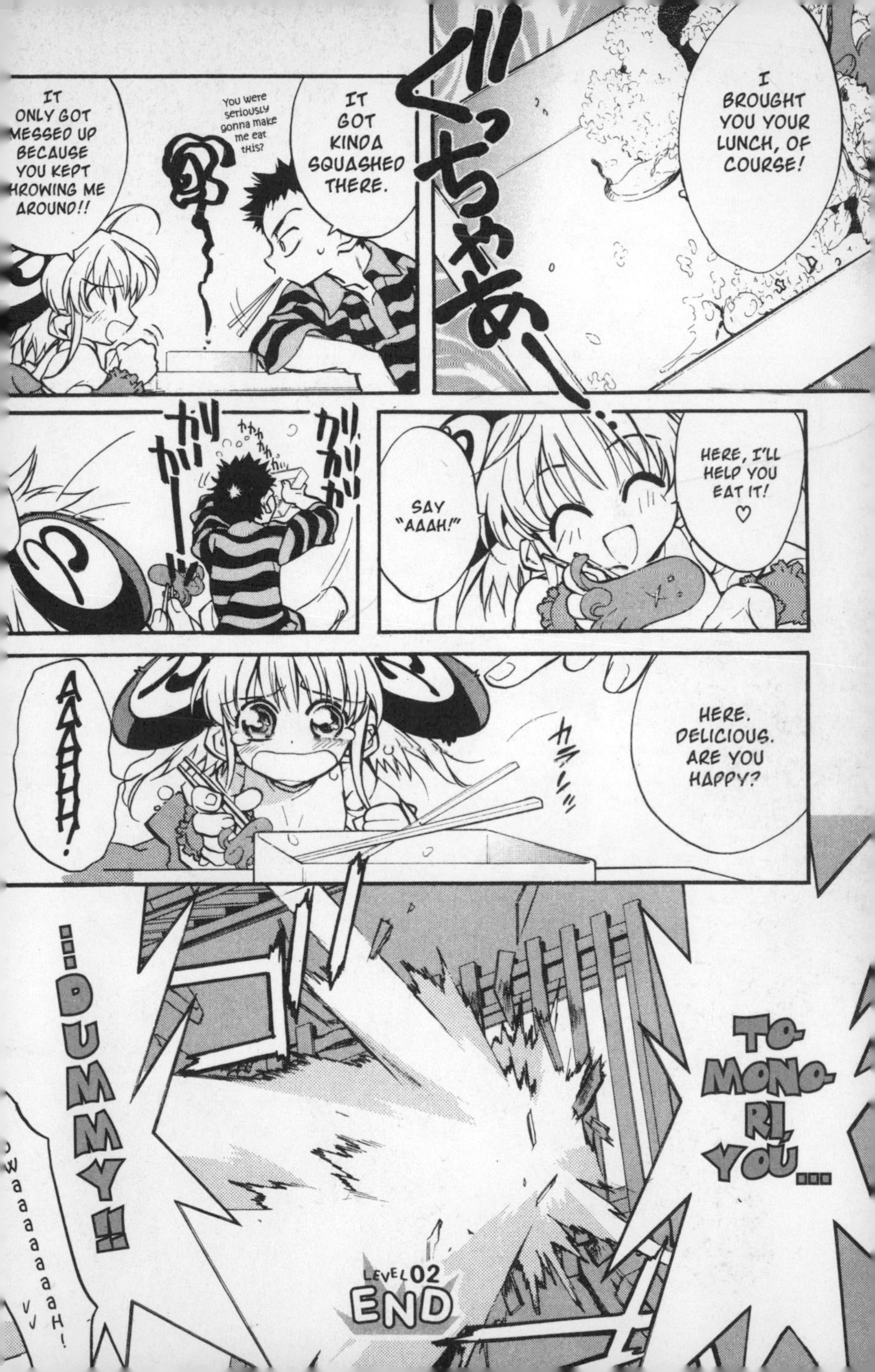
I BROUGHT YOU YOUR LUNCH, OF COURSE!
ぐっちゃぁ〜…
IT GOT KINDA SQUASHED THERE.
You were seriously gonna make me eat this?
IT ONLY GOT MESSED UP BECAUSE YOU KEPT HROWING ME AROUND!!
HERE, I'LL HELP YOU EAT IT! ♡
SAY "AAAH!"
ガリガリガリ
がりがりー
HERE. DELICIOUS. ARE YOU HAPPY?
AAAHHH!
TO-MONO-RI, YOU...
...DUMMY!!
Waaaaaaaaaah!
LEVEL 02 END

LEVEL 03 Love Comes with a Misunderstanding

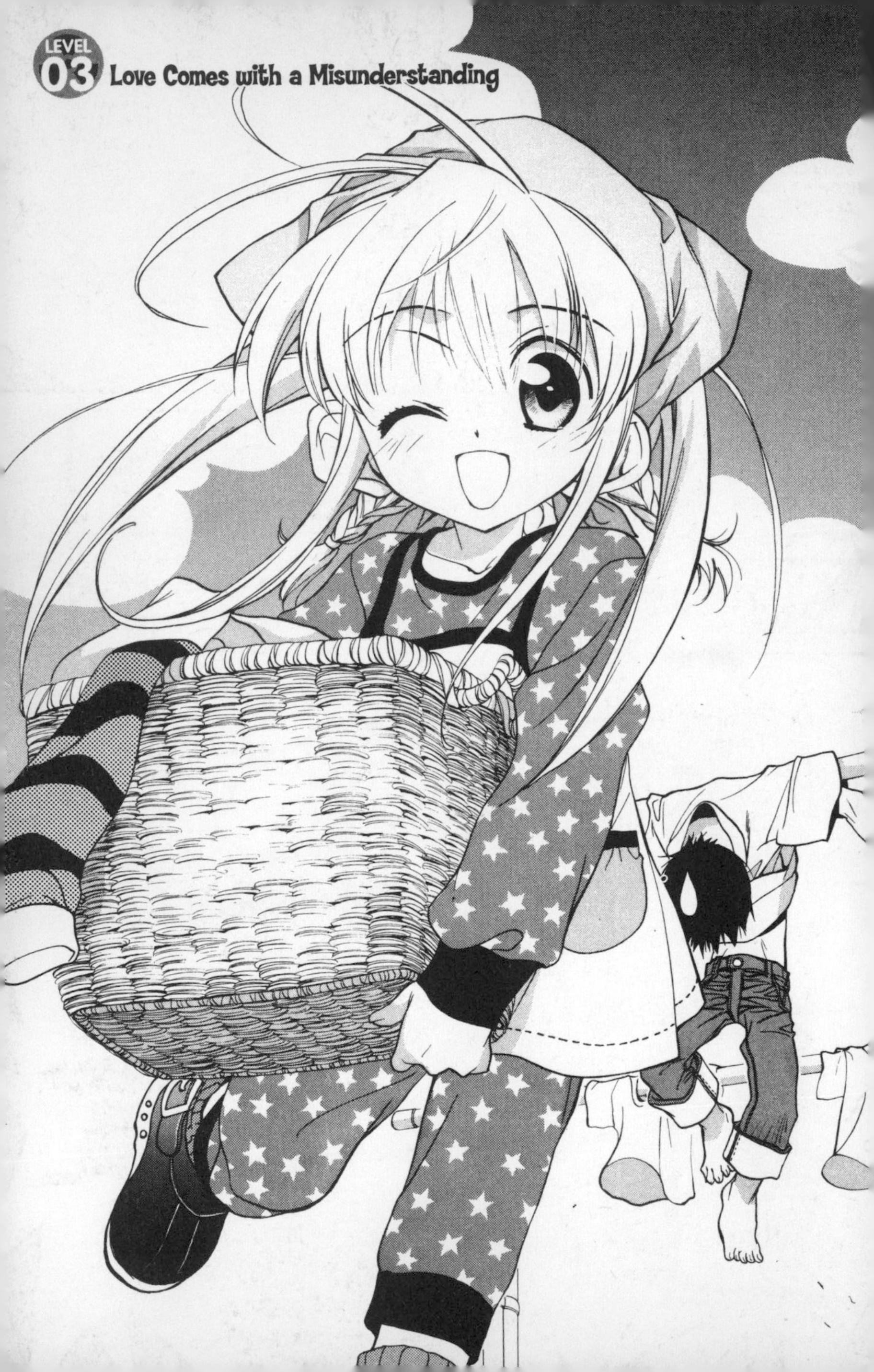

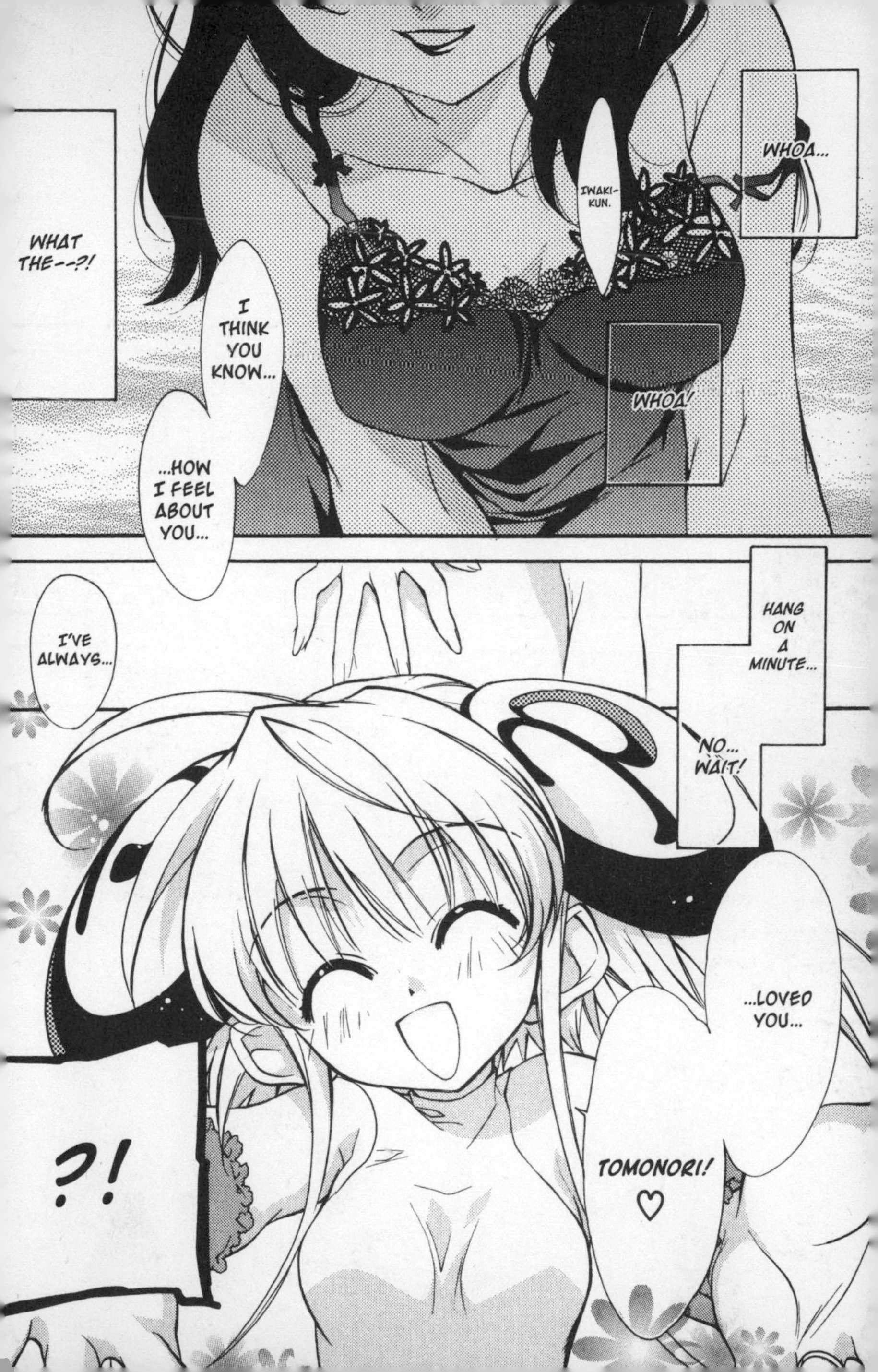
WHOA...
IWAKI-KUN.
WHOA!
I THINK YOU KNOW...
...HOW I FEEL ABOUT YOU...
WHAT THE--?!
HANG ON A MINUTE...
NO... WAIT!
I'VE ALWAYS...
...LOVED YOU...
TOMONORI! ♡
?!

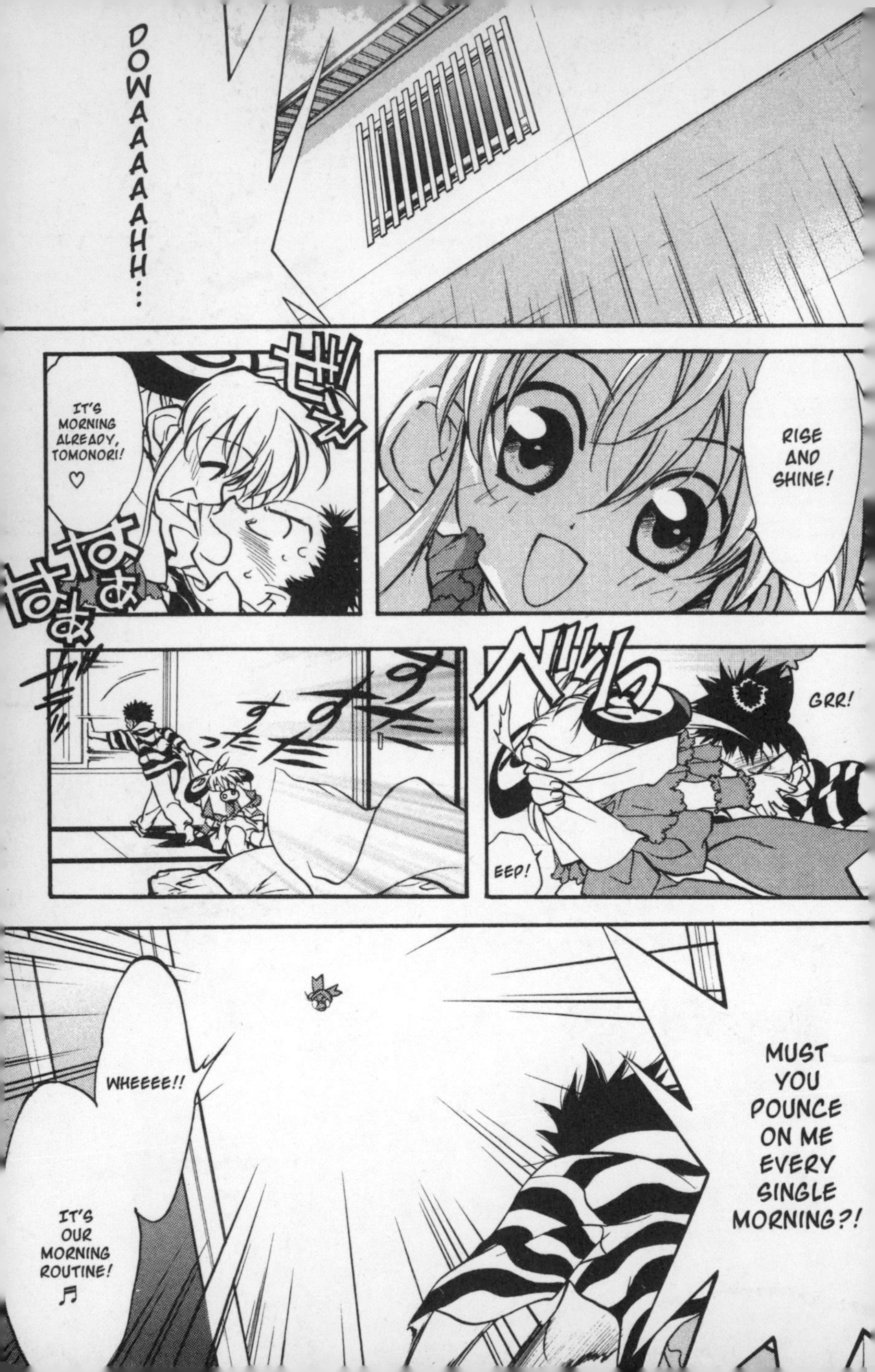
DOWAAAAAAAHH...
RISE AND SHINE!
IT'S MORNING ALREADY, TOMONORI! ♡
GRR!
EEP!
MUST YOU POUNCE ON ME EVERY SINGLE MORNING?!
WHEEEE!!
IT'S OUR MORNING ROUTINE! ♬

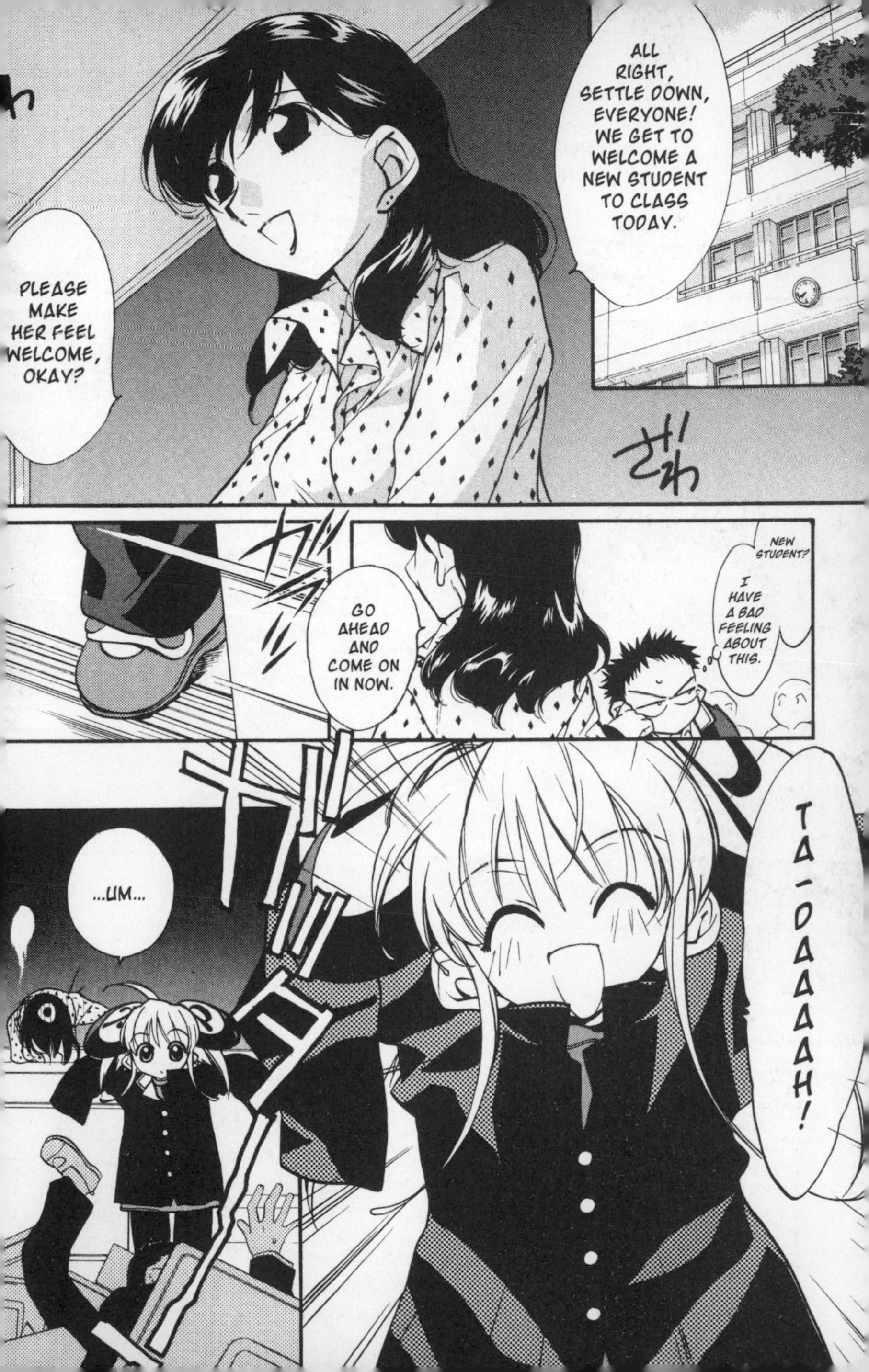
ALL RIGHT, SETTLE DOWN, EVERYONE! WE GET TO WELCOME A NEW STUDENT TO CLASS TODAY.
PLEASE MAKE HER FEEL WELCOME, OKAY?
NEW STUDENT?
I HAVE A BAD FEELING ABOUT THIS.
GO AHEAD AND COME ON IN NOW.
TA-DAAAAAH!
...UM...

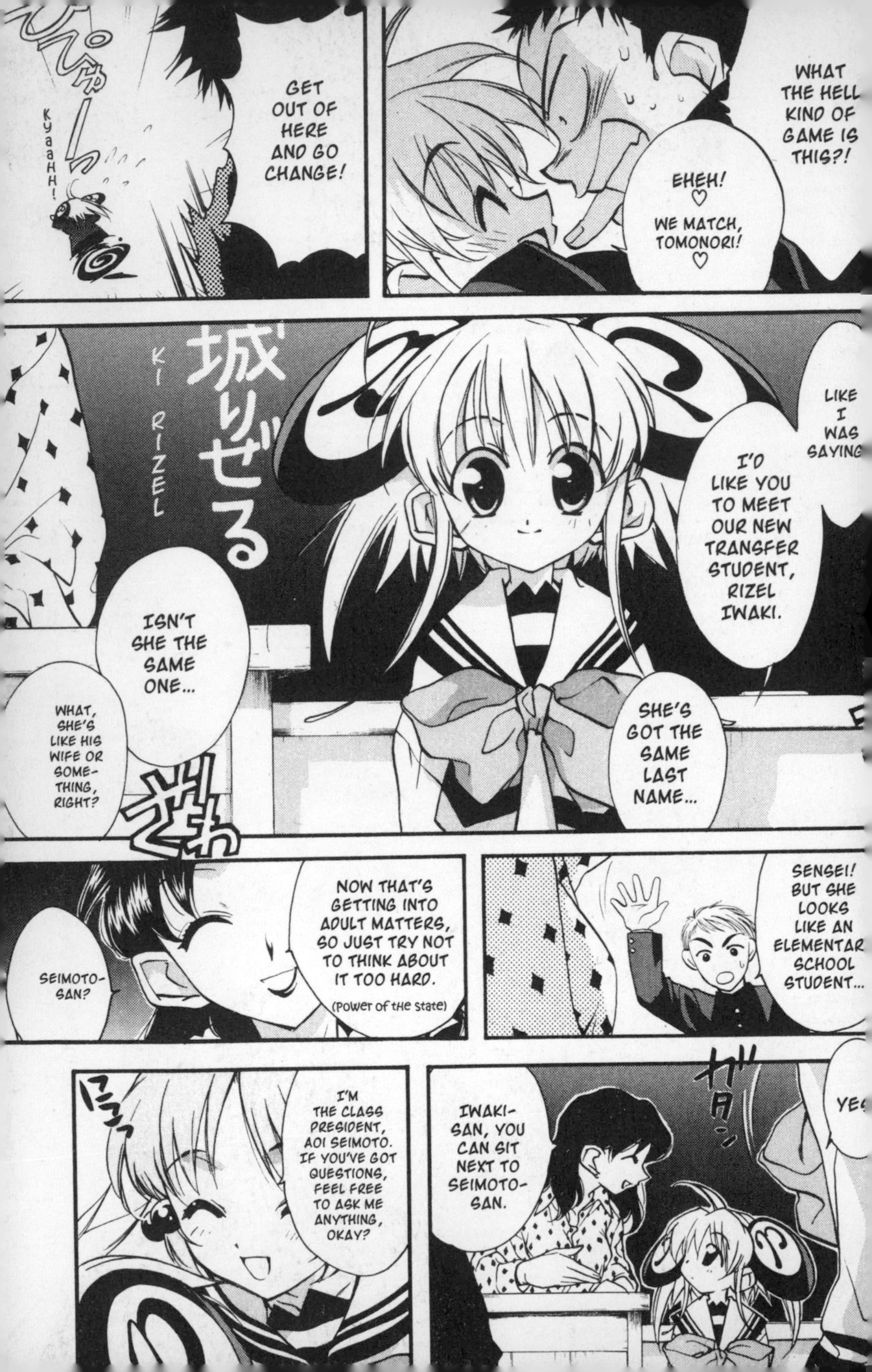
WHAT THE HELL KIND OF GAME IS THIS?!
EHEH! ♡ WE MATCH, TOMONORI! ♡
GET OUT OF HERE AND GO CHANGE!
ぴゅーっ
KYAAHH!
LIKE I WAS SAYING
I'D LIKE YOU TO MEET OUR NEW TRANSFER STUDENT, RIZEL IWAKI.
城りぜる
KI RIZEL
SHE'S GOT THE SAME LAST NAME...
ISN'T SHE THE SAME ONE...
WHAT, SHE'S LIKE HIS WIFE OR SOMETHING, RIGHT?
ざわ
SENSEI! BUT SHE LOOKS LIKE AN ELEMENTAR SCHOOL STUDENT...
NOW THAT'S GETTING INTO ADULT MATTERS, SO JUST TRY NOT TO THINK ABOUT IT TOO HARD.
(Power of the state)
SEIMOTO-SAN?
YE
ガタン
IWAKI-SAN, YOU CAN SIT NEXT TO SEIMOTO-SAN.
I'M THE CLASS PRESIDENT, AOI SEIMOTO. IF YOU'VE GOT QUESTIONS, FEEL FREE TO ASK ME ANYTHING, OKAY?
にこっ

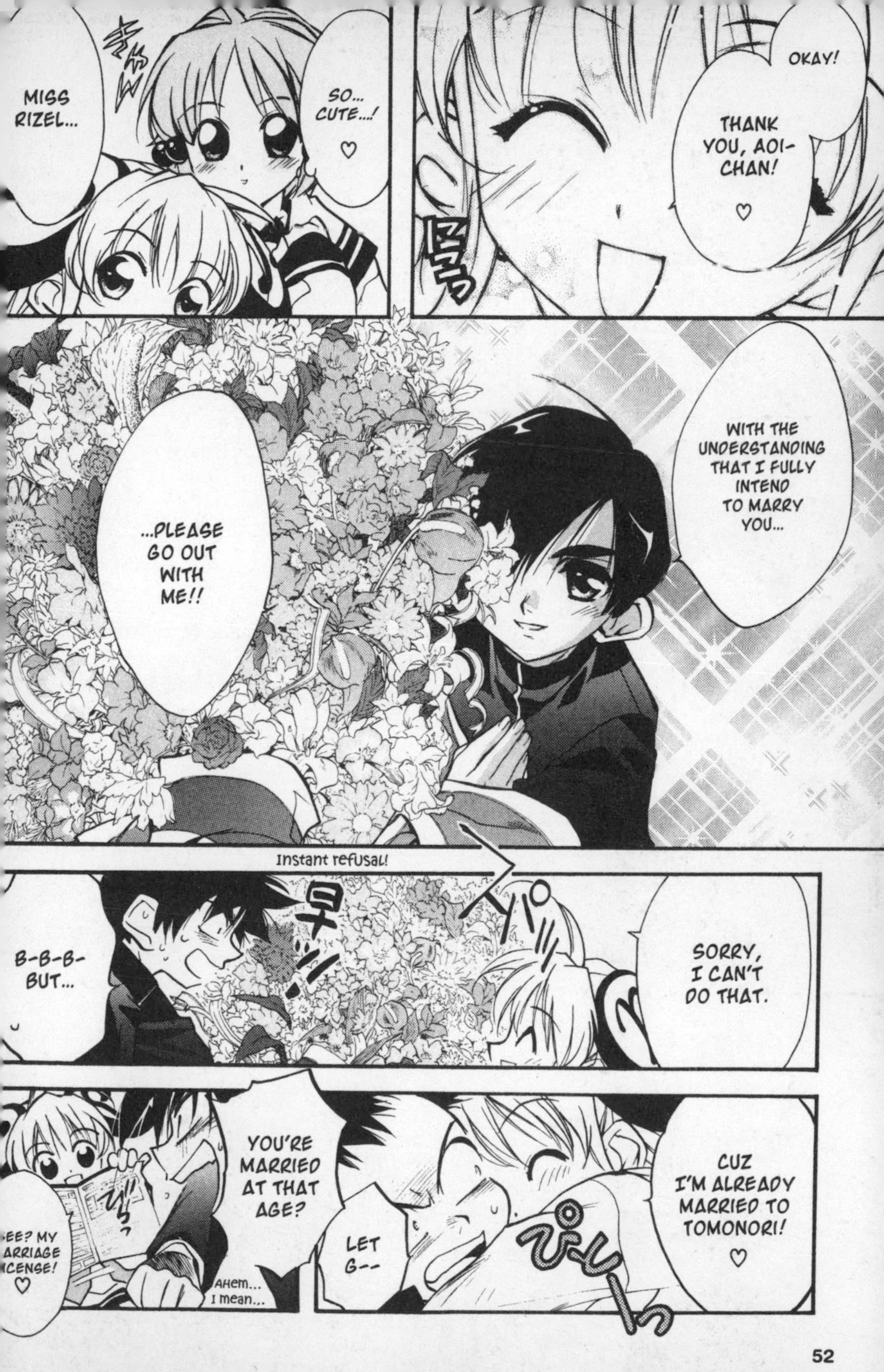
OKAY!
THANK YOU, AOI-CHAN! ♡
SO... CUTE...! ♡
MISS RIZEL...
WITH THE UNDERSTANDING THAT I FULLY INTEND TO MARRY YOU...
...PLEASE GO OUT WITH ME!!
Instant refusal!
SORRY, I CAN'T DO THAT.
B-B-B-BUT...
CUZ I'M ALREADY MARRIED TO TOMONORI! ♡
LET G--
YOU'RE MARRIED AT THAT AGE?
Ahem... I mean...
EE? MY ARRIAGE ICENSE! ♡

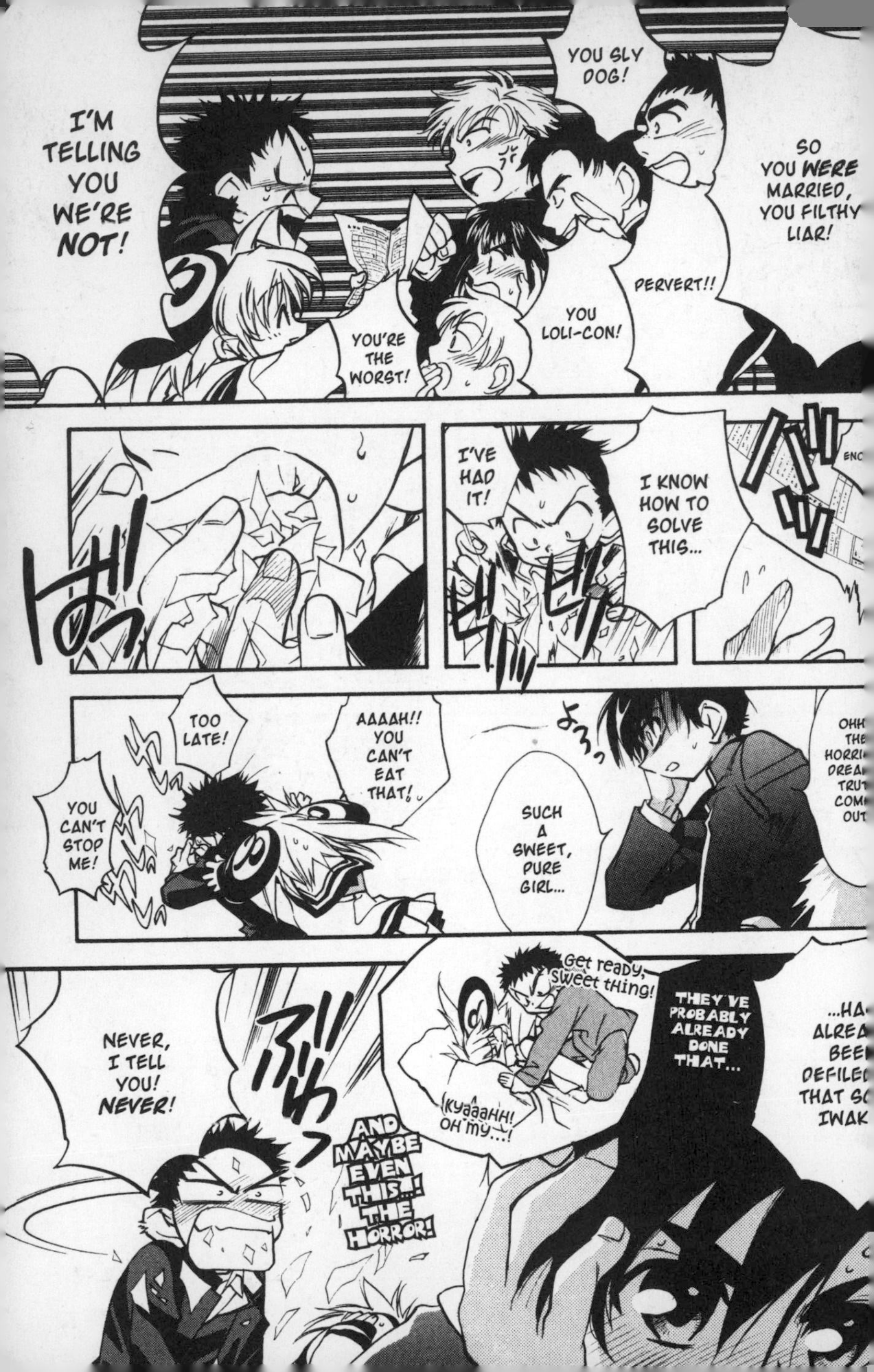
SO YOU WERE MARRIED, YOU FILTHY LIAR!
YOU SLY DOG!
PERVERT!!
YOU LOLI-CON!
YOU'RE THE WORST!
I'M TELLING YOU WE'RE NOT!
I KNOW HOW TO SOLVE THIS...
I'VE HAD IT!
SUCH A SWEET, PURE GIRL...
AAAAH!! YOU CAN'T EAT THAT!
TOO LATE!
YOU CAN'T STOP ME!
THEY'VE PROBABLY ALREADY DONE THAT...
Get ready, sweet thing!
Kyaaahh! Oh my...!
AND MAYBE EVEN THIS...! THE HORROR!
NEVER, I TELL YOU! NEVER!

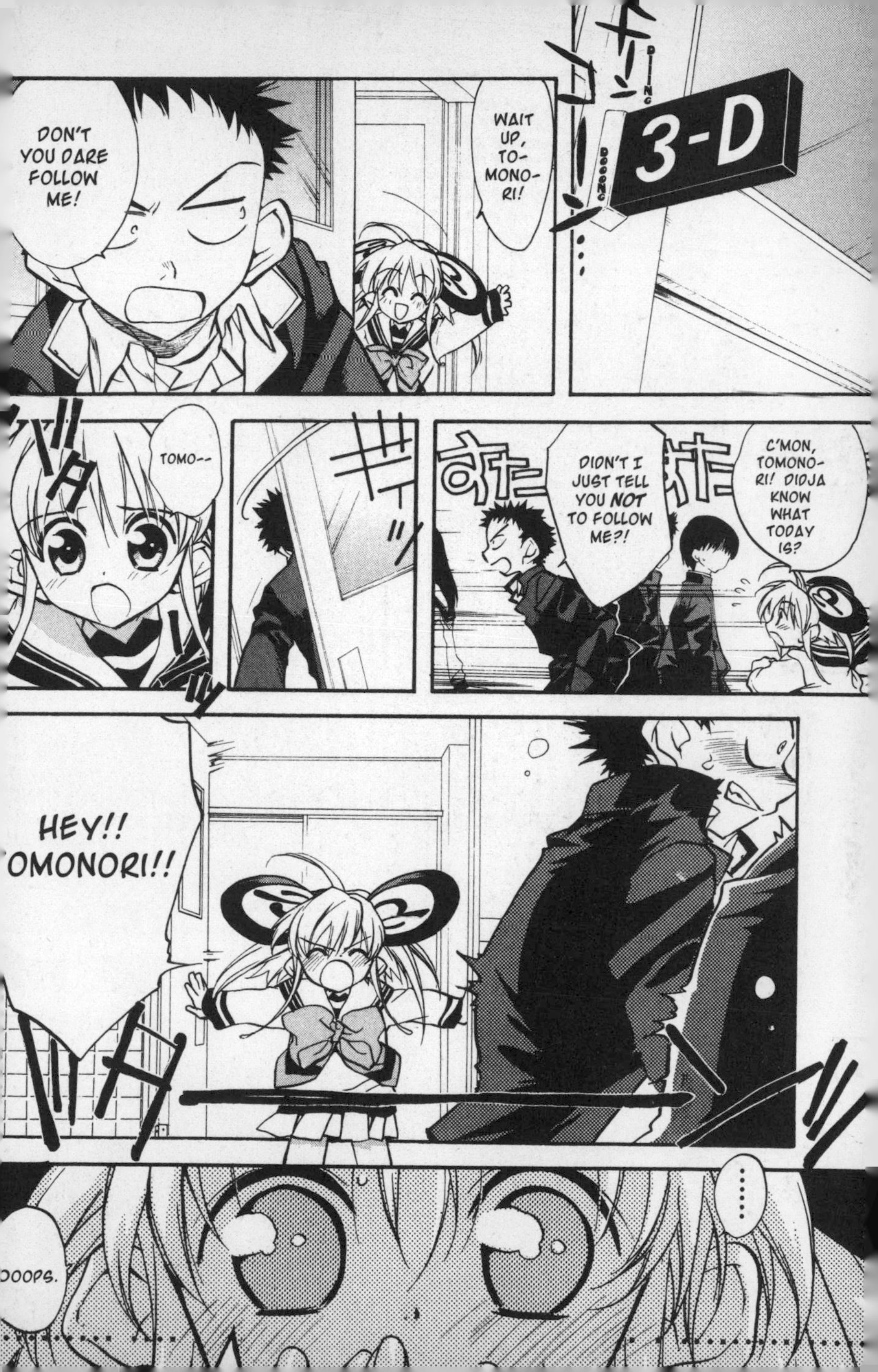
DIING
DOONG
3-D
WAIT UP, TO-MONO-RI!
DON'T YOU DARE FOLLOW ME!
C'MON, TOMONO-RI! DIDJA KNOW WHAT TODAY IS?
DIDN'T I JUST TELL YOU **NOT** TO FOLLOW ME?!
TOMO--
HEY!! TOMONORI!!
......
OOPS.

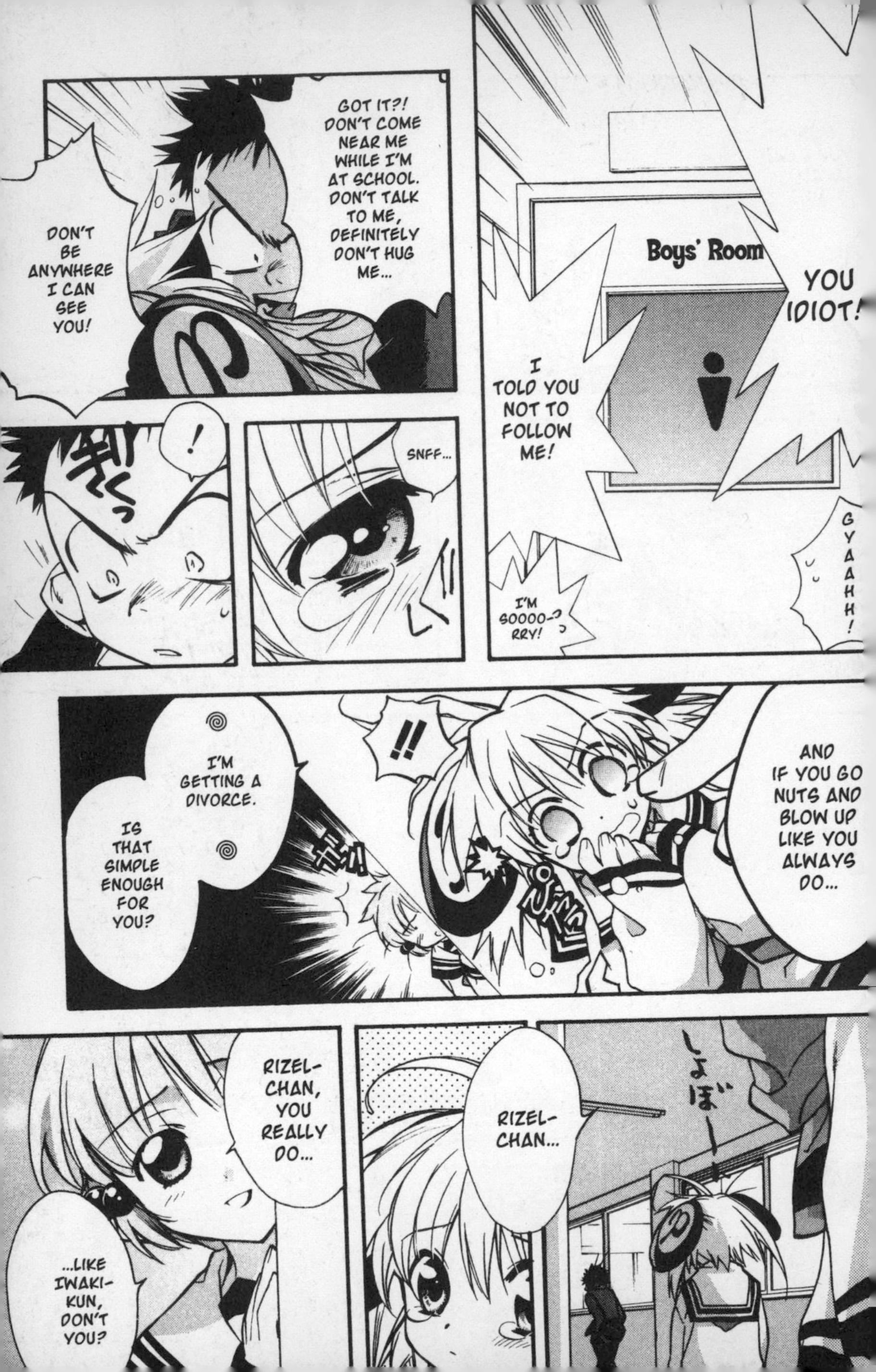
Boys' Room
YOU IDIOT!
I TOLD YOU NOT TO FOLLOW ME!
GYAAHH!
I'M SOOOO-RRY!
GOT IT?! DON'T COME NEAR ME WHILE I'M AT SCHOOL. DON'T TALK TO ME, DEFINITELY DON'T HUG ME...
DON'T BE ANYWHERE I CAN SEE YOU!
SNFF...
!
ぎくっ
AND IF YOU GO NUTS AND BLOW UP LIKE YOU ALWAYS DO...
!!
I'M GETTING A DIVORCE.
IS THAT SIMPLE ENOUGH FOR YOU?
しょぼー
RIZEL-CHAN...
RIZEL-CHAN, YOU REALLY DO...
...LIKE IWAKI-KUN, DON'T YOU?

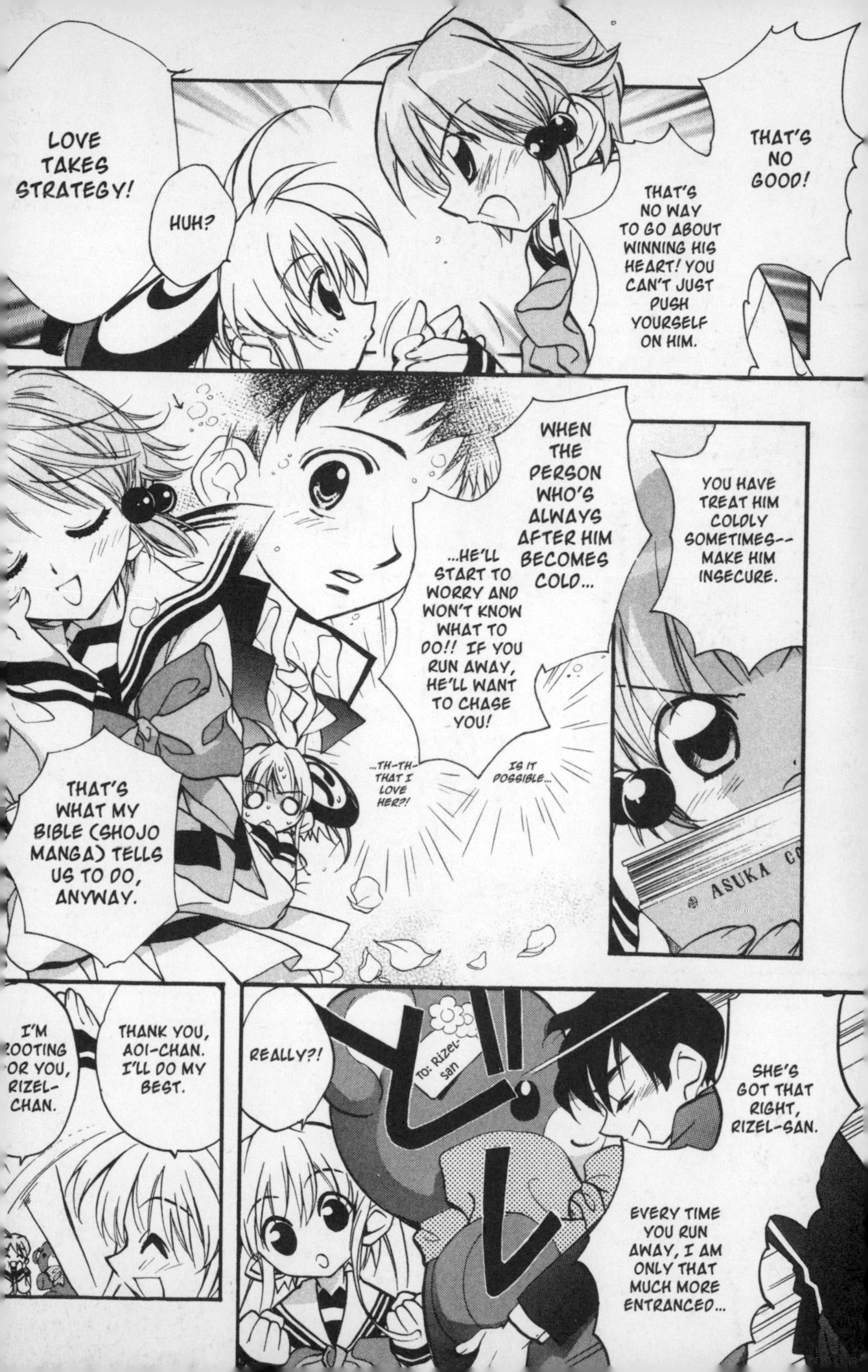
THAT'S NO GOOD!
THAT'S NO WAY TO GO ABOUT WINNING HIS HEART! YOU CAN'T JUST PUSH YOURSELF ON HIM.
HUH?
LOVE TAKES STRATEGY!
YOU HAVE TREAT HIM COLDLY SOMETIMES--MAKE HIM INSECURE.
ASUKA CO
WHEN THE PERSON WHO'S ALWAYS AFTER HIM BECOMES COLD...
...HE'LL START TO WORRY AND WON'T KNOW WHAT TO DO!! IF YOU RUN AWAY, HE'LL WANT TO CHASE YOU!
IS IT POSSIBLE...
...TH-TH-THAT I LOVE HER?!
THAT'S WHAT MY BIBLE (SHOJO MANGA) TELLS US TO DO, ANYWAY.
SHE'S GOT THAT RIGHT, RIZEL-SAN.
EVERY TIME YOU RUN AWAY, I AM ONLY THAT MUCH MORE ENTRANCED...
TO: Rizel-san
REALLY?!
THANK YOU, AOI-CHAN. I'LL DO MY BEST.
I'M ROOTING FOR YOU, RIZEL-CHAN.

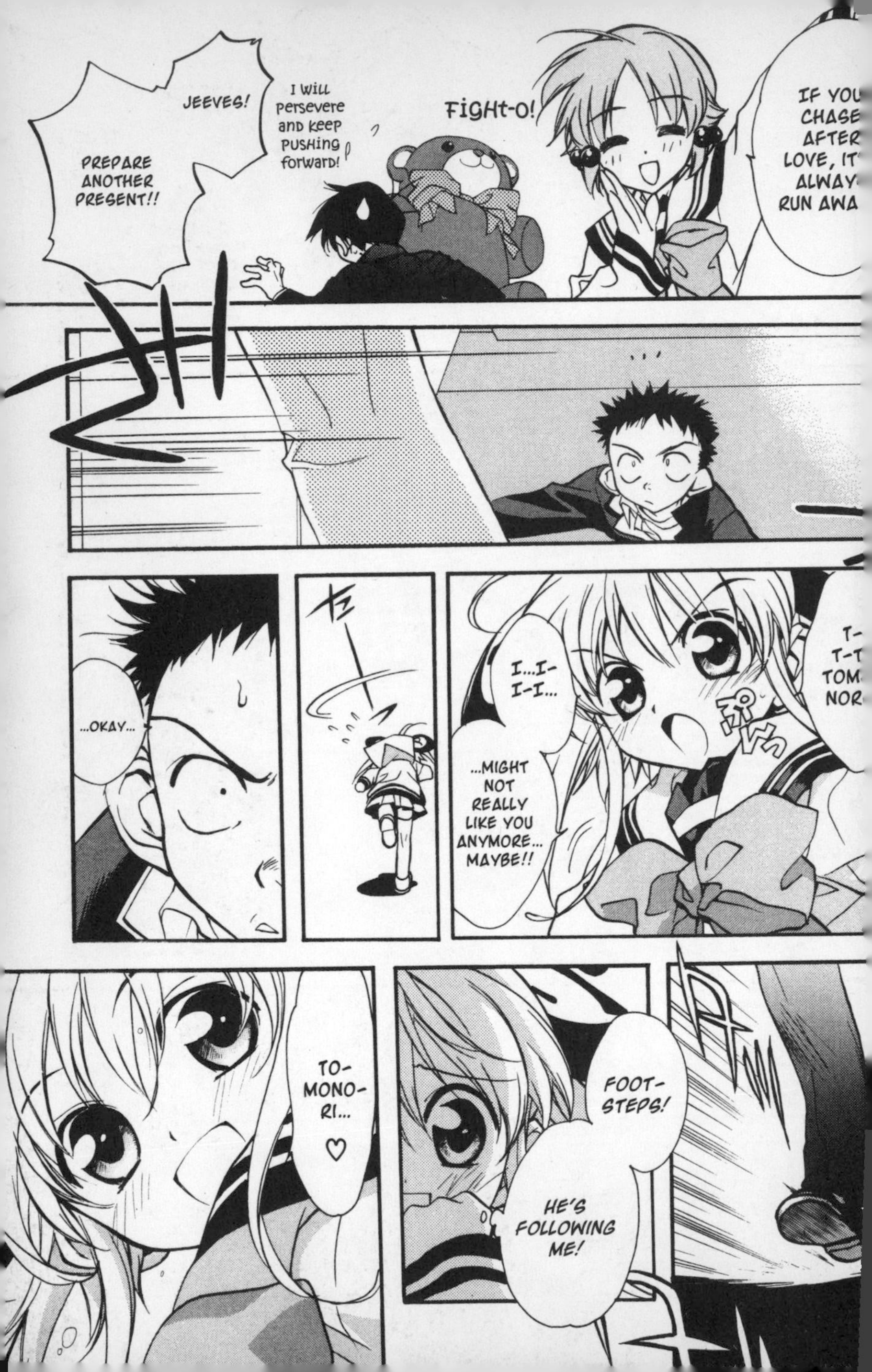
IF YOU CHASE AFTER LOVE, IT' ALWAY RUN AWA
FiGHt-O!
I will persevere and keep pushing forward!
JEEVES!
PREPARE ANOTHER PRESENT!!
T- T-T TOM NOR
I...I- I-I...
...MIGHT NOT REALLY LIKE YOU ANYMORE... MAYBE!!
...OKAY...
FOOT-STEPS!
HE'S FOLLOWING ME!
TO-MONO-RI... ♡

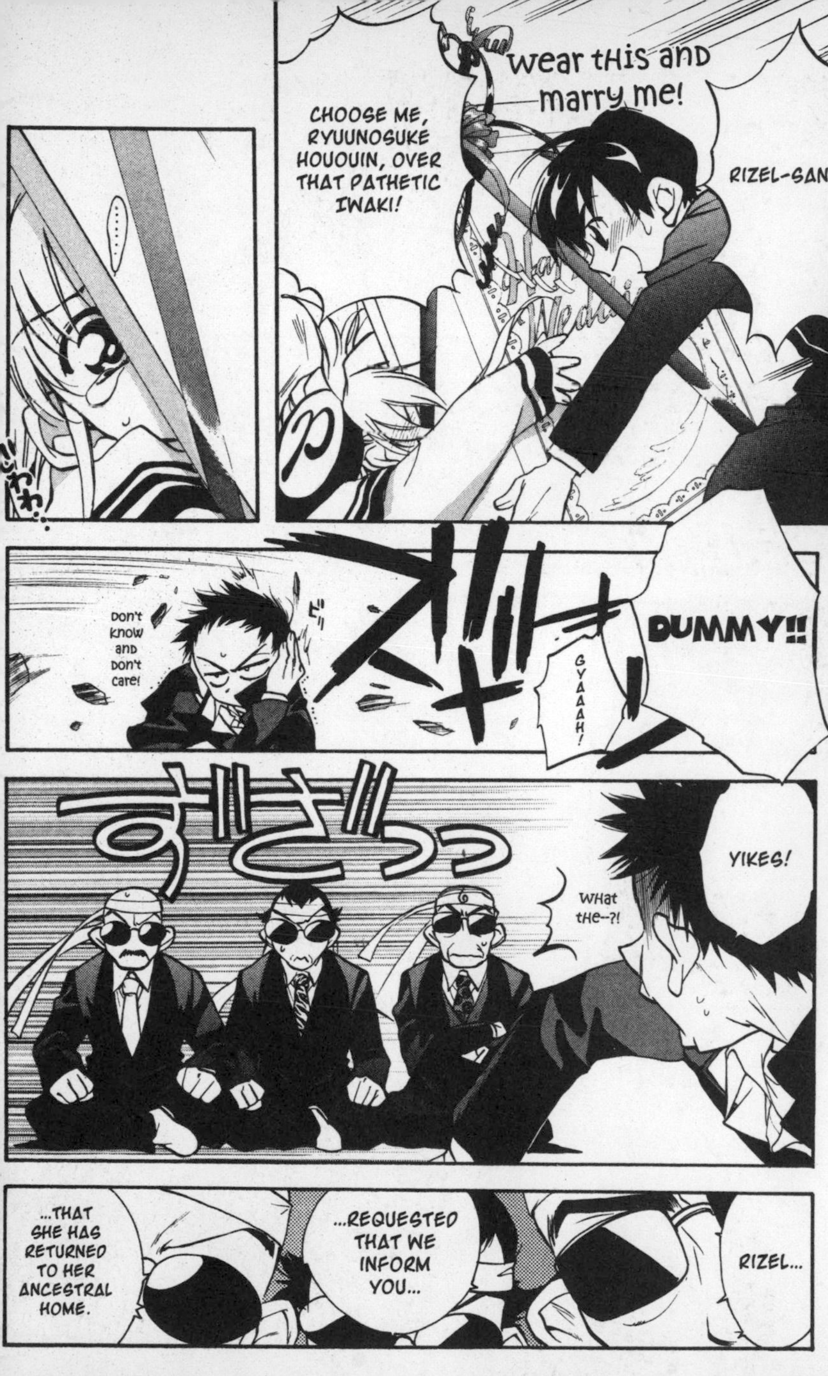
RIZEL-SAN!
CHOOSE ME, RYUUNOSUKE HOUOUIN, OVER THAT PATHETIC IWAKI!
Wear tHIS and marry me!
......
DUMMY!!
GYAAAAH!
Don't know and Don't care!
YIKES!
WHat tHe--?!
RIZEL...
...REQUESTED THAT WE INFORM YOU...
...THAT SHE HAS RETURNED TO HER ANCESTRAL HOME.

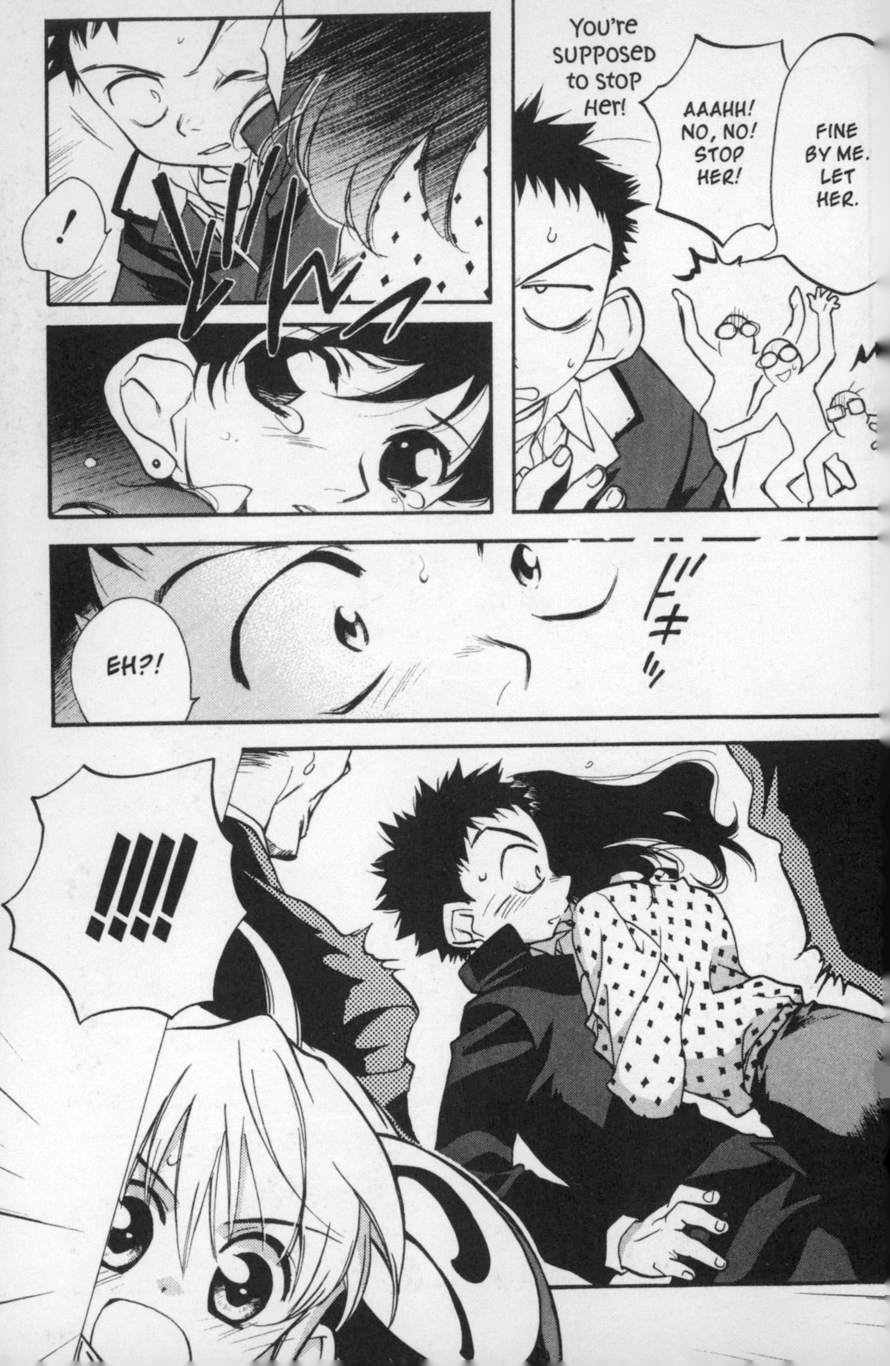
FINE BY ME. LET HER.
AAAHH! NO, NO! STOP HER!
You're SUPPOSED to STOP Her!
!
ドキッ
EH?!
!!!!!

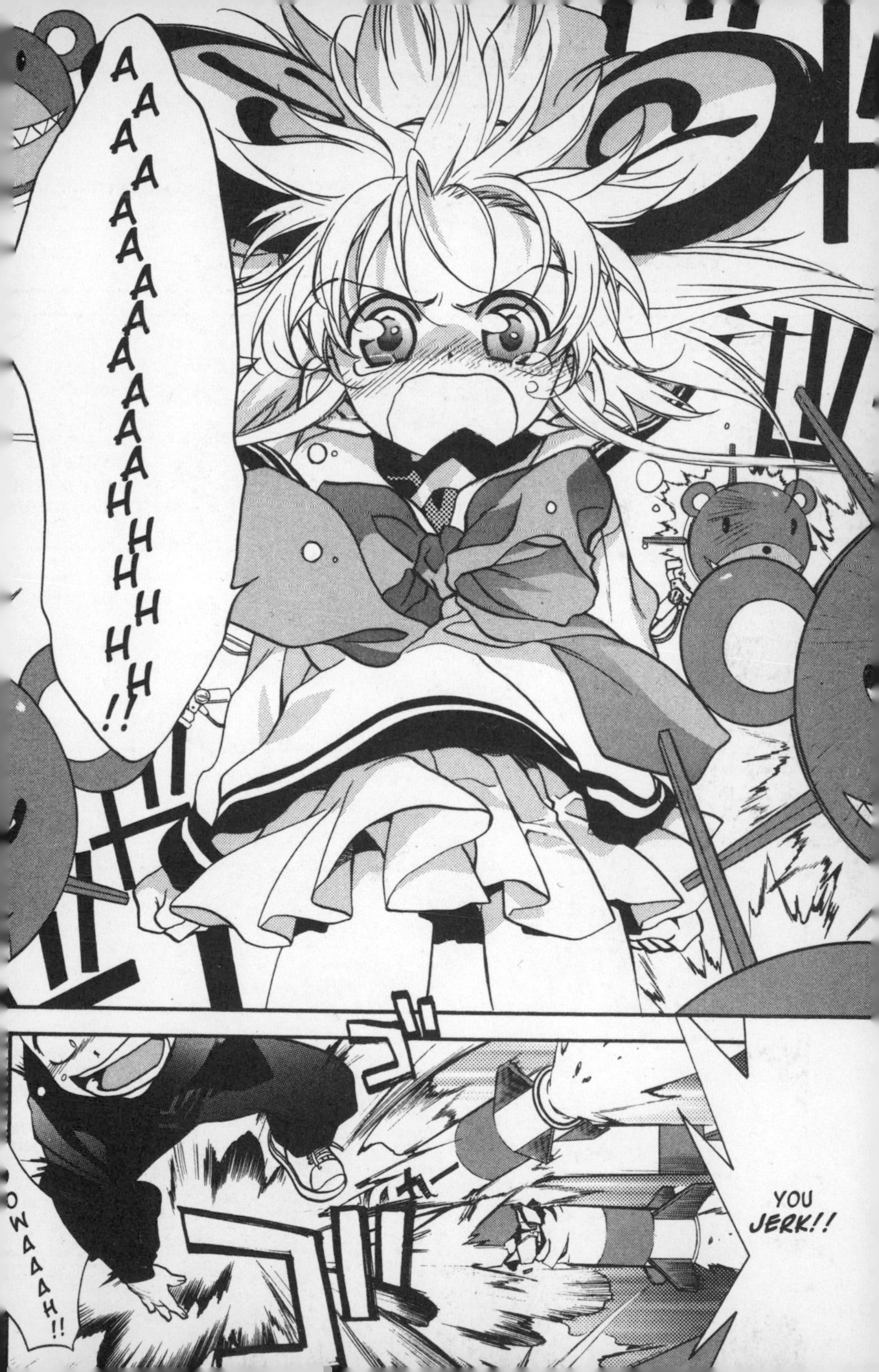
AAAAAAAAAAAAAAAAHHHHHH!!
YOU JERK!!
OWAAAAH!!

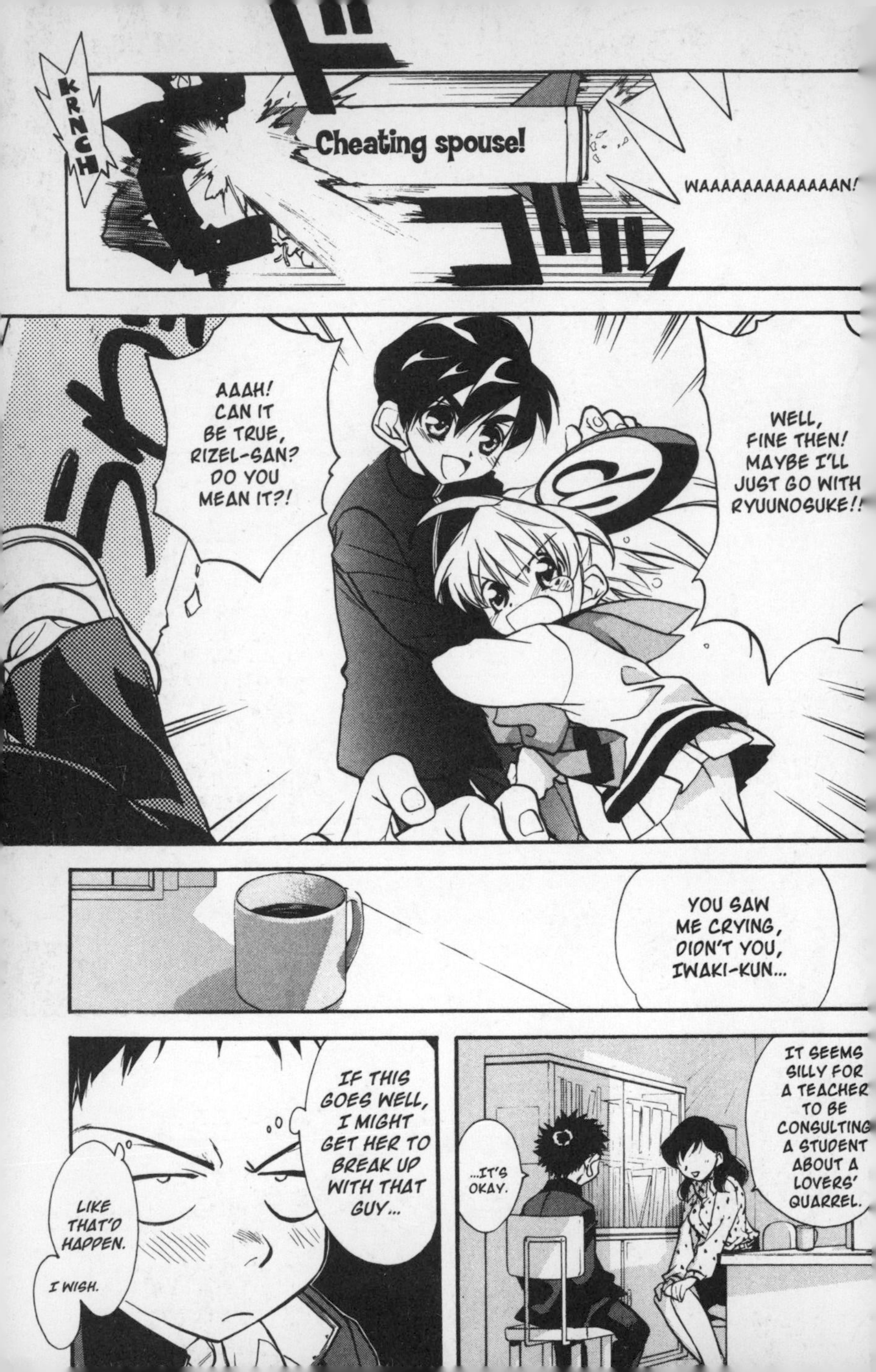
WAAAAAAAAAAAAAN!
Cheating spouse!
KRNCH
WELL, FINE THEN! MAYBE I'LL JUST GO WITH RYUUNOSUKE!!
AAAH! CAN IT BE TRUE, RIZEL-SAN? DO YOU MEAN IT?!
YOU SAW ME CRYING, DIDN'T YOU, IWAKI-KUN...
IT SEEMS SILLY FOR A TEACHER TO BE CONSULTING A STUDENT ABOUT A LOVERS' QUARREL.
...IT'S OKAY.
IF THIS GOES WELL, I MIGHT GET HER TO BREAK UP WITH THAT GUY...
LIKE THAT'D HAPPEN.
I WISH.

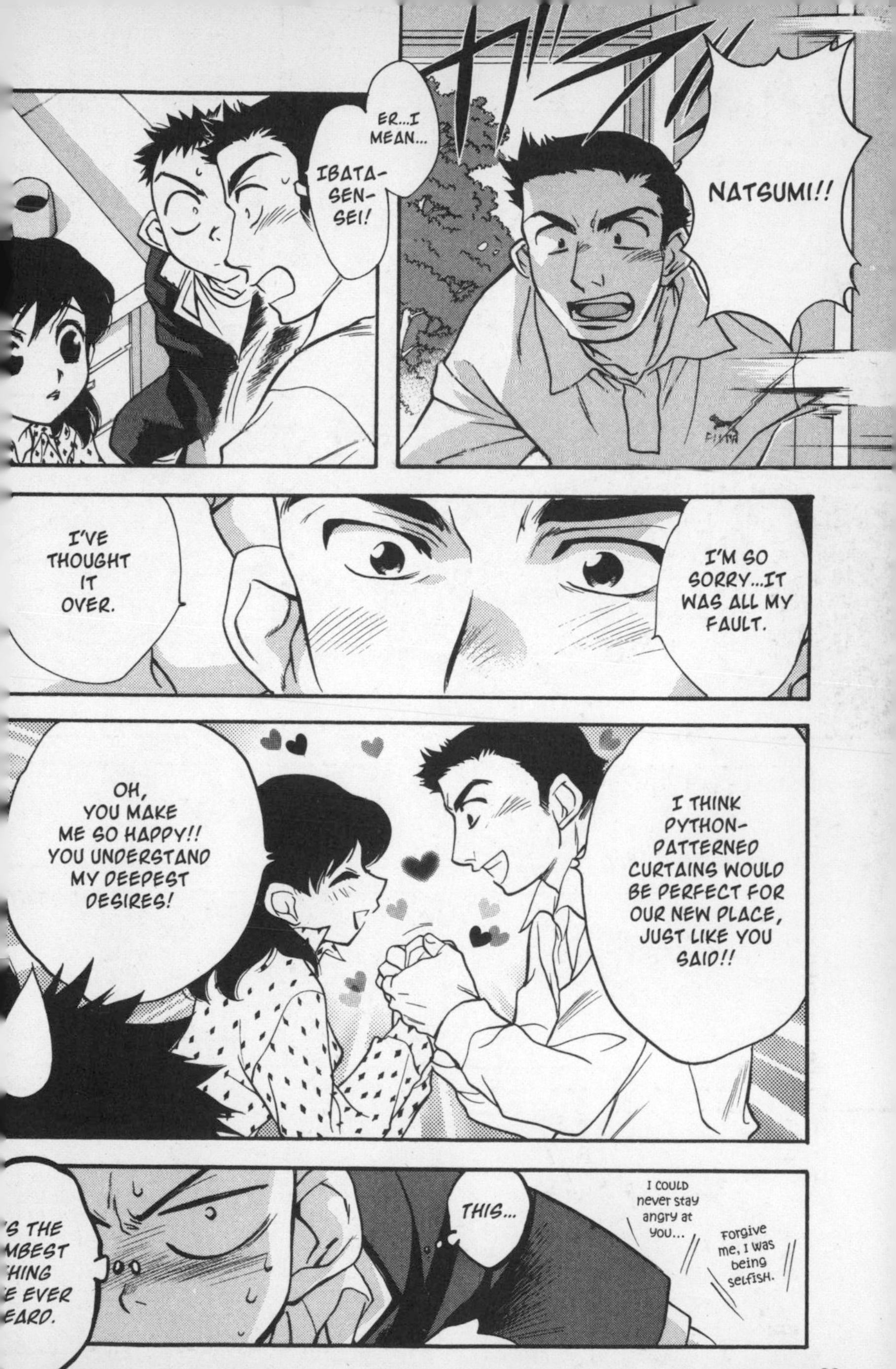
NATSUMI!!
ER...I MEAN...
IBATA-SENSEI!
I'M SO SORRY...IT WAS ALL MY FAULT.
I'VE THOUGHT IT OVER.
I THINK PYTHON-PATTERNED CURTAINS WOULD BE PERFECT FOR OUR NEW PLACE, JUST LIKE YOU SAID!!
OH, YOU MAKE ME SO HAPPY!! YOU UNDERSTAND MY DEEPEST DESIRES!
Forgive me, I was being selfish.
I could never stay angry at you...
THIS...
'S THE MBEST HING E EVER EARD.

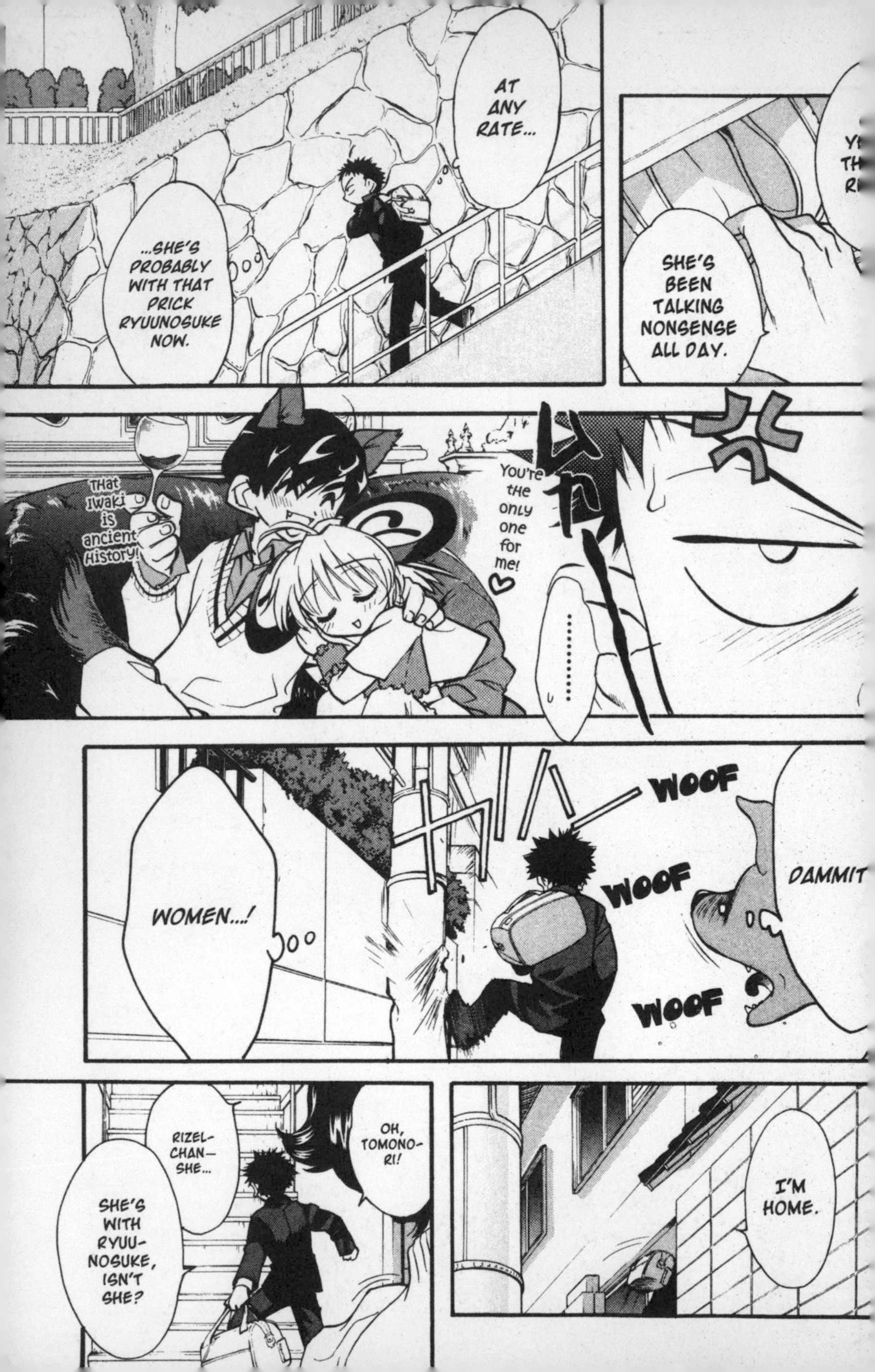
SHE'S BEEN TALKING NONSENSE ALL DAY.
AT ANY RATE...
...SHE'S PROBABLY WITH THAT PRICK RYUUNOSUKE NOW.
......
You're the only one for me!
That Iwaki is ancient History!
DAMMIT
WOOF
WOOF
WOOF
WOMEN...!
I'M HOME.
OH, TOMONO-RI!
RIZEL-CHAN—SHE...
SHE'S WITH RYUU-NOSUKE, ISN'T SHE?

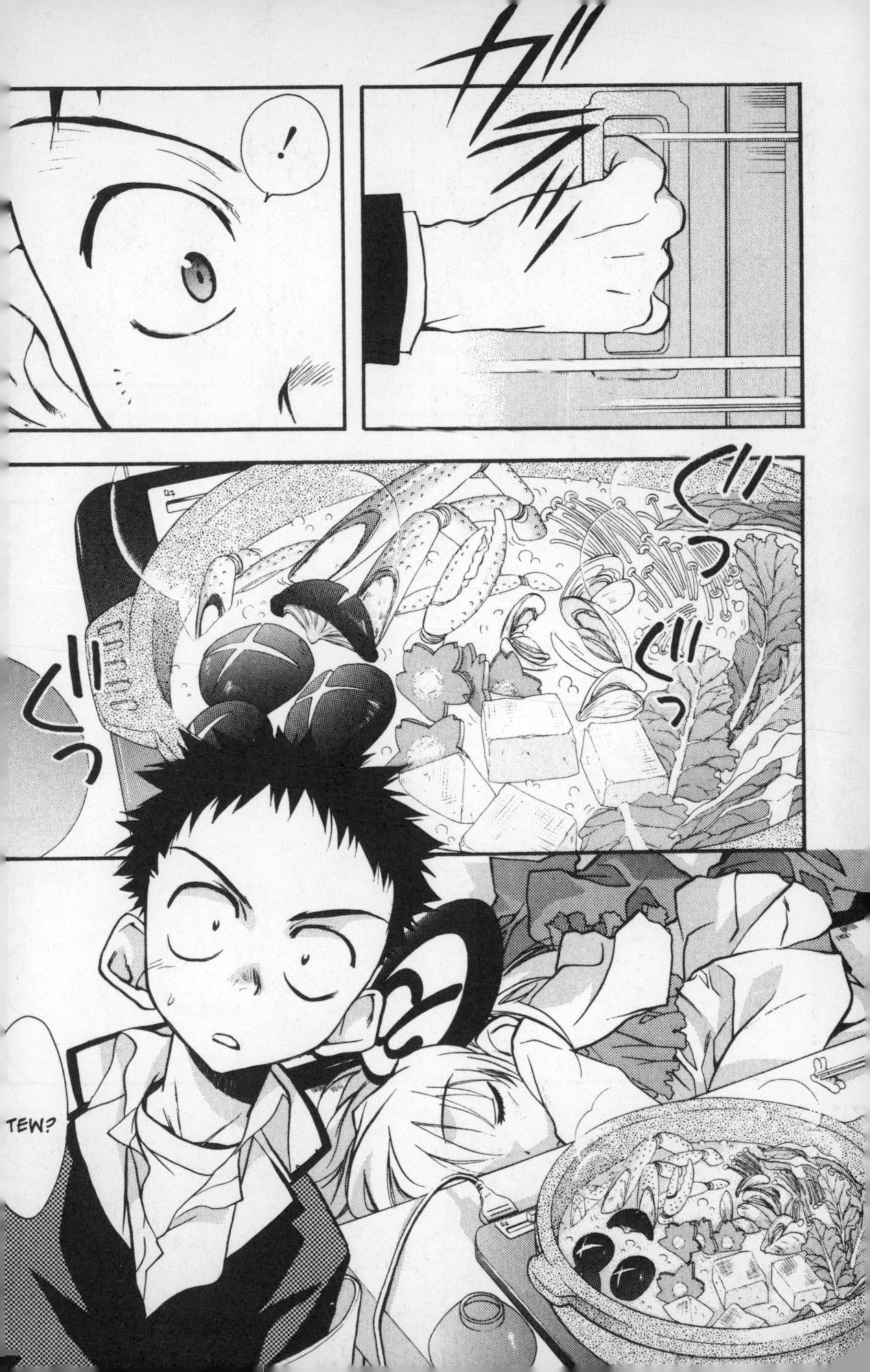
!
ぐつ
ぐつ
ぐつ
TEW?

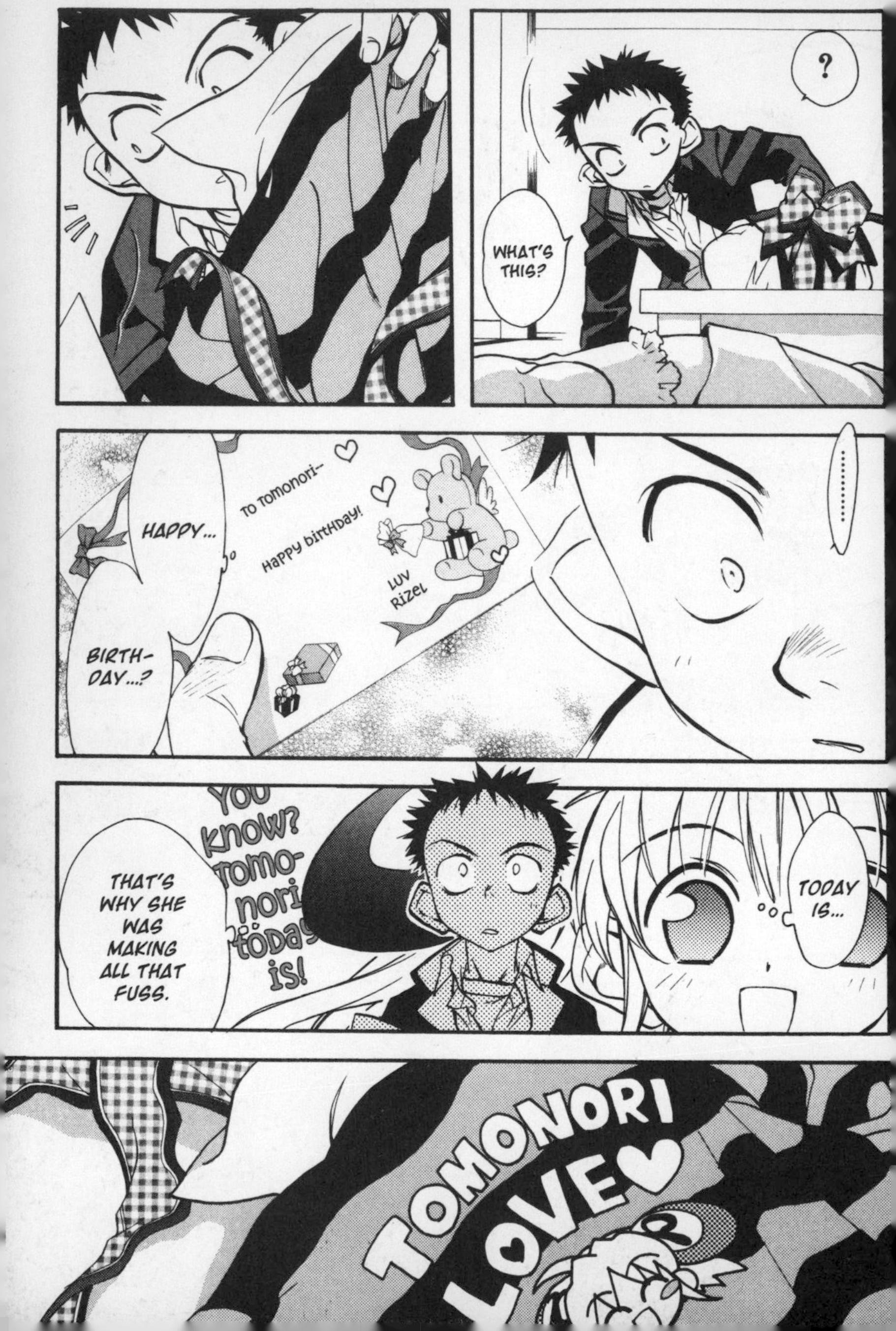
?
WHAT'S THIS?
......
TO TOMONORI~
HAPPY BIRTHDAY!
LUV RIZEL
HAPPY...
BIRTHDAY...?
TODAY IS...
YOU KNOW? TOMONORI TODAY IS!
THAT'S WHY SHE WAS MAKING ALL THAT FUSS.
TOMONORI LOVE♥

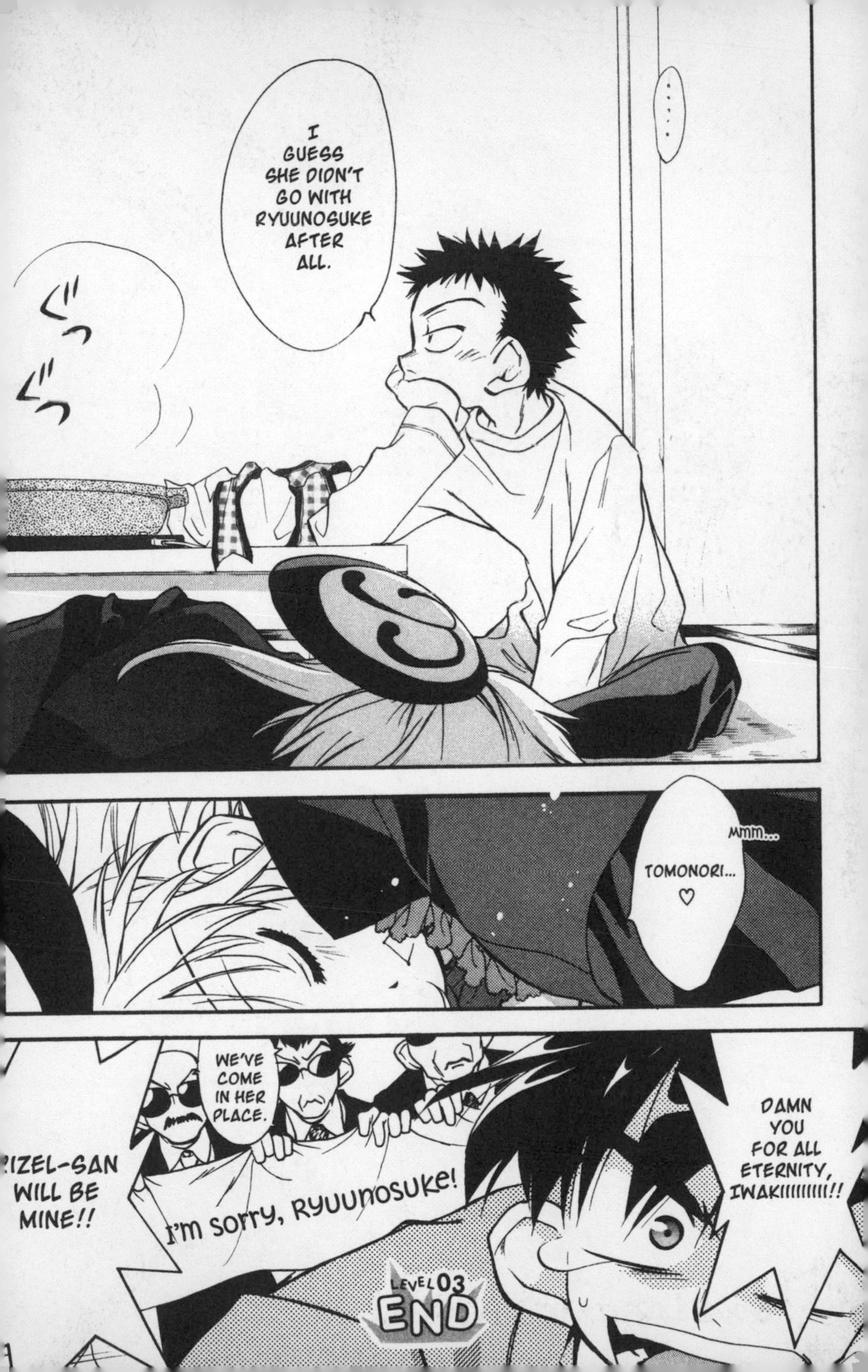
......
I GUESS SHE DIDN'T GO WITH RYUUNOSUKE AFTER ALL.
ぐつぐつ
Mmm...
TOMONORI... ♡
DAMN YOU FOR ALL ETERNITY, IWAKIIIIIIIII!!
WE'VE COME IN HER PLACE.
I'm sorry, Ryuunosuke!
IZEL-SAN WILL BE MINE!!
LEVEL 03 END

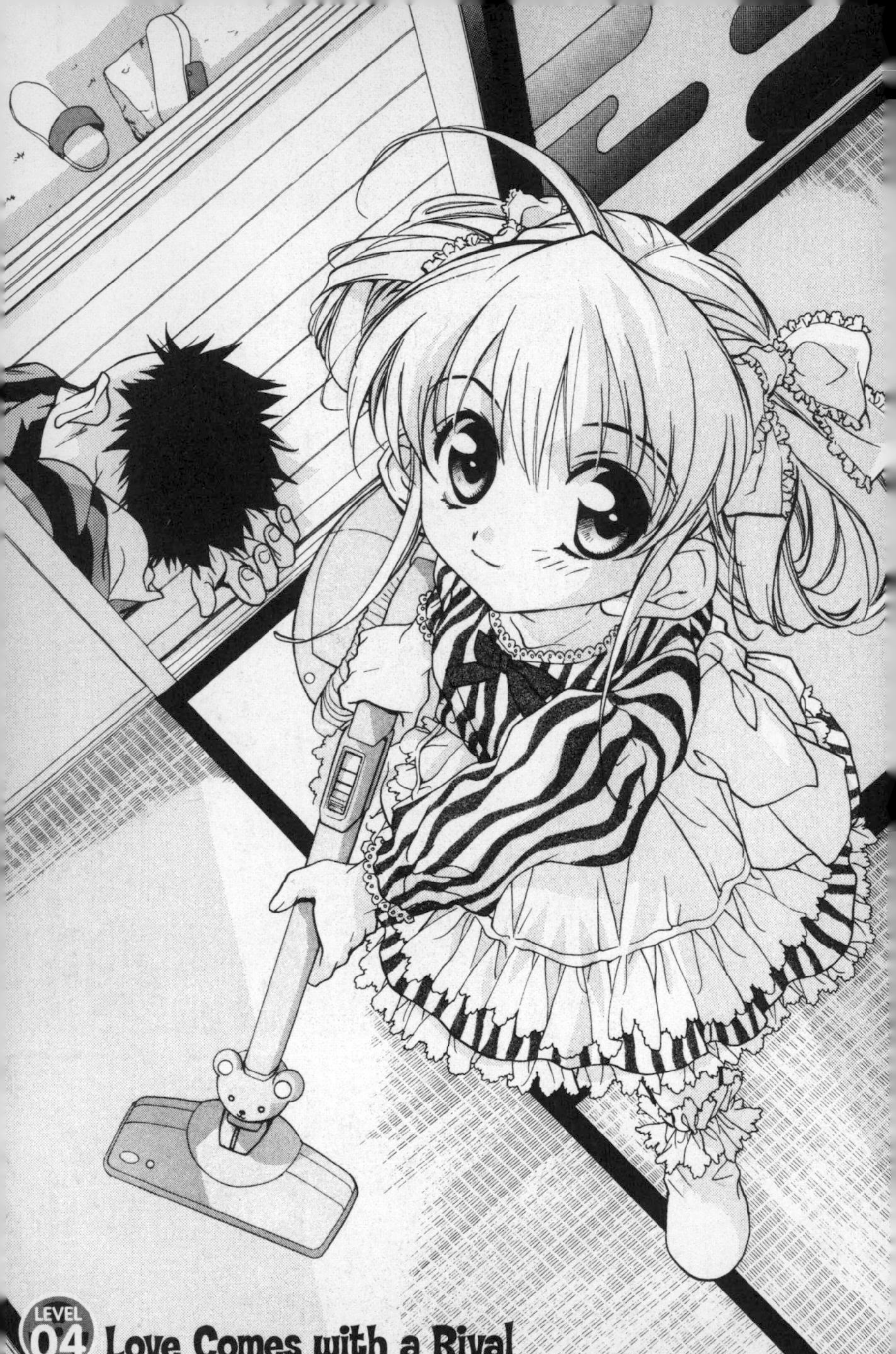

LEVEL 04 Love Comes with a Rival

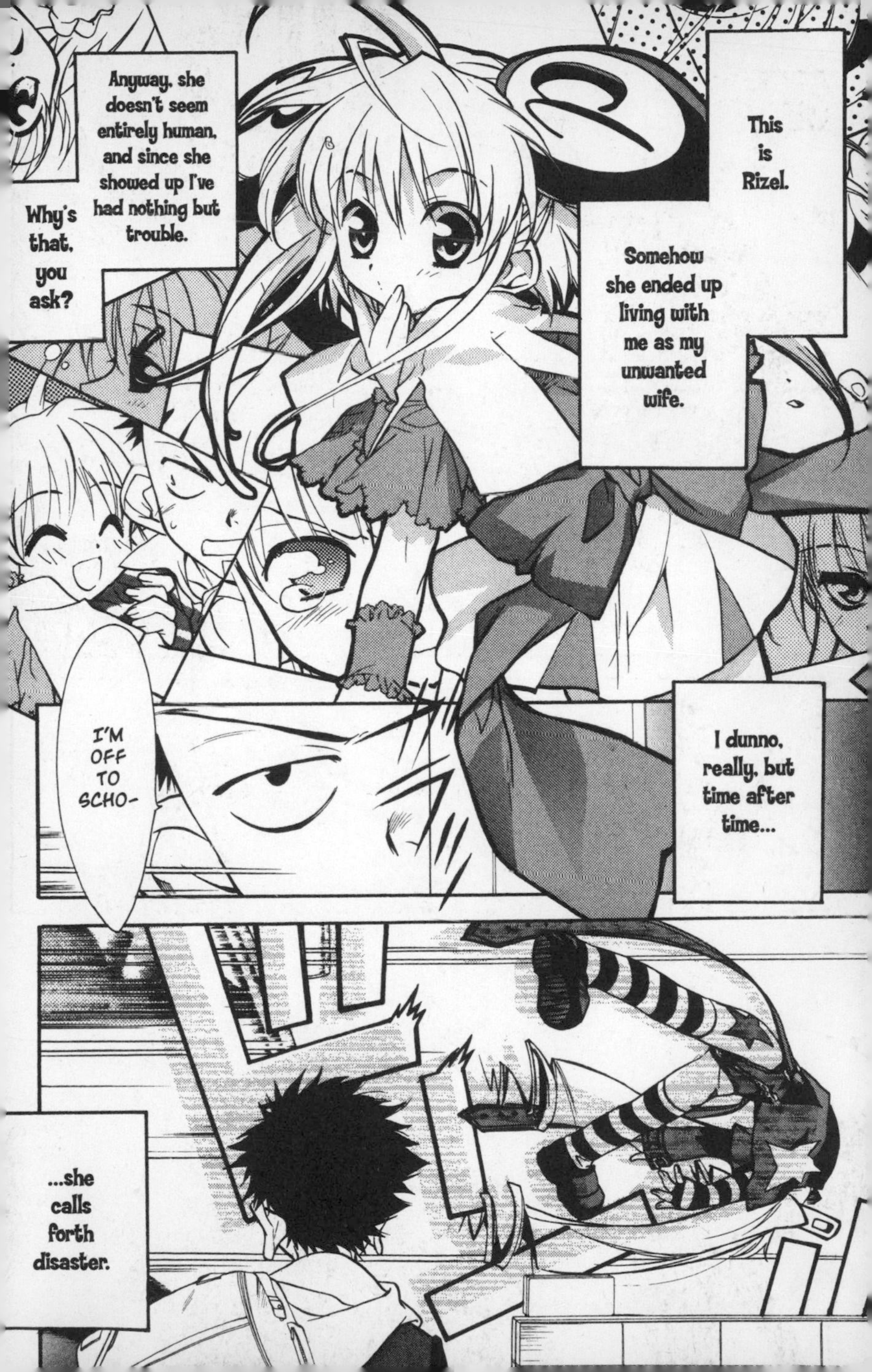
This is Rizel.
Somehow she ended up living with me as my unwanted wife.
Anyway, she doesn't seem entirely human, and since she showed up I've had nothing but trouble.
Why's that, you ask?
I dunno, really, but time after time...
I'M OFF TO SCHO-
...she calls forth disaster.

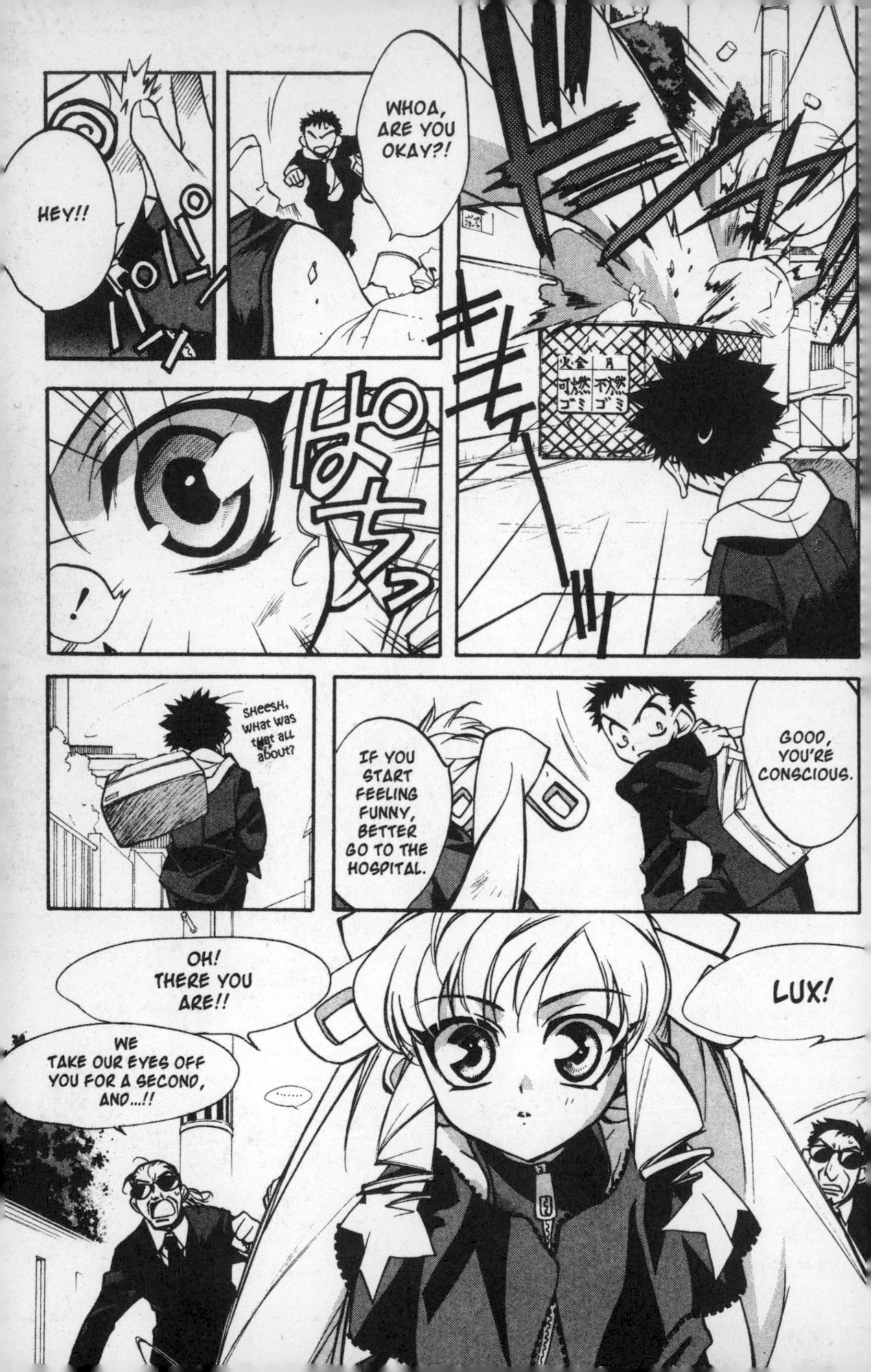
火・金 可燃ゴミ
月 不燃ゴミ
WHOA, ARE YOU OKAY?!
HEY!!
!
ぱちっ
GOOD, YOU'RE CONSCIOUS.
IF YOU START FEELING FUNNY, BETTER GO TO THE HOSPITAL.
SHEESH, WHAT WAS THAT ALL ABOUT?
LUX!
OH! THERE YOU ARE!!
WE TAKE OUR EYES OFF YOU FOR A SECOND, AND...!!
......

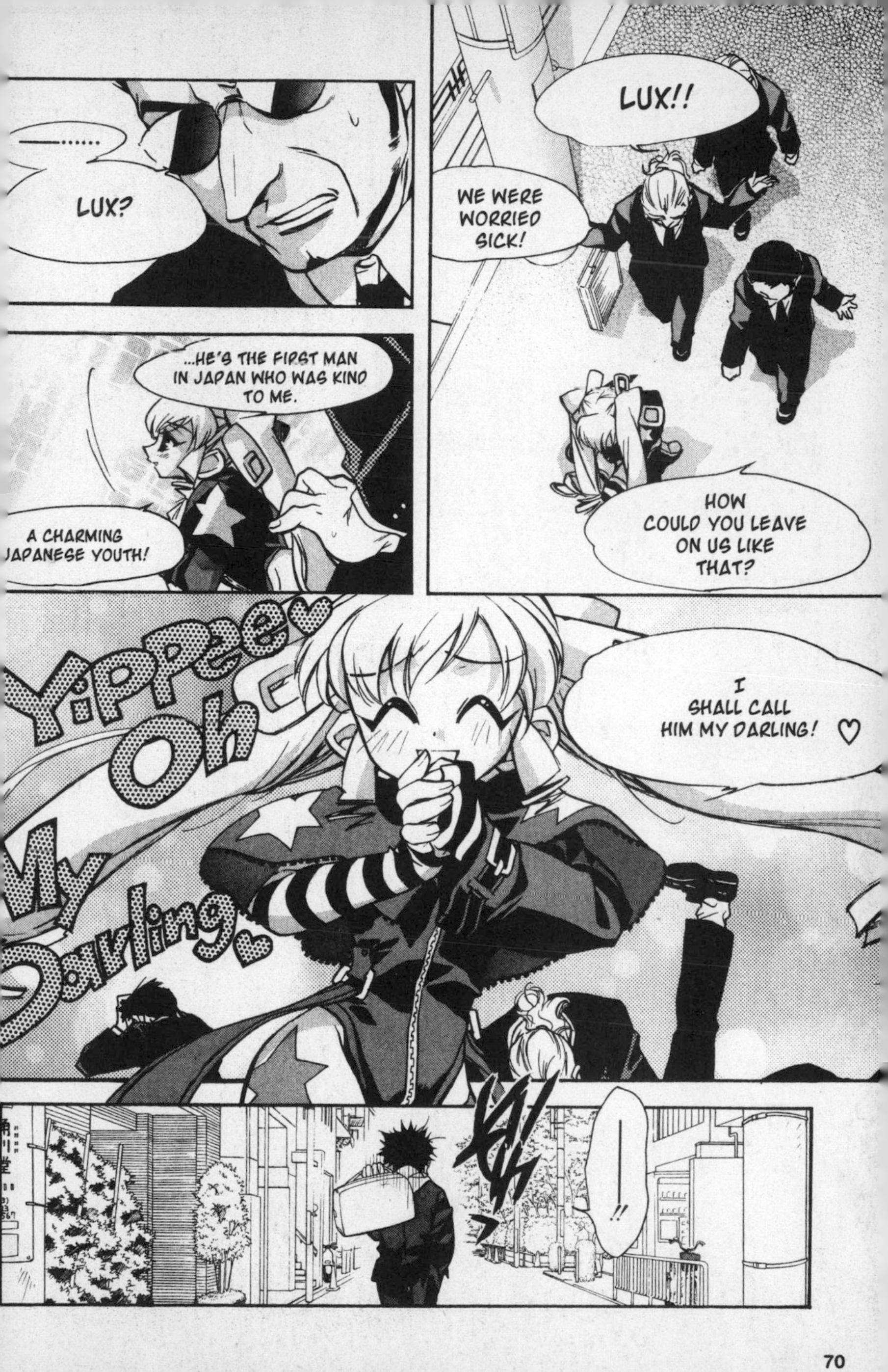
LUX!!
WE WERE WORRIED SICK!
HOW COULD YOU LEAVE ON US LIKE THAT?
——......
LUX?
...HE'S THE FIRST MAN IN JAPAN WHO WAS KIND TO ME.
A CHARMING JAPANESE YOUTH!
I SHALL CALL HIM MY DARLING! ♡
Yippee ♡ Oh My Darling ♡
!!

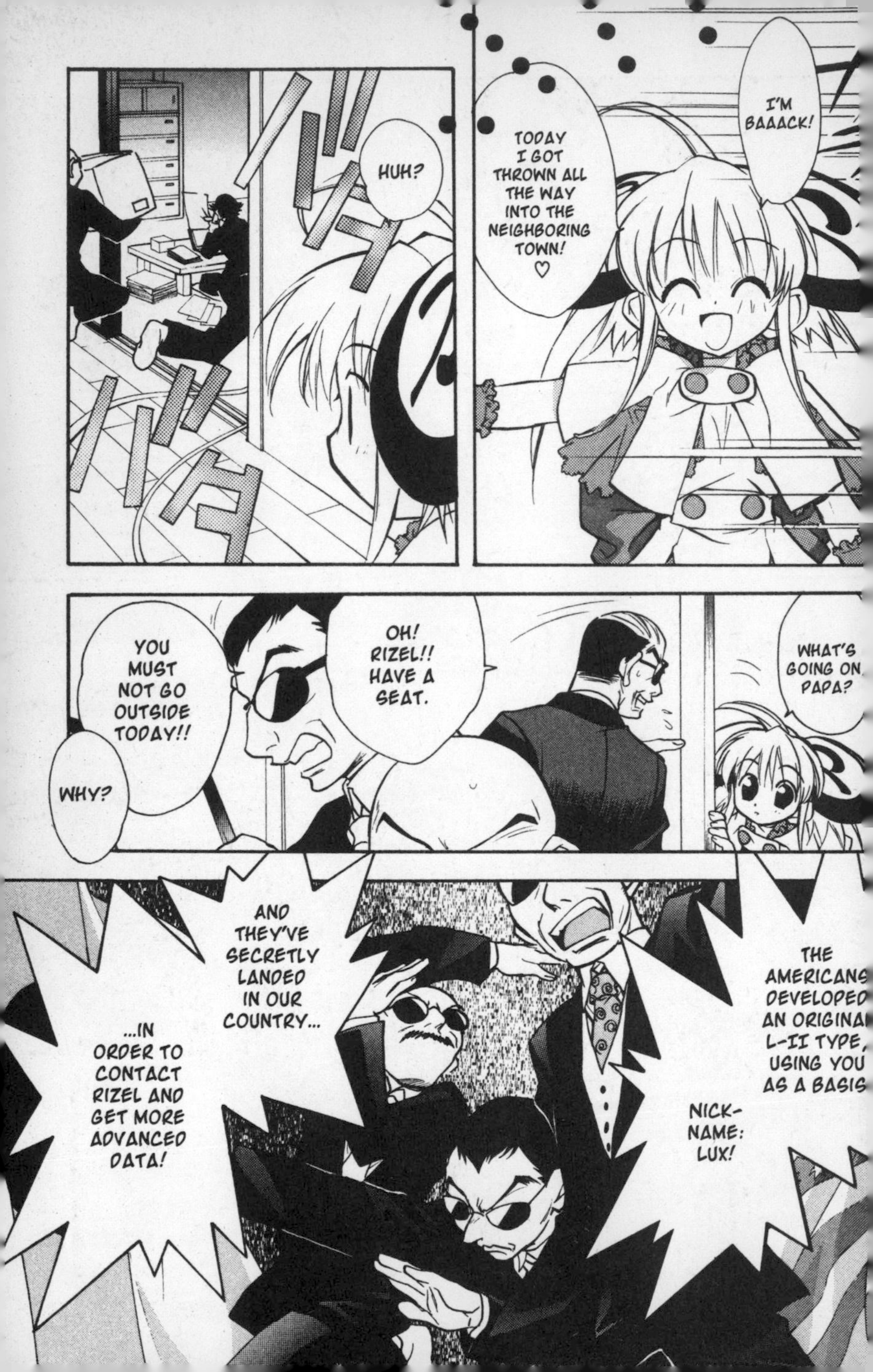
I'M BAAACK!
TODAY I GOT THROWN ALL THE WAY INTO THE NEIGHBORING TOWN! ♡
HUH?
WHAT'S GOING ON, PAPA?
OH! RIZEL!! HAVE A SEAT.
YOU MUST NOT GO OUTSIDE TODAY!!
WHY?
THE AMERICANS DEVELOPED AN ORIGINA L-II TYPE, USING YOU AS A BASIS
NICK-NAME: LUX!
AND THEY'VE SECRETLY LANDED IN OUR COUNTRY...
...IN ORDER TO CONTACT RIZEL AND GET MORE ADVANCED DATA!

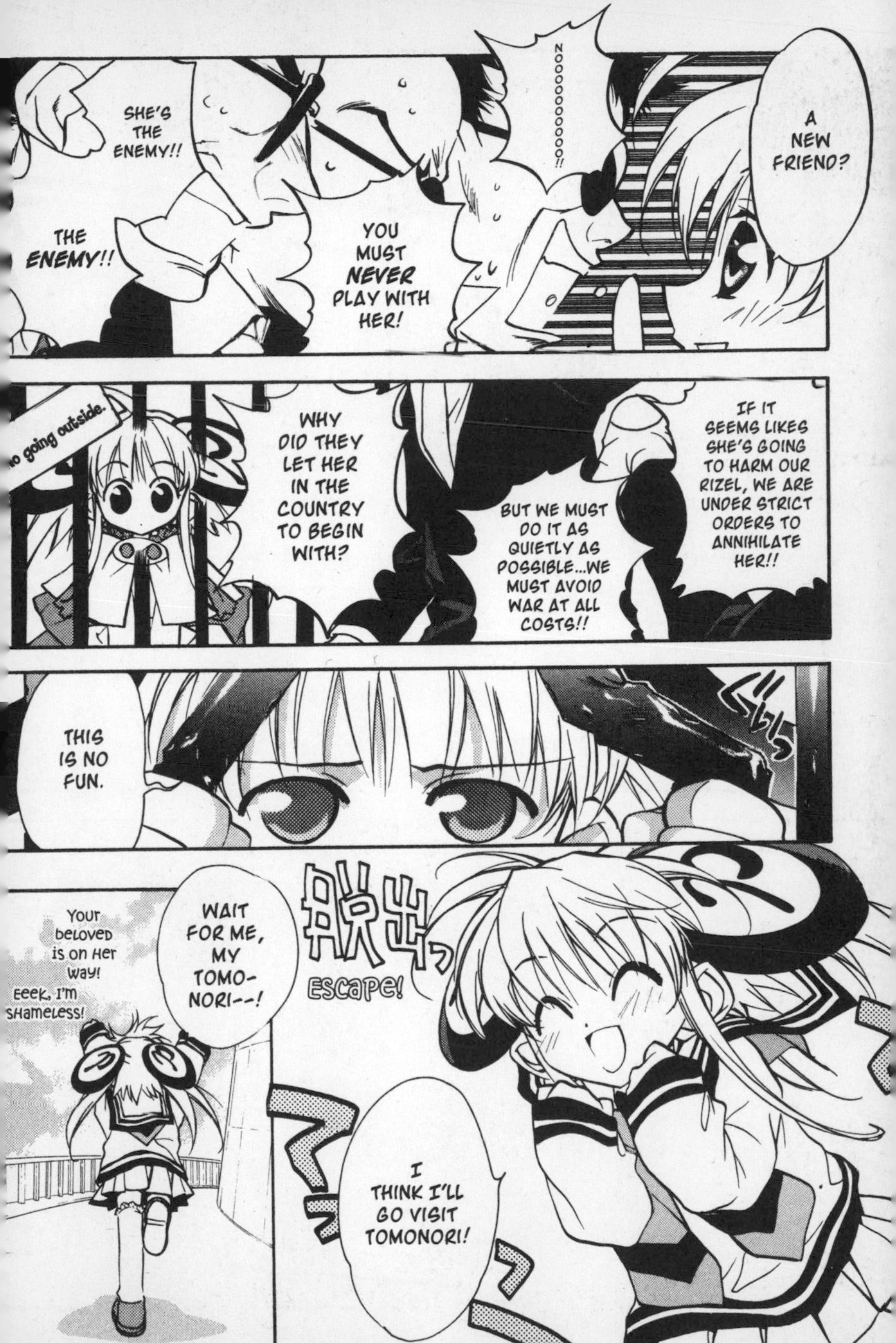
A NEW FRIEND?
NOOOOOOOOOOOO!!
YOU MUST NEVER PLAY WITH HER!
SHE'S THE ENEMY!!
THE ENEMY!!
IF IT SEEMS LIKES SHE'S GOING TO HARM OUR RIZEL, WE ARE UNDER STRICT ORDERS TO ANNIHILATE HER!!
BUT WE MUST DO IT AS QUIETLY AS POSSIBLE...WE MUST AVOID WAR AT ALL COSTS!!
WHY DID THEY LET HER IN THE COUNTRY TO BEGIN WITH?
no going outside.
THIS IS NO FUN.
I THINK I'LL GO VISIT TOMONORI!
ESCAPE!
WAIT FOR ME, MY TOMO-NORI--!
Your beloved is on her way!
Eeek, I'm shameless!

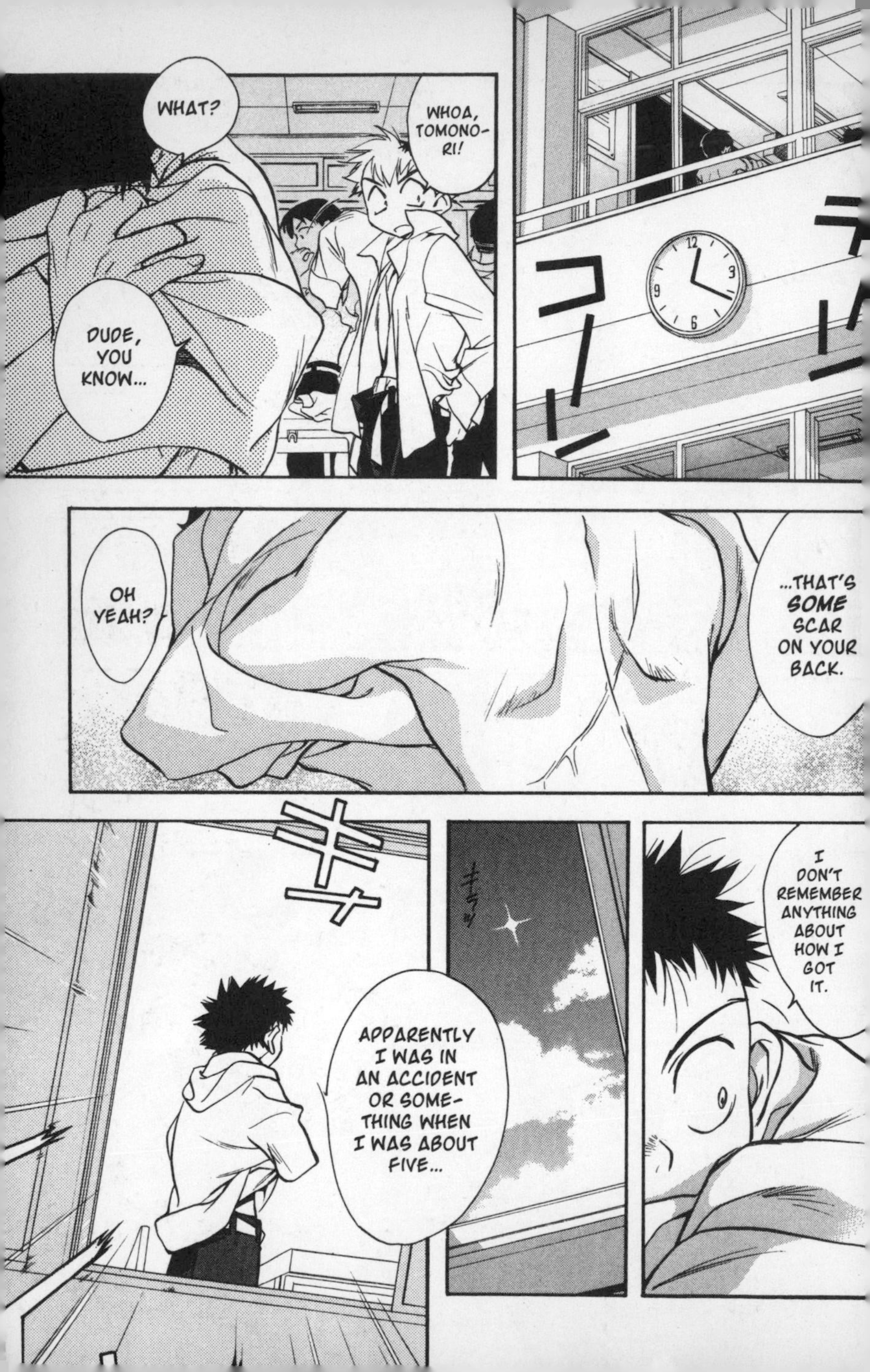
WHOA, TOMONO-RI!
WHAT?
DUDE, YOU KNOW...
...THAT'S SOME SCAR ON YOUR BACK.
OH YEAH?
I DON'T REMEMBER ANYTHING ABOUT HOW I GOT IT.
APPARENTLY I WAS IN AN ACCIDENT OR SOME-THING WHEN I WAS ABOUT FIVE...

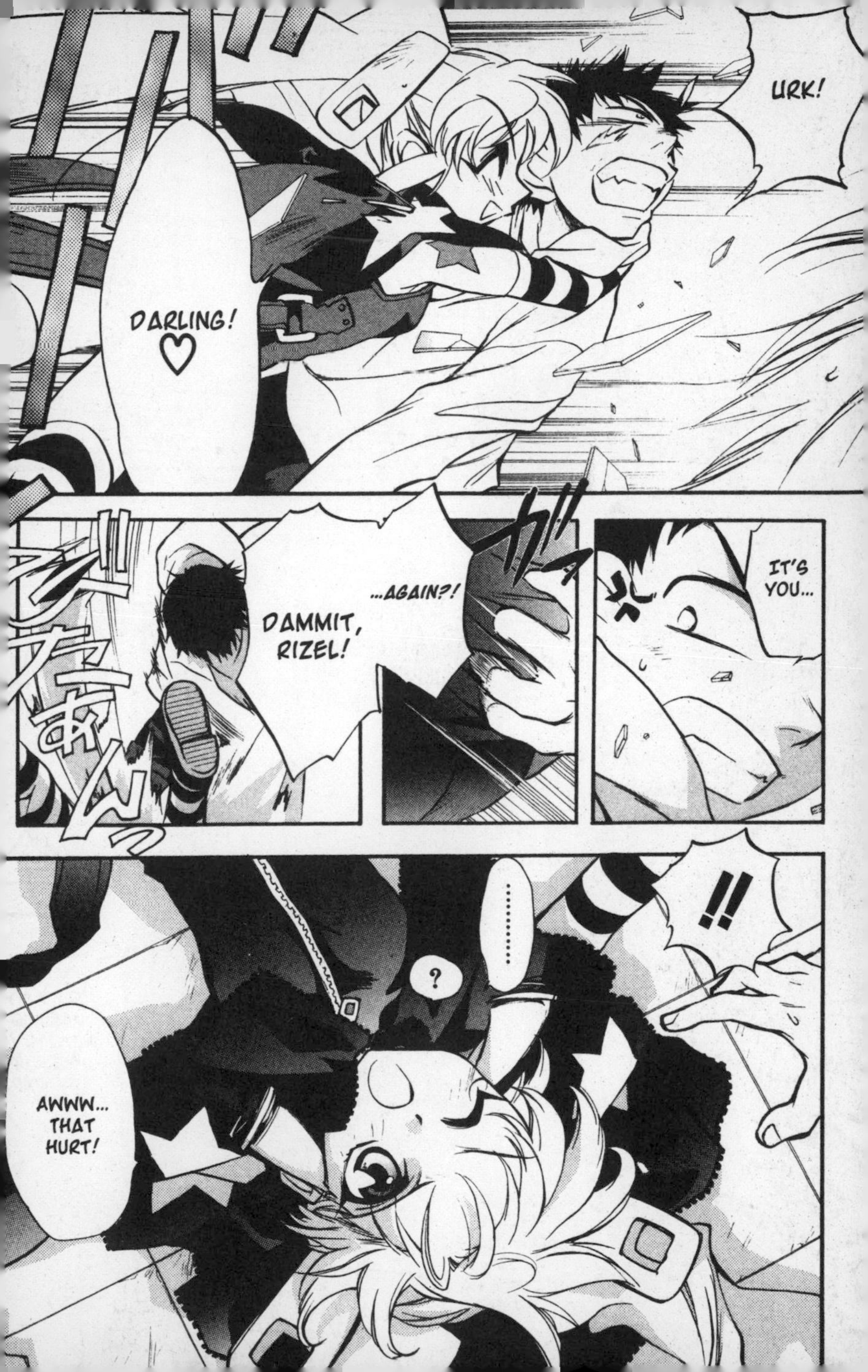
URK!
DARLING! ♥
IT'S YOU...
...AGAIN?!
DAMMIT, RIZEL!
!!
......
?
AWWW... THAT HURT!

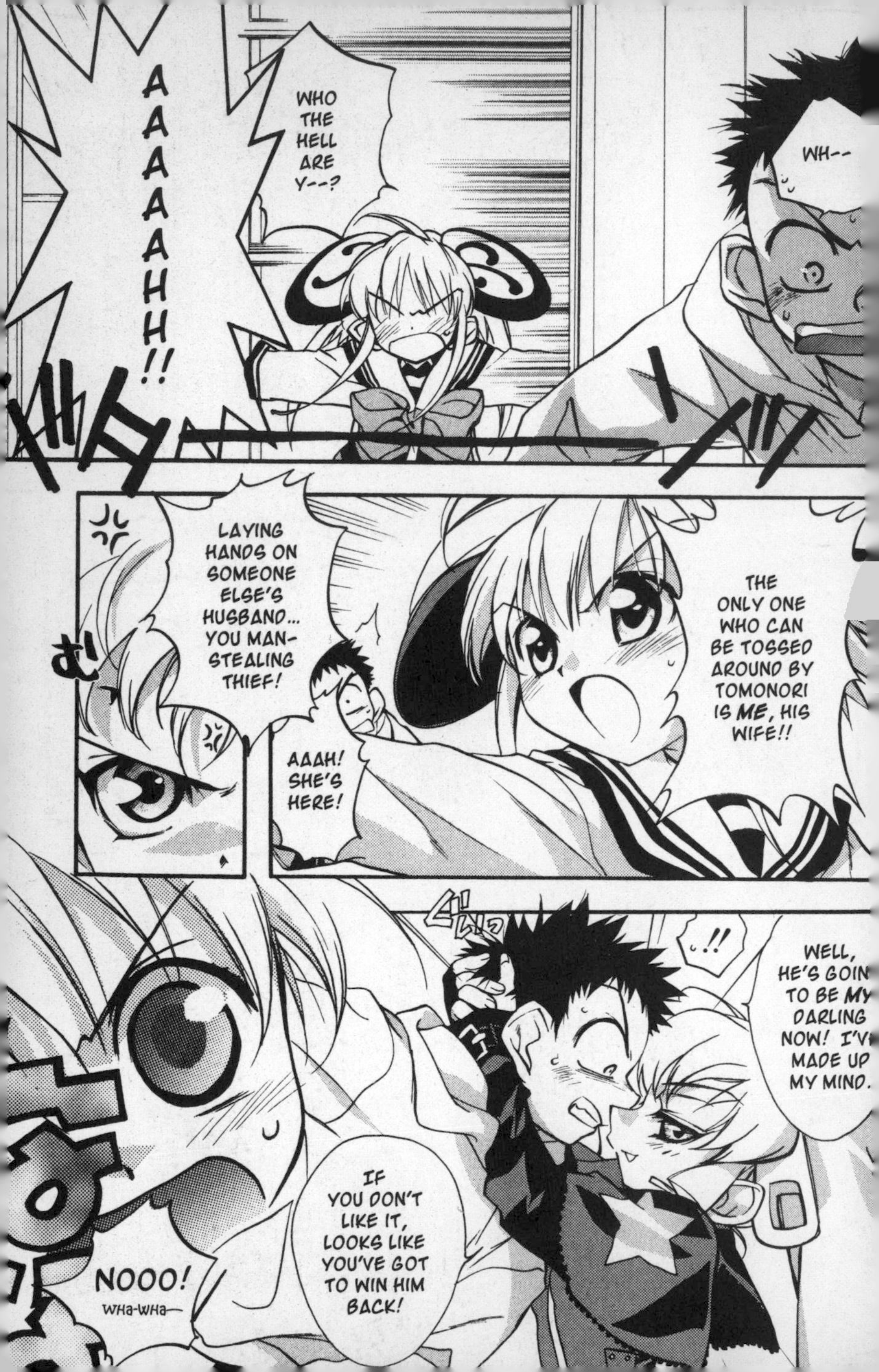
WH--
WHO THE HELL ARE Y--?
AAAAAHH!!
THE ONLY ONE WHO CAN BE TOSSED AROUND BY TOMONORI IS *ME*, HIS WIFE!!
AAAH! SHE'S HERE!
LAYING HANDS ON SOMEONE ELSE'S HUSBAND... YOU MAN-STEALING THIEF!
..!!
WELL, HE'S GOIN TO BE *MY* DARLING NOW! I'V MADE UP MY MIND.
IF YOU DON'T LIKE IT, LOOKS LIKE YOU'VE GOT TO WIN HIM BACK!
NOOO!
WHA-WHA—

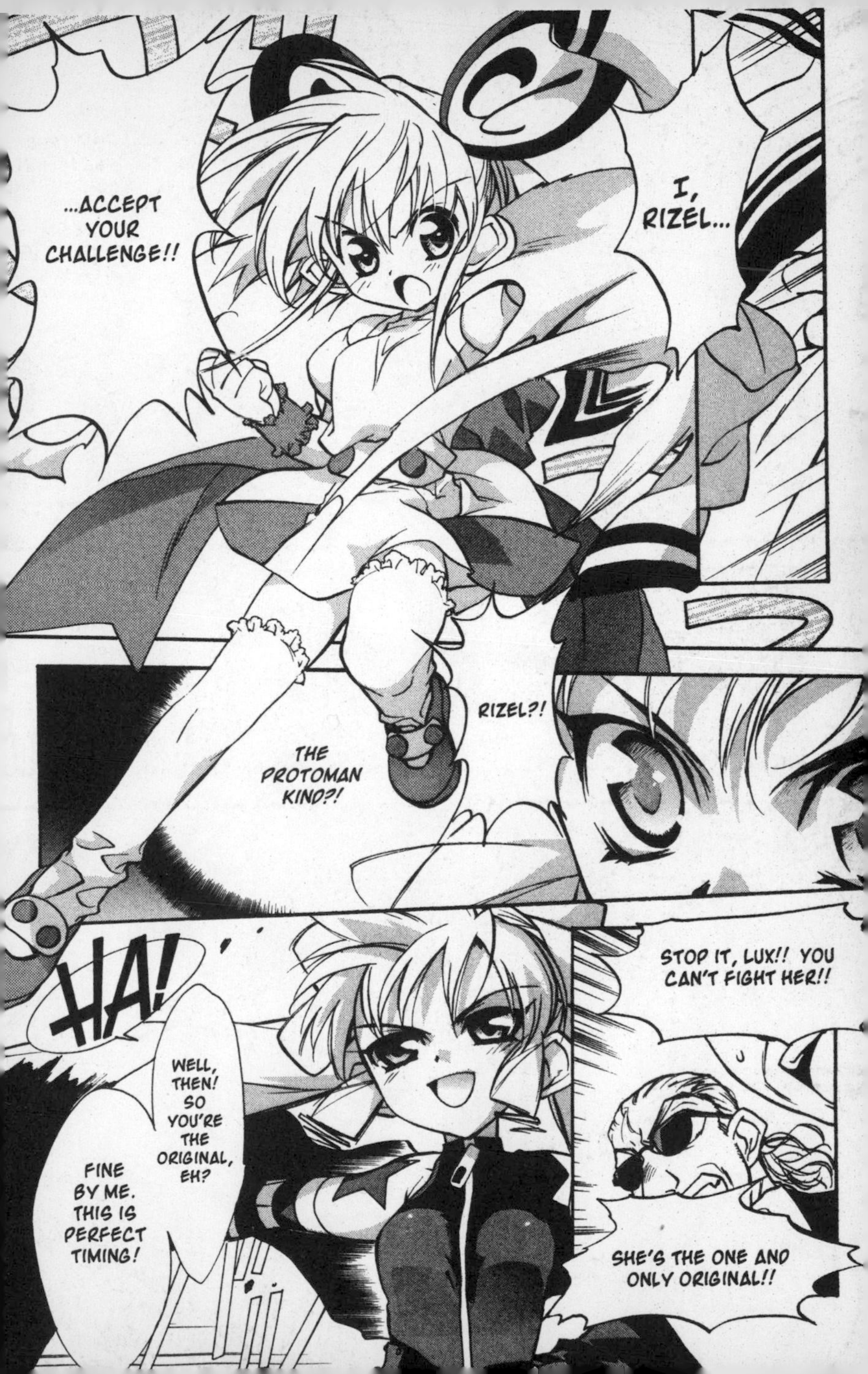
I, RIZEL...
...ACCEPT YOUR CHALLENGE!!
RIZEL?!
THE PROTOMAN KIND?!
STOP IT, LUX!! YOU CAN'T FIGHT HER!!
SHE'S THE ONE AND ONLY ORIGINAL!!
HA!
WELL, THEN! SO YOU'RE THE ORIGINAL, EH?
FINE BY ME. THIS IS PERFECT TIMING!

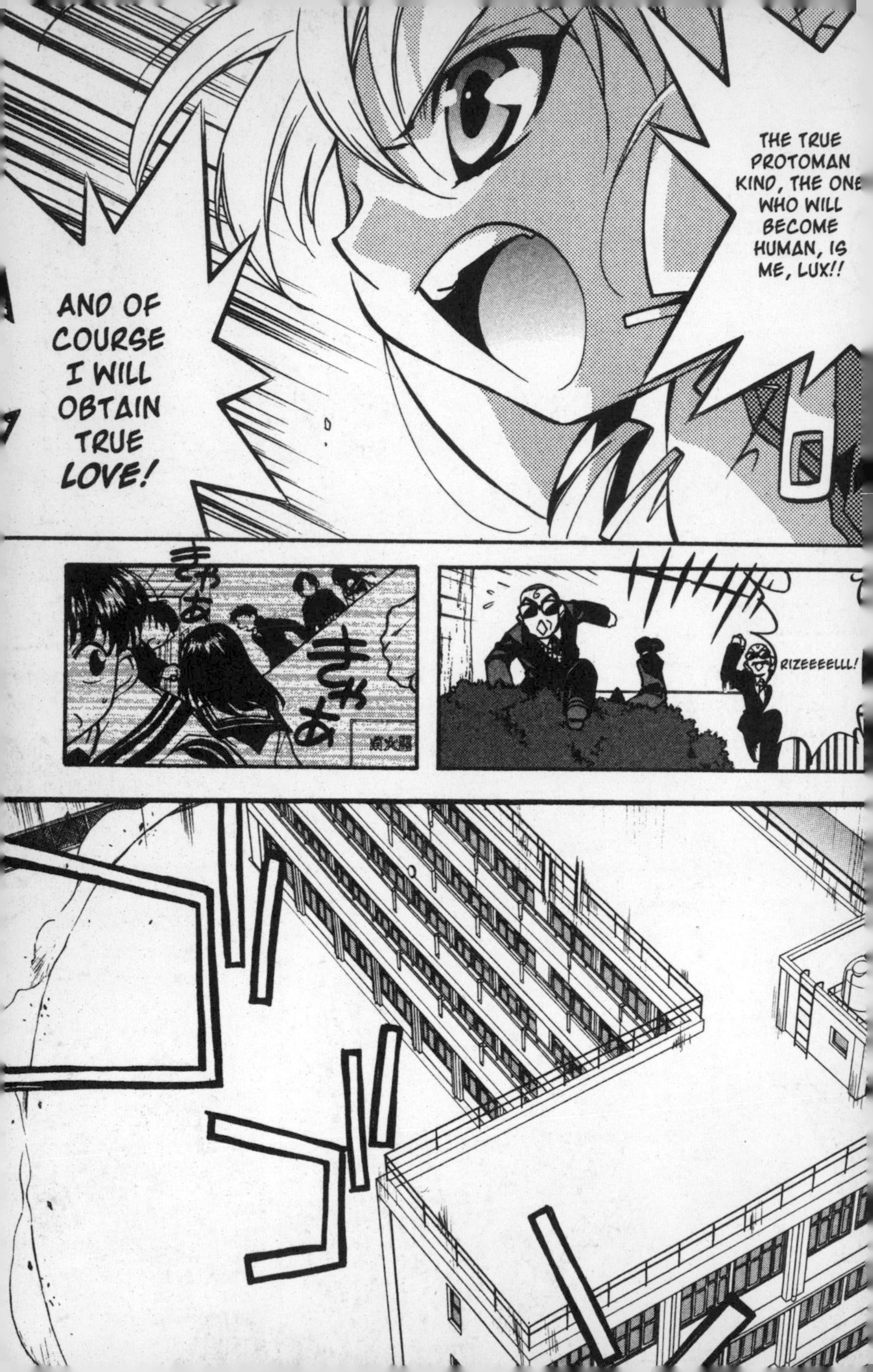
THE TRUE PROTOMAN KIND, THE ONE WHO WILL BECOME HUMAN, IS ME, LUX!!
AND OF COURSE I WILL OBTAIN TRUE LOVE!
RIZEEEELLL!
きゃあ
きゃあ
消火器

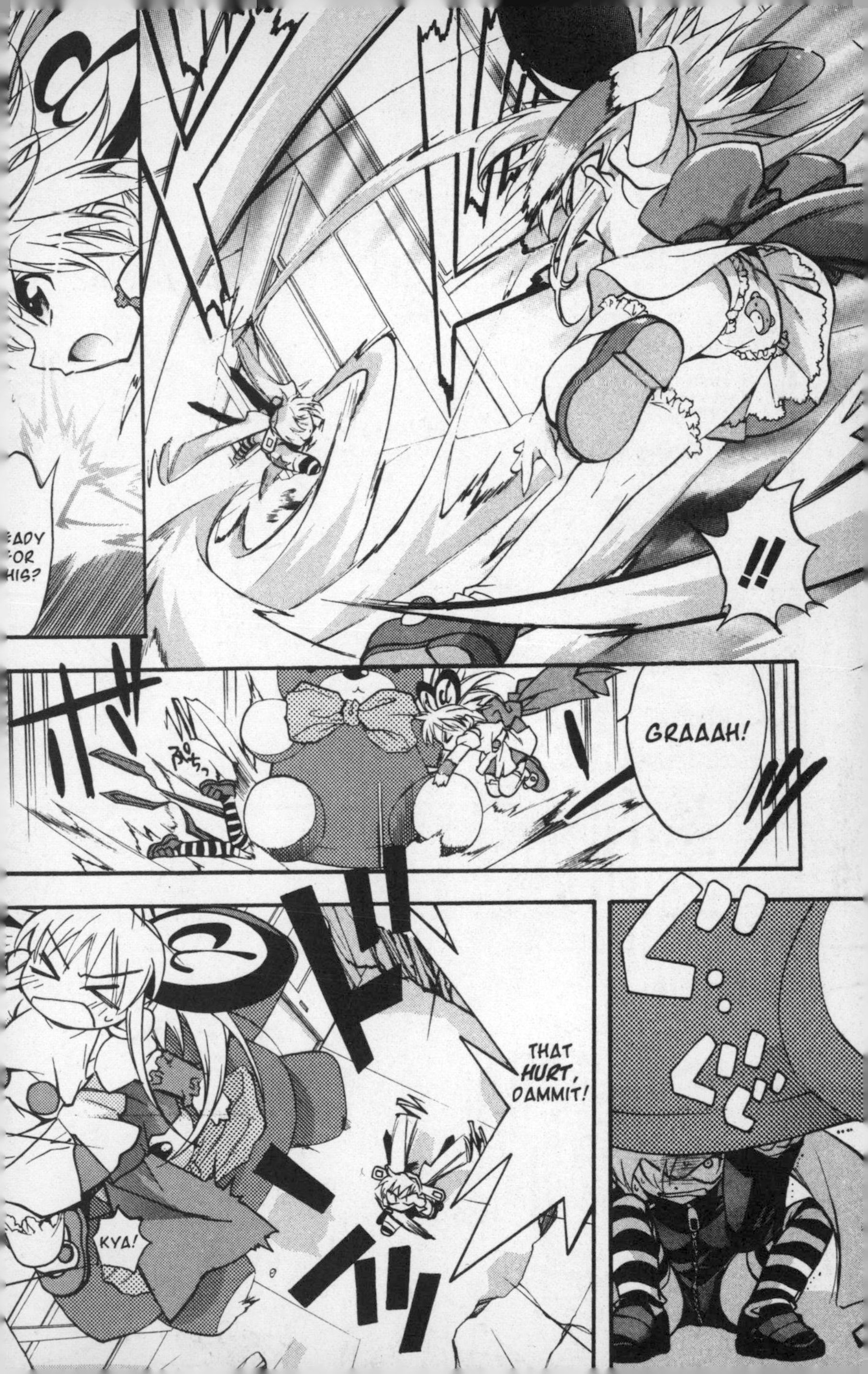
!!
EADY FOR HIS?
GRAAAH!
THAT HURT, DAMMIT!
KYA!

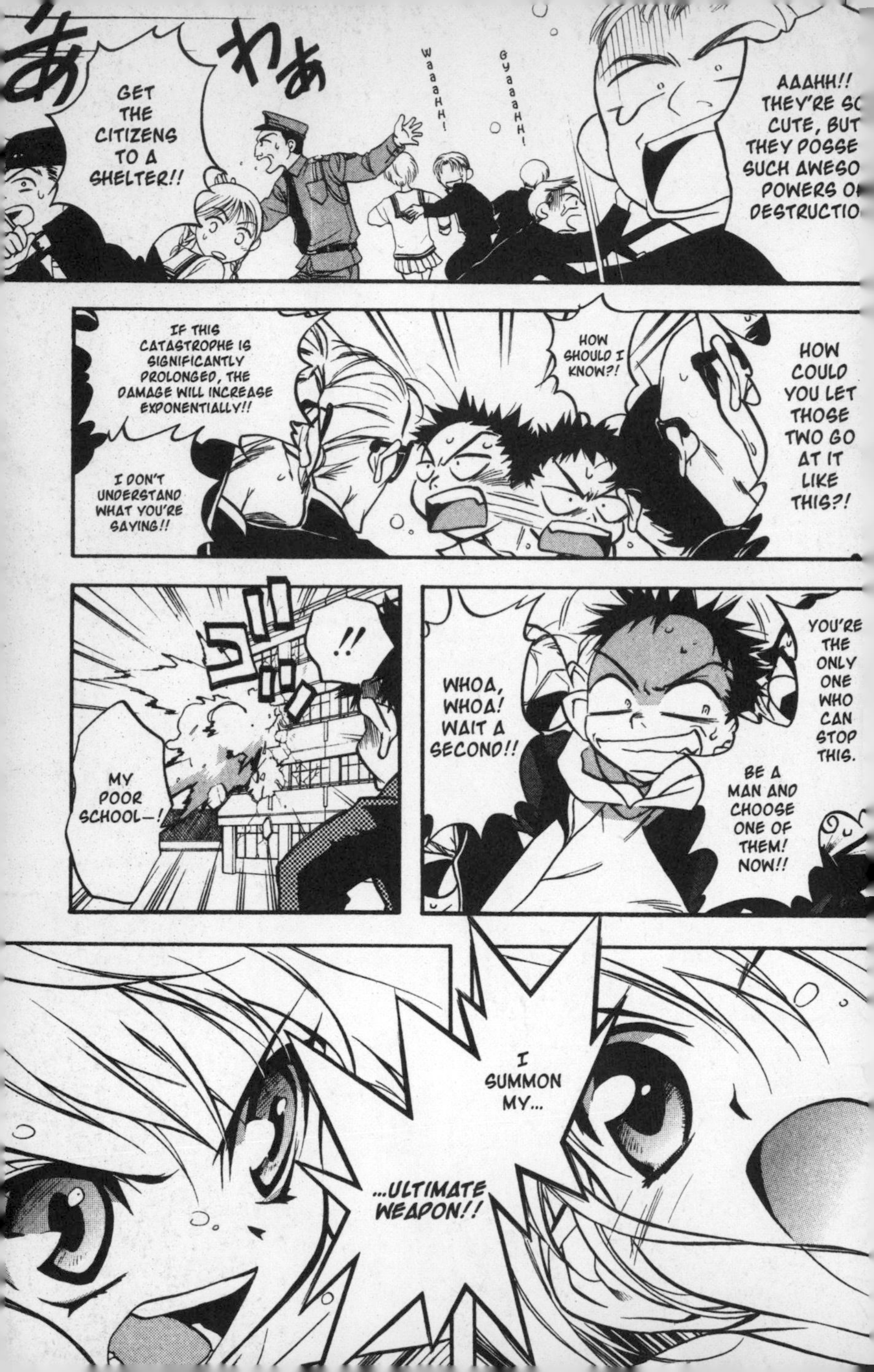
AAAHH!! THEY'RE SO CUTE, BUT THEY POSSE SUCH AWESO POWERS OF DESTRUCTIO
GYAAAAHH!
WAAAAHH!
わぁ
あ〜
GET THE CITIZENS TO A SHELTER!!
HOW COULD YOU LET THOSE TWO GO AT IT LIKE THIS?!
HOW SHOULD I KNOW?!
IF THIS CATASTROPHE IS SIGNIFICANTLY PROLONGED, THE DAMAGE WILL INCREASE EXPONENTIALLY!!
I DON'T UNDERSTAND WHAT YOU'RE SAYING!!
YOU'RE THE ONLY ONE WHO CAN STOP THIS.
BE A MAN AND CHOOSE ONE OF THEM! NOW!!
WHOA, WHOA! WAIT A SECOND!!
!!
MY POOR SCHOOL—!
I SUMMON MY...
...ULTIMATE WEAPON!!

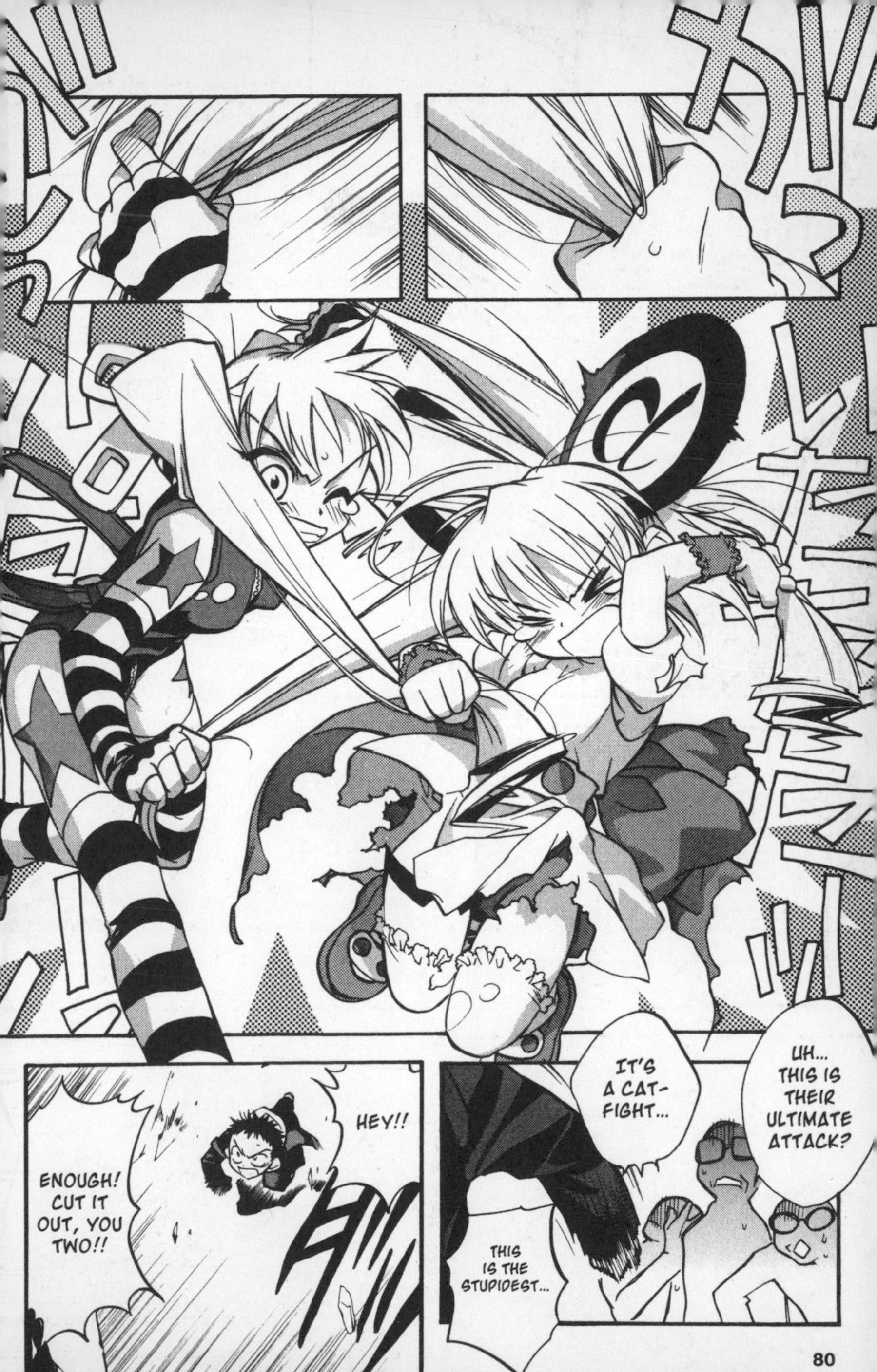
UH... THIS IS THEIR ULTIMATE ATTACK?
IT'S A CAT-FIGHT...
THIS IS THE STUPIDEST...
HEY!!
ENOUGH! CUT IT OUT, YOU TWO!!

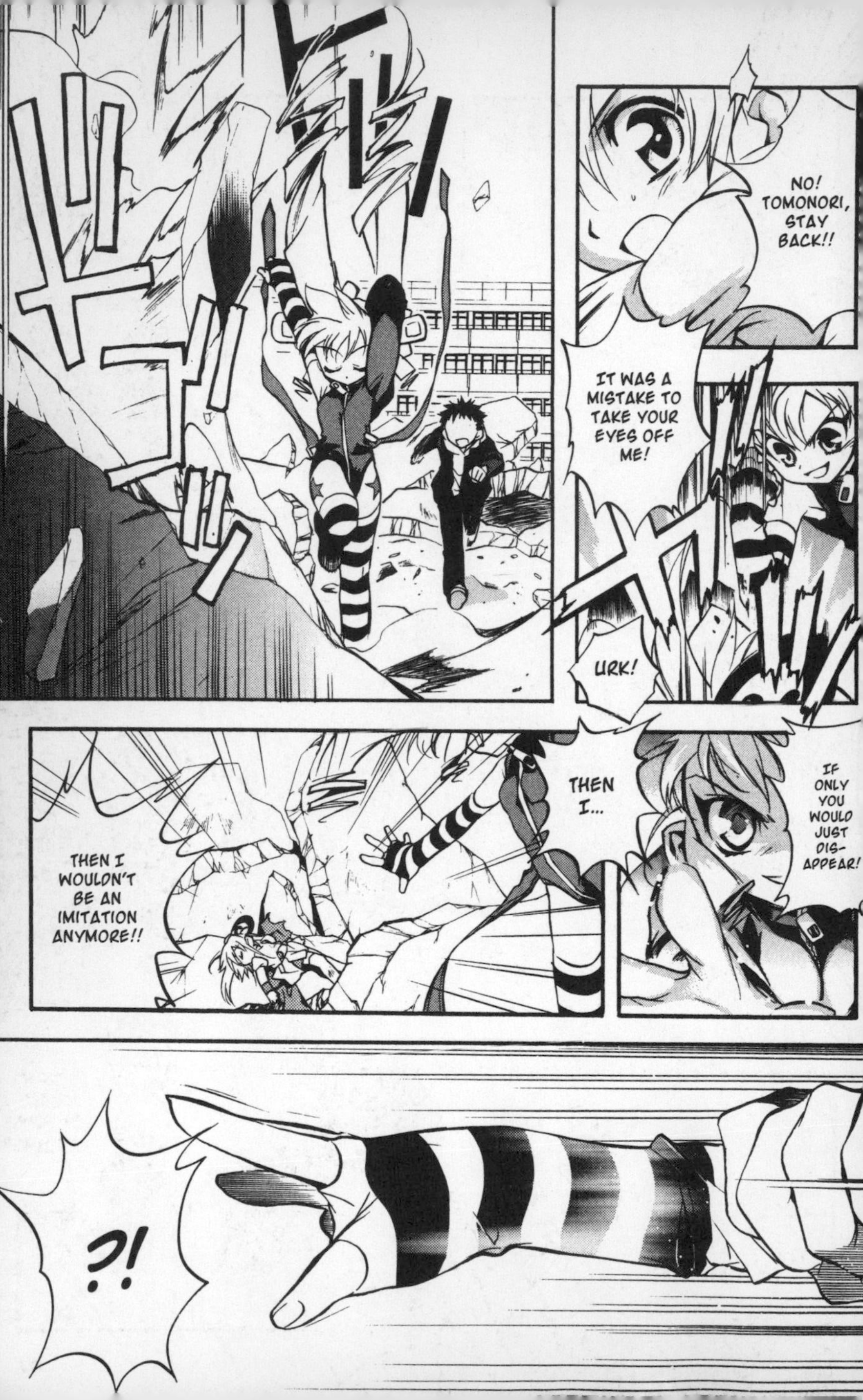
NO! TOMONORI, STAY BACK!!
IT WAS A MISTAKE TO TAKE YOUR EYES OFF ME!
URK!
IF ONLY YOU WOULD JUST DIS-APPEAR!
THEN I...
THEN I WOULDN'T BE AN IMITATION ANYMORE!!
?!

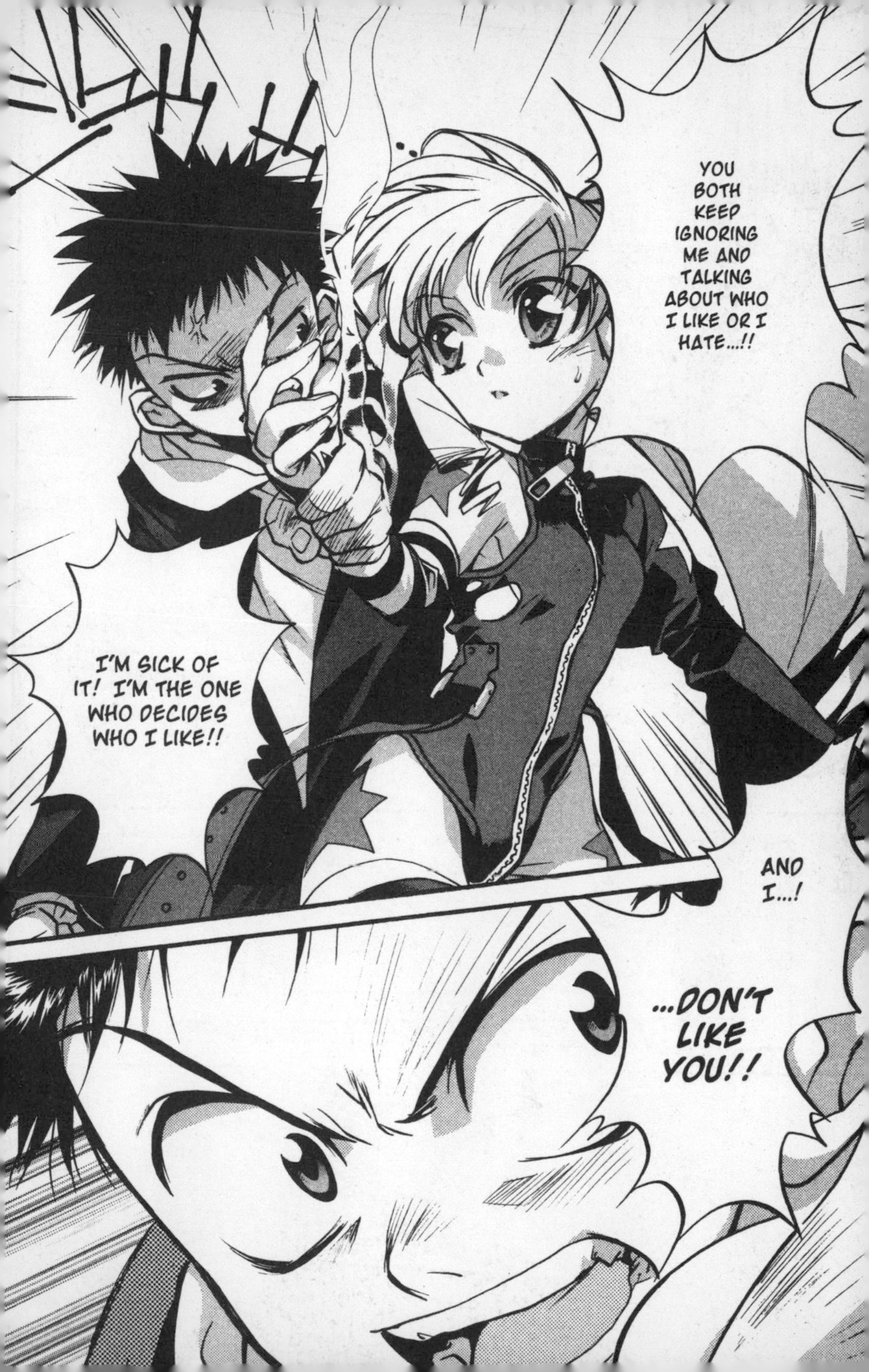
YOU BOTH KEEP IGNORING ME AND TALKING ABOUT WHO I LIKE OR I HATE...!!
I'M SICK OF IT! I'M THE ONE WHO DECIDES WHO I LIKE!!
AND I...!
...DON'T LIKE YOU!!

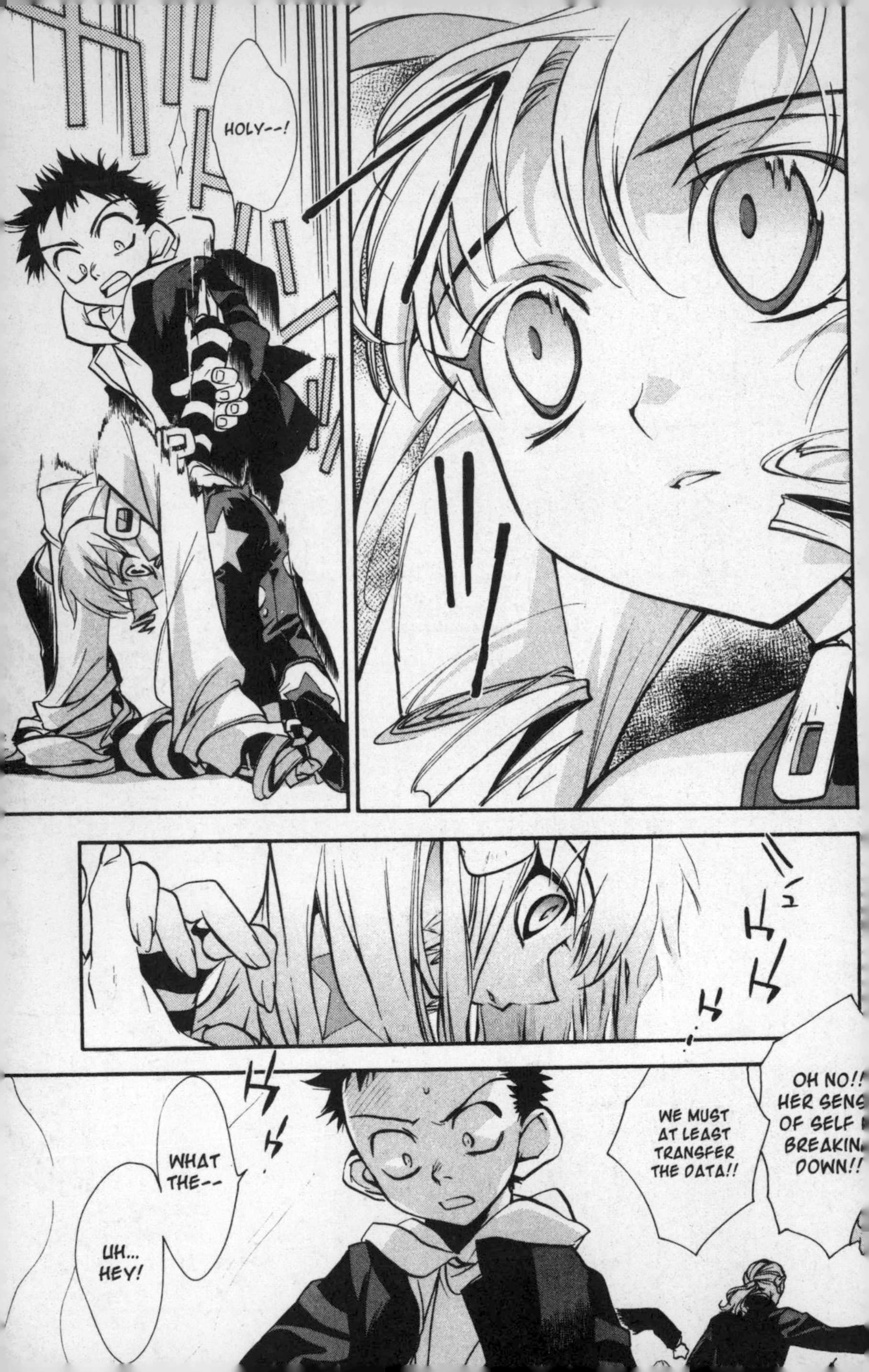
HOLY--!
OH NO!! HER SENS OF SELF BREAKIN DOWN!!
WE MUST AT LEAST TRANSFER THE DATA!!
WHAT THE--
UH... HEY!

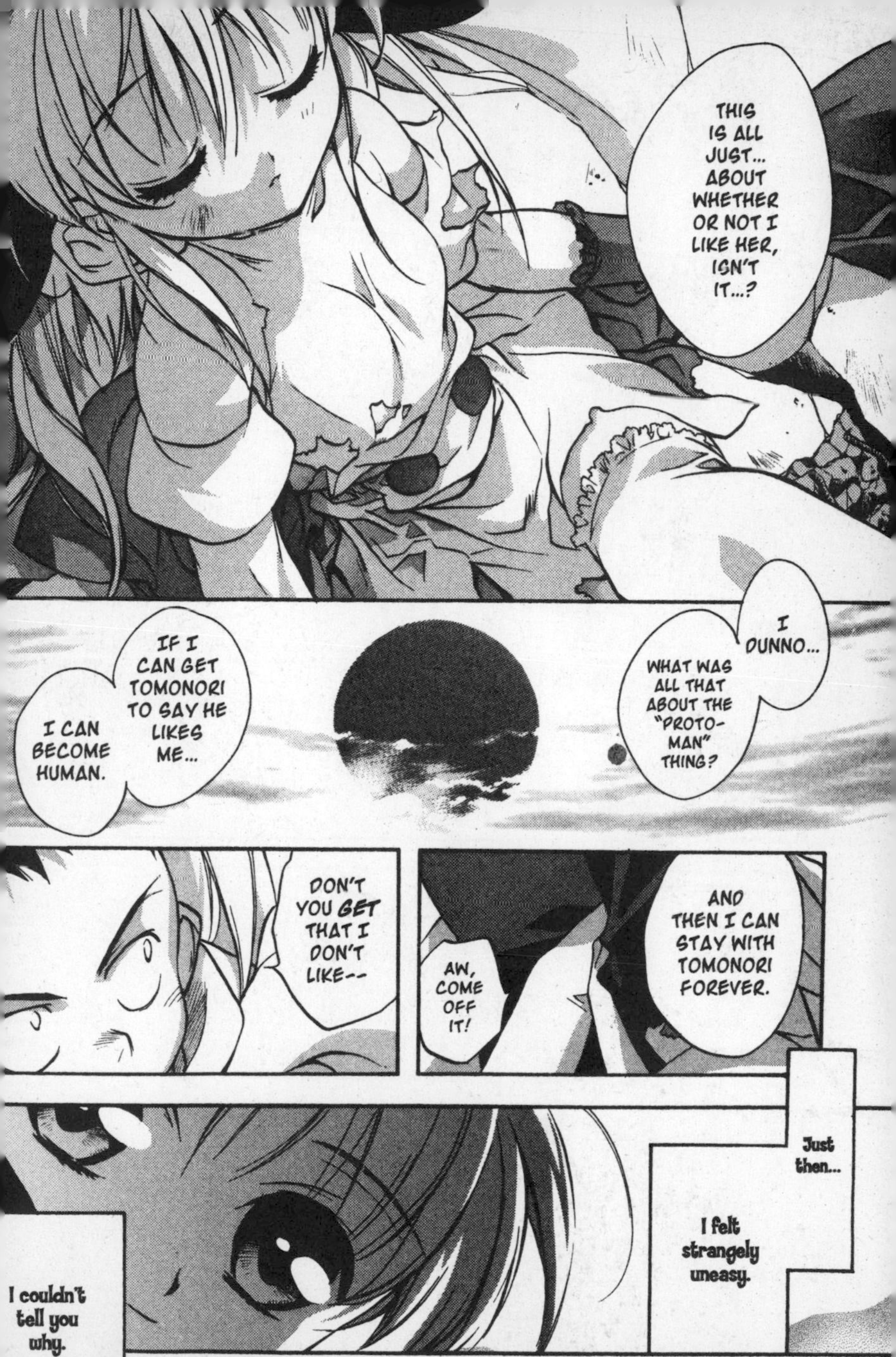
THIS IS ALL JUST... ABOUT WHETHER OR NOT I LIKE HER, ISN'T IT...?
I DUNNO...
WHAT WAS ALL THAT ABOUT THE "PROTO-MAN" THING?
IF I CAN GET TOMONORI TO SAY HE LIKES ME...
I CAN BECOME HUMAN.
AND THEN I CAN STAY WITH TOMONORI FOREVER.
AW, COME OFF IT!
DON'T YOU GET THAT I DON'T LIKE--
Just then...
I felt strangely uneasy.
I couldn't tell you why.

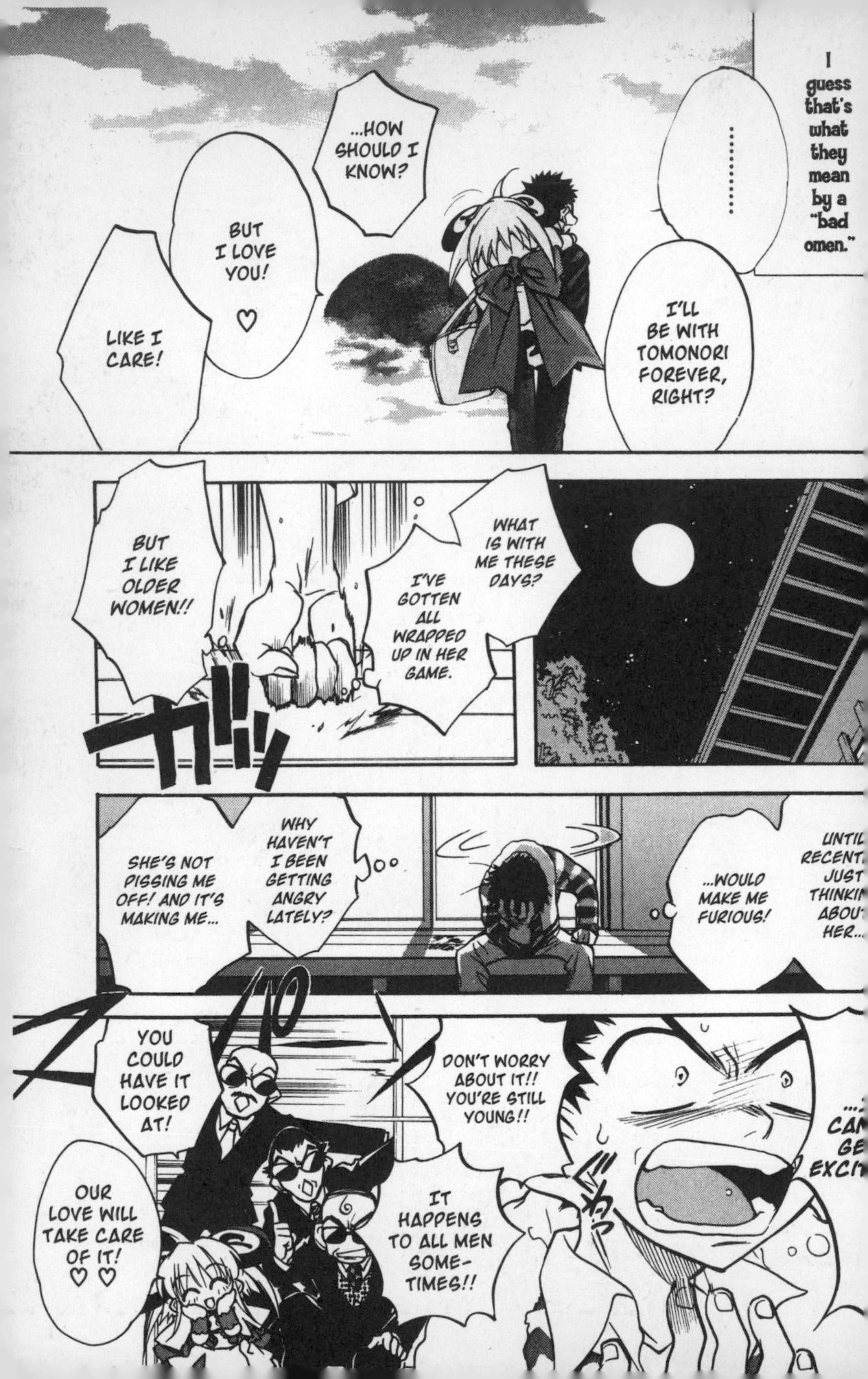
I guess that's what they mean by a "bad omen."
......
I'LL BE WITH TOMONORI FOREVER, RIGHT?
...HOW SHOULD I KNOW?
BUT I LOVE YOU! ♡
LIKE I CARE!
WHAT IS WITH ME THESE DAYS?
I'VE GOTTEN ALL WRAPPED UP IN HER GAME.
BUT I LIKE OLDER WOMEN!!
UNTIL RECENT JUST THINKI ABOUT HER...
...WOULD MAKE ME FURIOUS!
WHY HAVEN'T I BEEN GETTING ANGRY LATELY?
SHE'S NOT PISSING ME OFF! AND IT'S MAKING ME...
...CA GE EXCIT
DON'T WORRY ABOUT IT!! YOU'RE STILL YOUNG!!
YOU COULD HAVE IT LOOKED AT!
IT HAPPENS TO ALL MEN SOME-TIMES!!
OUR LOVE WILL TAKE CARE OF IT! ♡ ♡

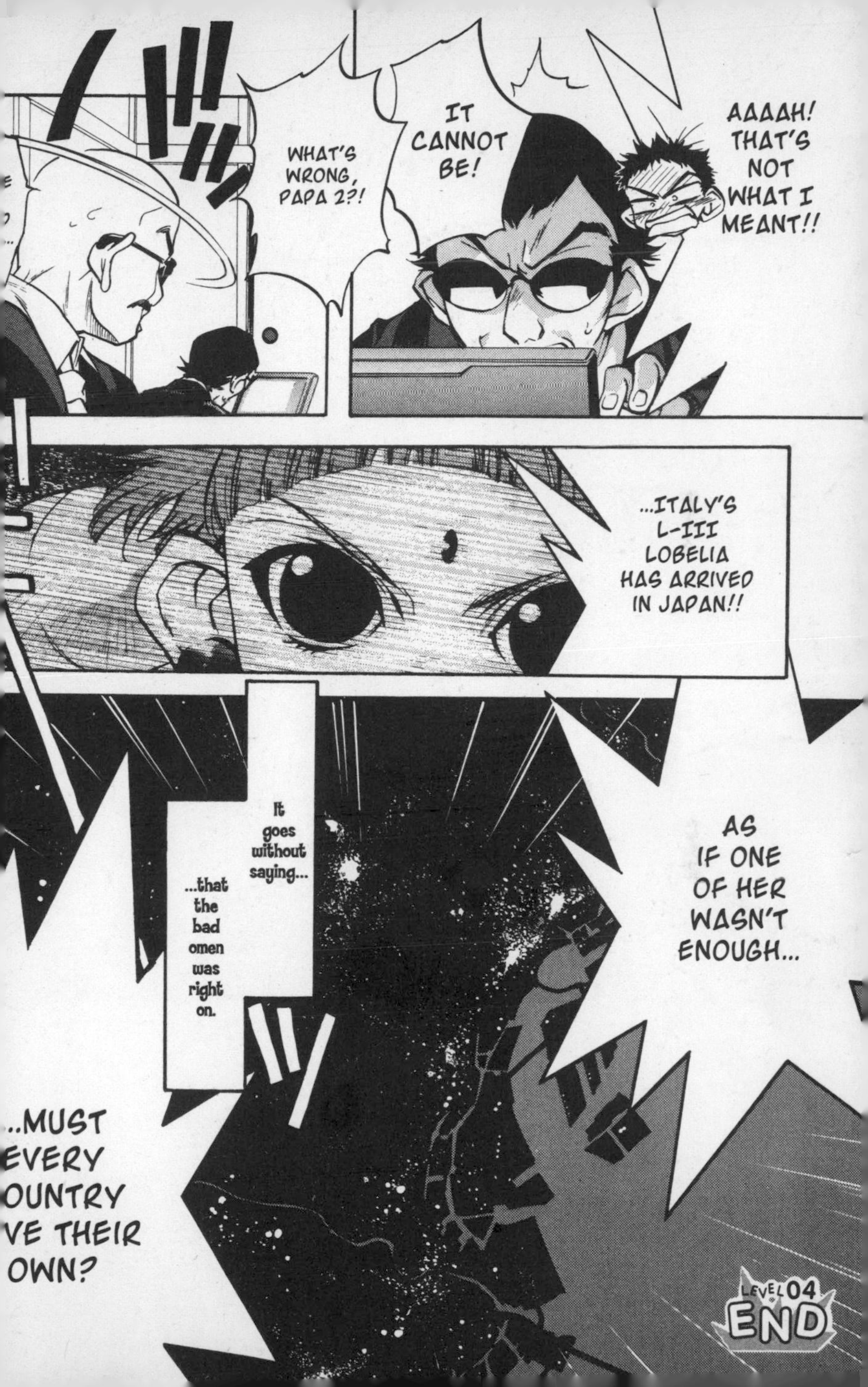
AAAAH! THAT'S NOT WHAT I MEANT!!
IT CANNOT BE!
WHAT'S WRONG, PAPA 2?!
...ITALY'S L-III LOBELIA HAS ARRIVED IN JAPAN!!
AS IF ONE OF HER WASN'T ENOUGH...
It goes without saying...
...that the bad omen was right on.
..MUST EVERY OUNTRY VE THEIR OWN?
LEVEL 04 END

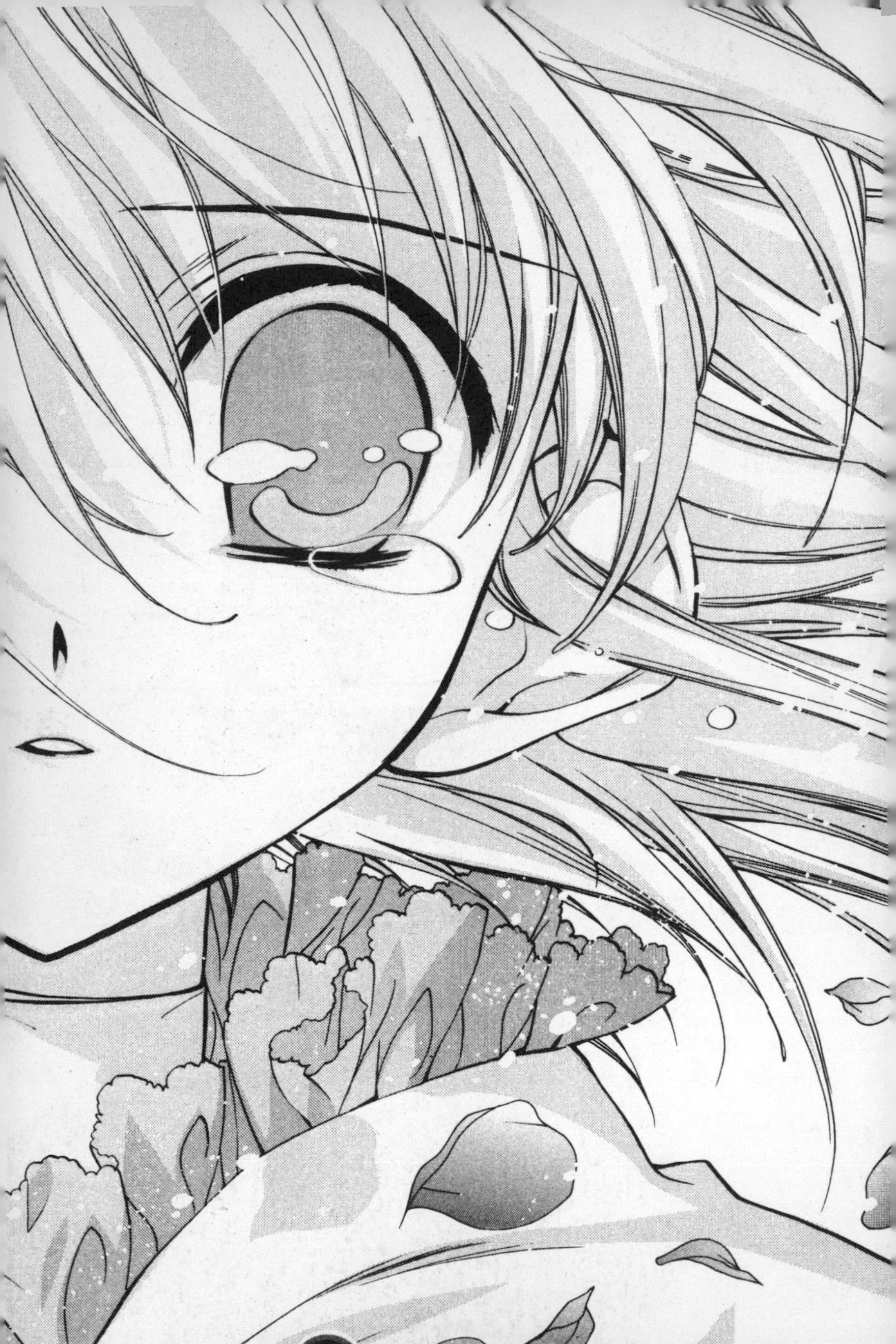

LEVEL 05 Love Comes with Tears

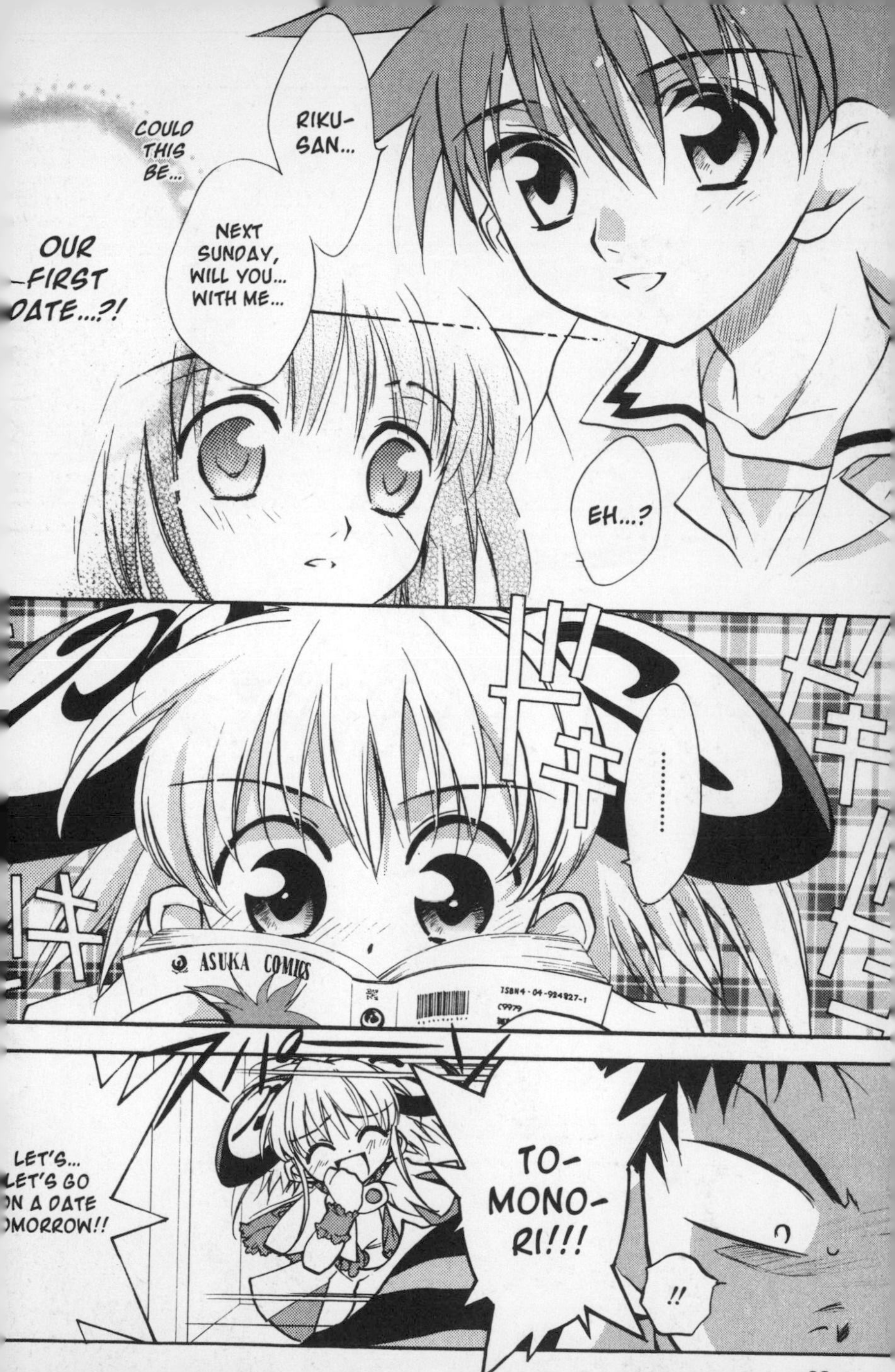
RIKU-SAN...
COULD THIS BE...
NEXT SUNDAY, WILL YOU... WITH ME...
OUR -FIRST DATE...?!
EH...?
......
ASUKA COMICS
ISBN4-04-924827-1
C9979
TO-MONO-RI!!!
!!
LET'S... LET'S GO ON A DATE OMORROW!!

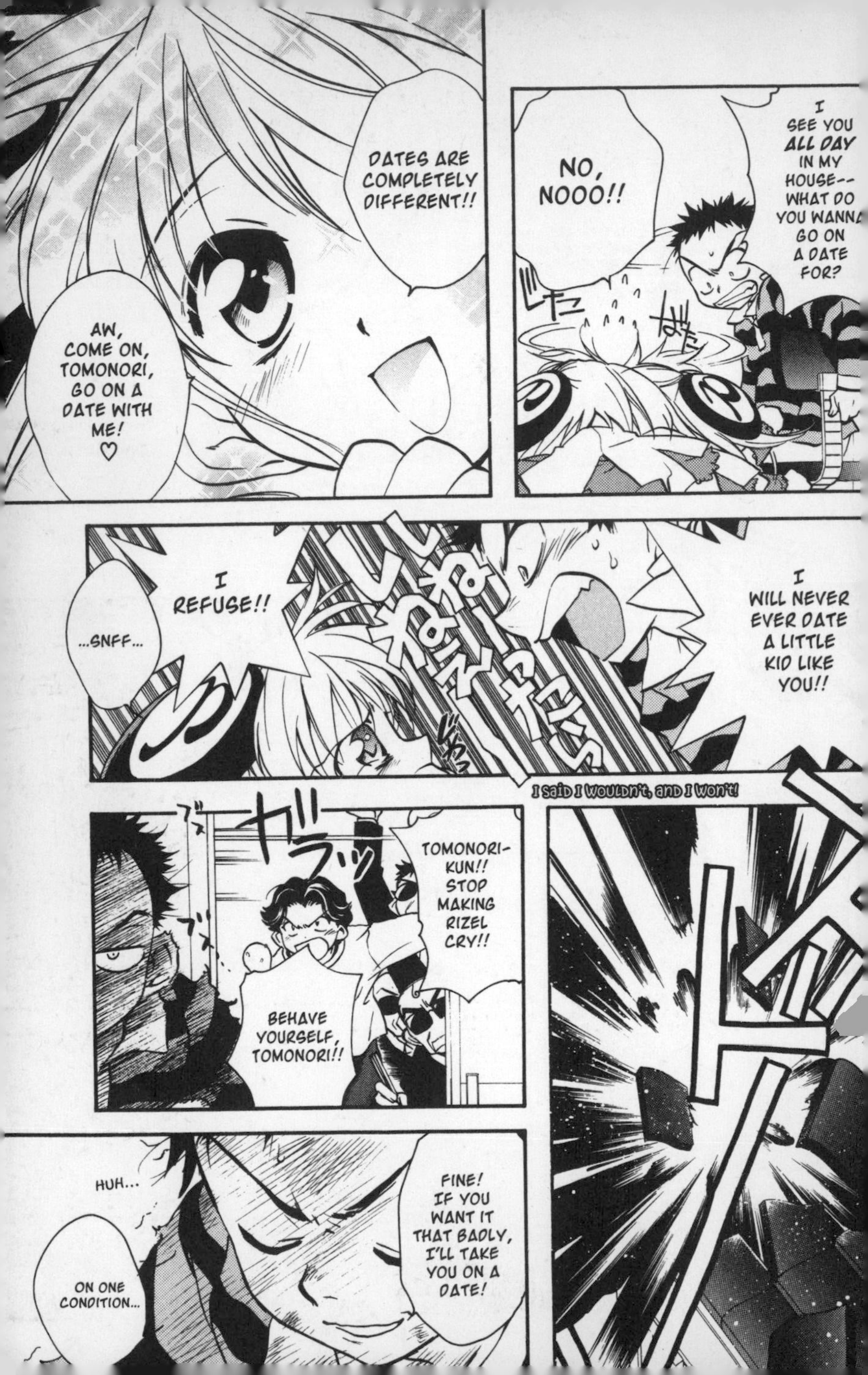
I SEE YOU ALL DAY IN MY HOUSE-- WHAT DO YOU WANNA GO ON A DATE FOR?
NO, NOOO!!
DATES ARE COMPLETELY DIFFERENT!!
AW, COME ON, TOMONORI, GO ON A DATE WITH ME! ♡
I WILL NEVER EVER DATE A LITTLE KID LIKE YOU!!
I REFUSE!!
...SNFF...
I said I wouldn't, and I won't!
TOMONORI-KUN!! STOP MAKING RIZEL CRY!!
BEHAVE YOURSELF, TOMONORI!!
FINE! IF YOU WANT IT THAT BADLY, I'LL TAKE YOU ON A DATE!
HUH...
ON ONE CONDITION...

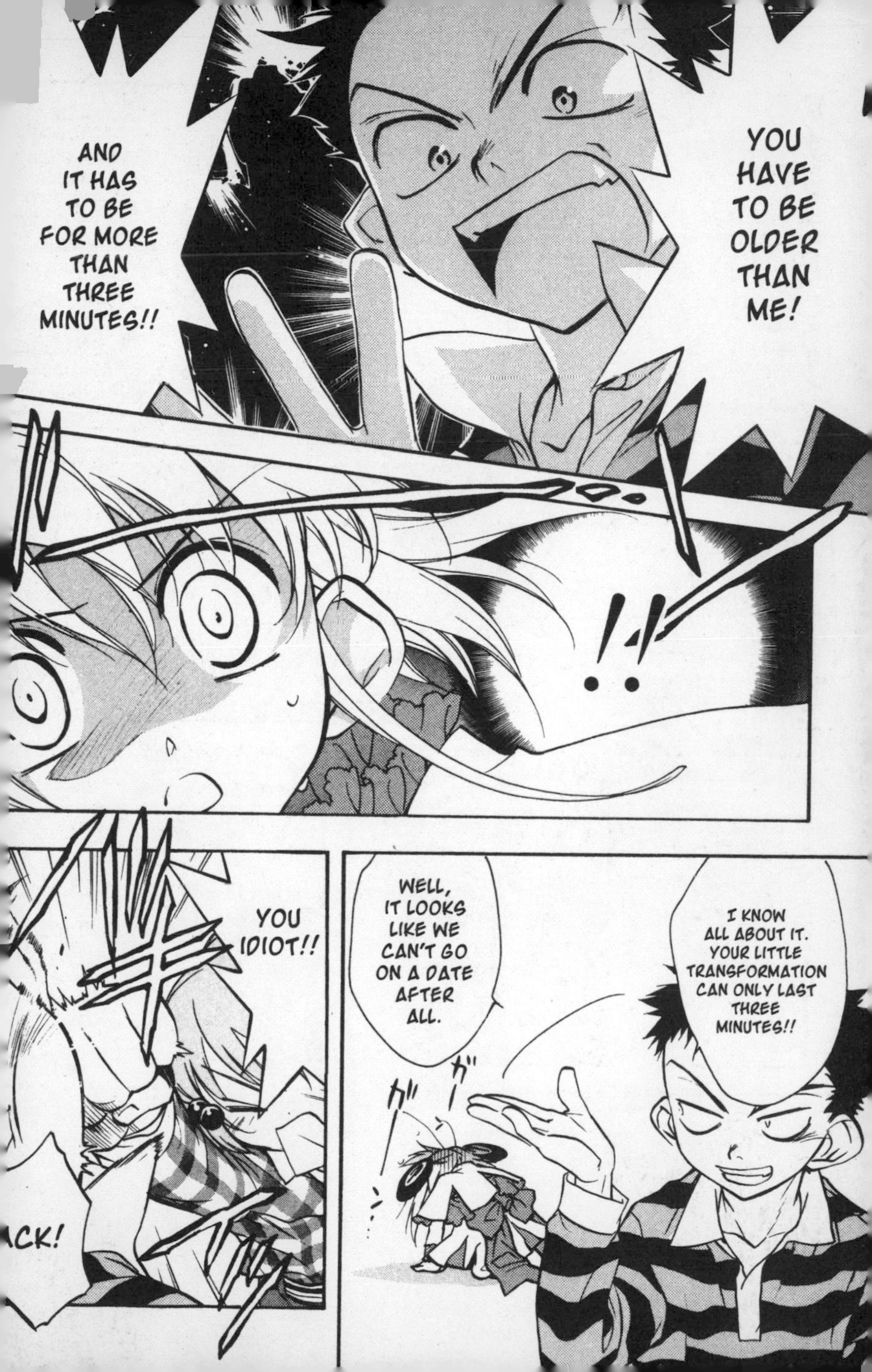
YOU HAVE TO BE OLDER THAN ME!
AND IT HAS TO BE FOR MORE THAN THREE MINUTES!!
!!
I KNOW ALL ABOUT IT. YOUR LITTLE TRANSFORMATION CAN ONLY LAST THREE MINUTES!!
WELL, IT LOOKS LIKE WE CAN'T GO ON A DATE AFTER ALL.
ガ
ガ
YOU IDIOT!!
ACK!

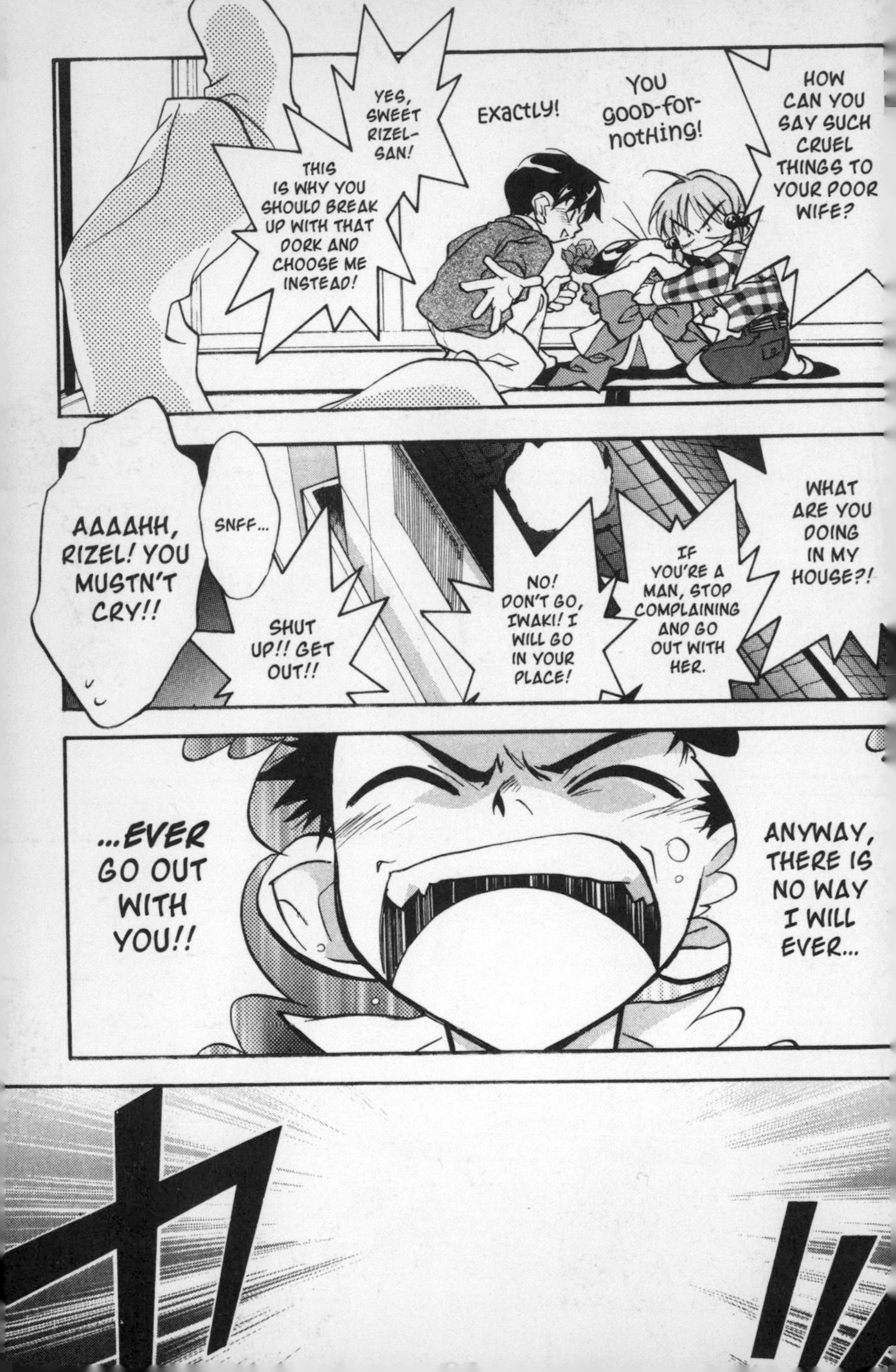
HOW CAN YOU SAY SUCH CRUEL THINGS TO YOUR POOR WIFE?
YOU good-for-nothing!
Exactly!
YES, SWEET RIZEL-SAN!
THIS IS WHY YOU SHOULD BREAK UP WITH THAT DORK AND CHOOSE ME INSTEAD!
WHAT ARE YOU DOING IN MY HOUSE?!
IF YOU'RE A MAN, STOP COMPLAINING AND GO OUT WITH HER.
NO! DON'T GO, IWAKI! I WILL GO IN YOUR PLACE!
SHUT UP!! GET OUT!!
SNFF...
AAAAHH, RIZEL! YOU MUSTN'T CRY!!
ANYWAY, THERE IS NO WAY I WILL EVER...
...EVER GO OUT WITH YOU!!

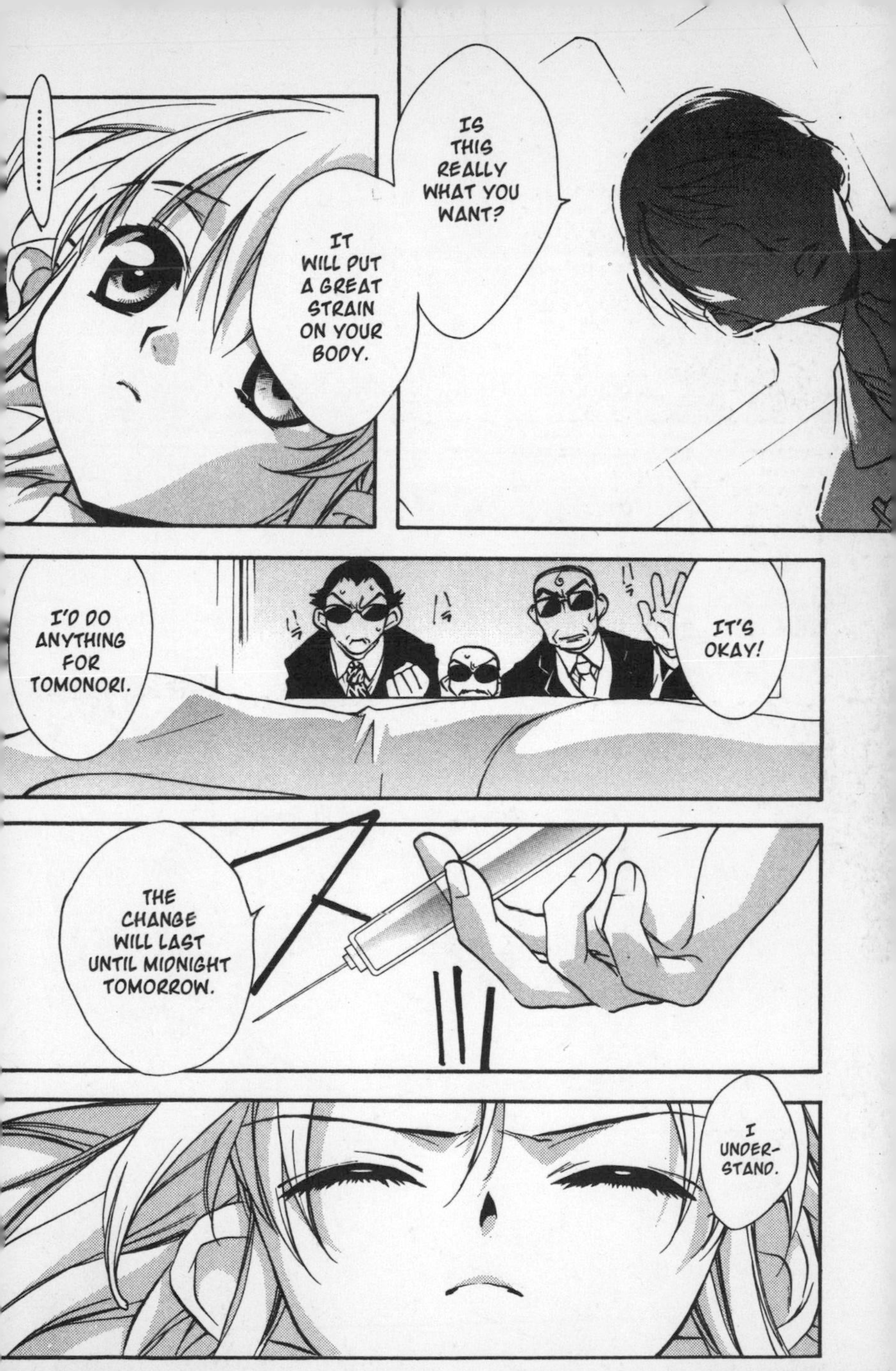
IS THIS REALLY WHAT YOU WANT?
IT WILL PUT A GREAT STRAIN ON YOUR BODY.
......
IT'S OKAY!
I'D DO ANYTHING FOR TOMONORI.
THE CHANGE WILL LAST UNTIL MIDNIGHT TOMORROW.
I UNDER-STAND.

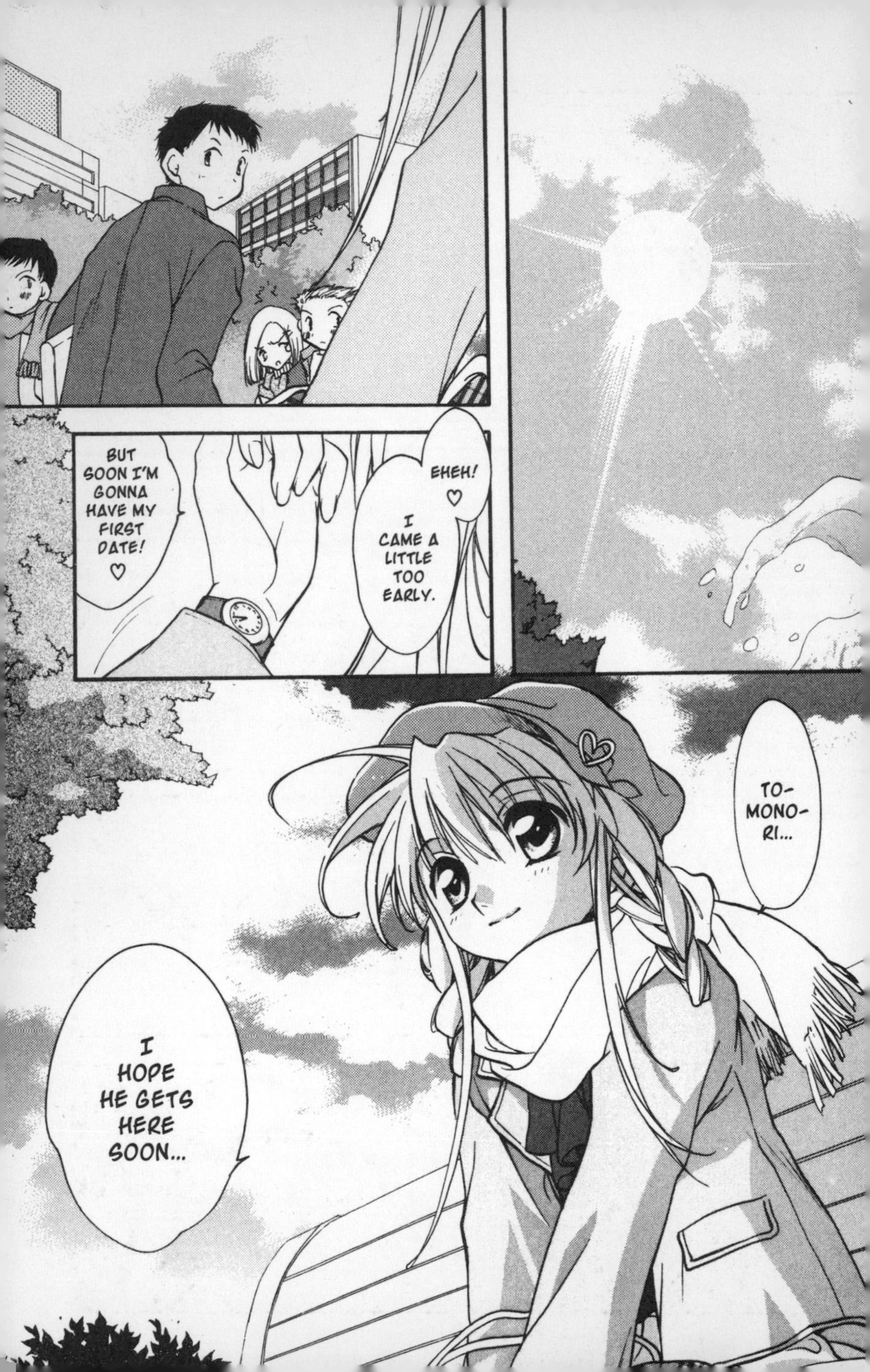
EHEH! ♡
I CAME A LITTLE TOO EARLY.
BUT SOON I'M GONNA HAVE MY FIRST DATE! ♡
TO-MONO-RI...
I HOPE HE GETS HERE SOON...

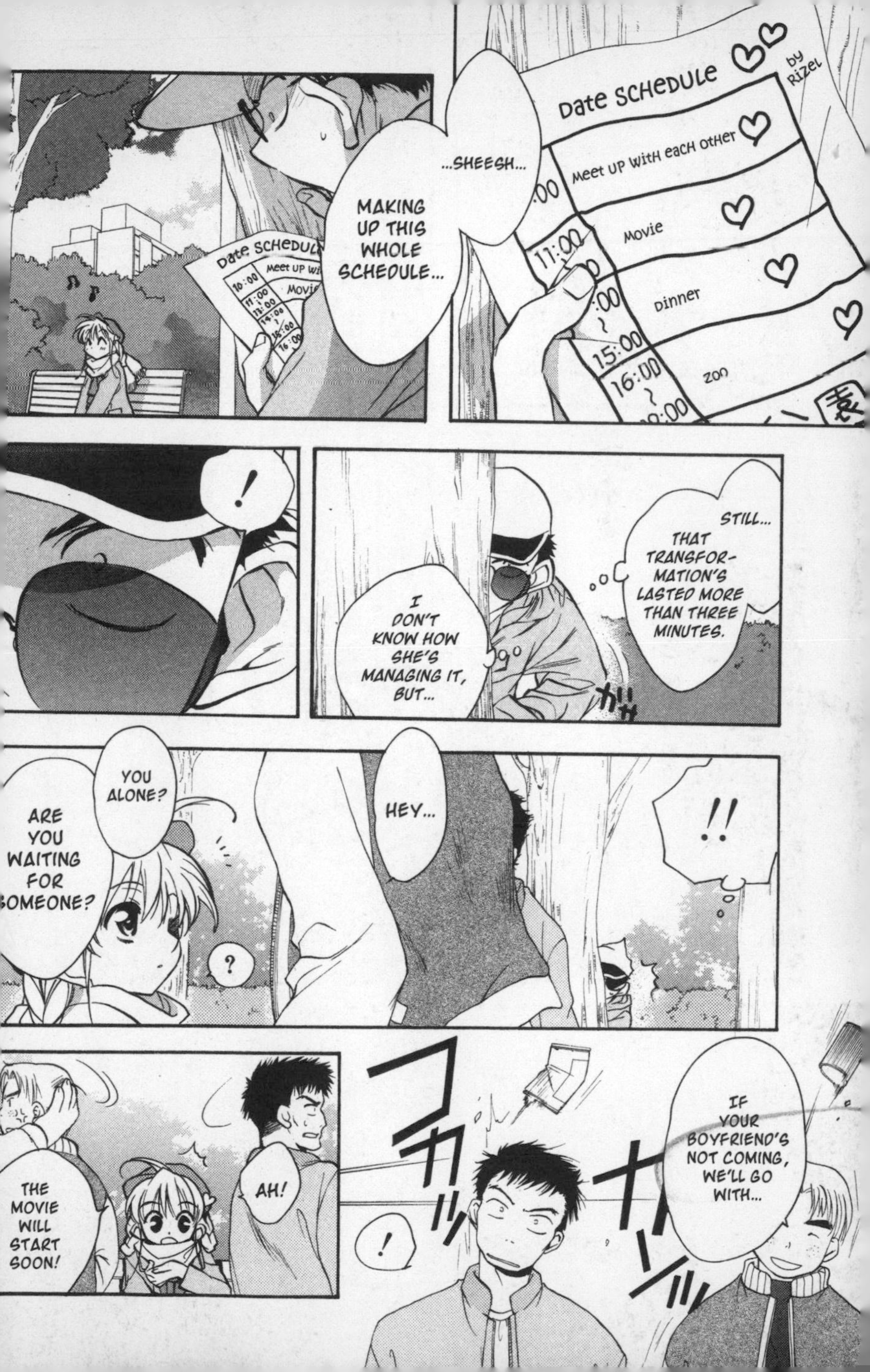
Date SCHEDULE
by Rizel
Meet up with each other
11:00
Movie
Dinner
15:00
16:00
Zoo
...SHEESH...
MAKING UP THIS WHOLE SCHEDULE...
STILL... THAT TRANSFOR-MATION'S LASTED MORE THAN THREE MINUTES.
I DON'T KNOW HOW SHE'S MANAGING IT, BUT...
!
!!
HEY...
YOU ALONE?
ARE YOU WAITING FOR SOMEONE?
?
IF YOUR BOYFRIEND'S NOT COMING, WE'LL GO WITH...
!
AH!
THE MOVIE WILL START SOON!

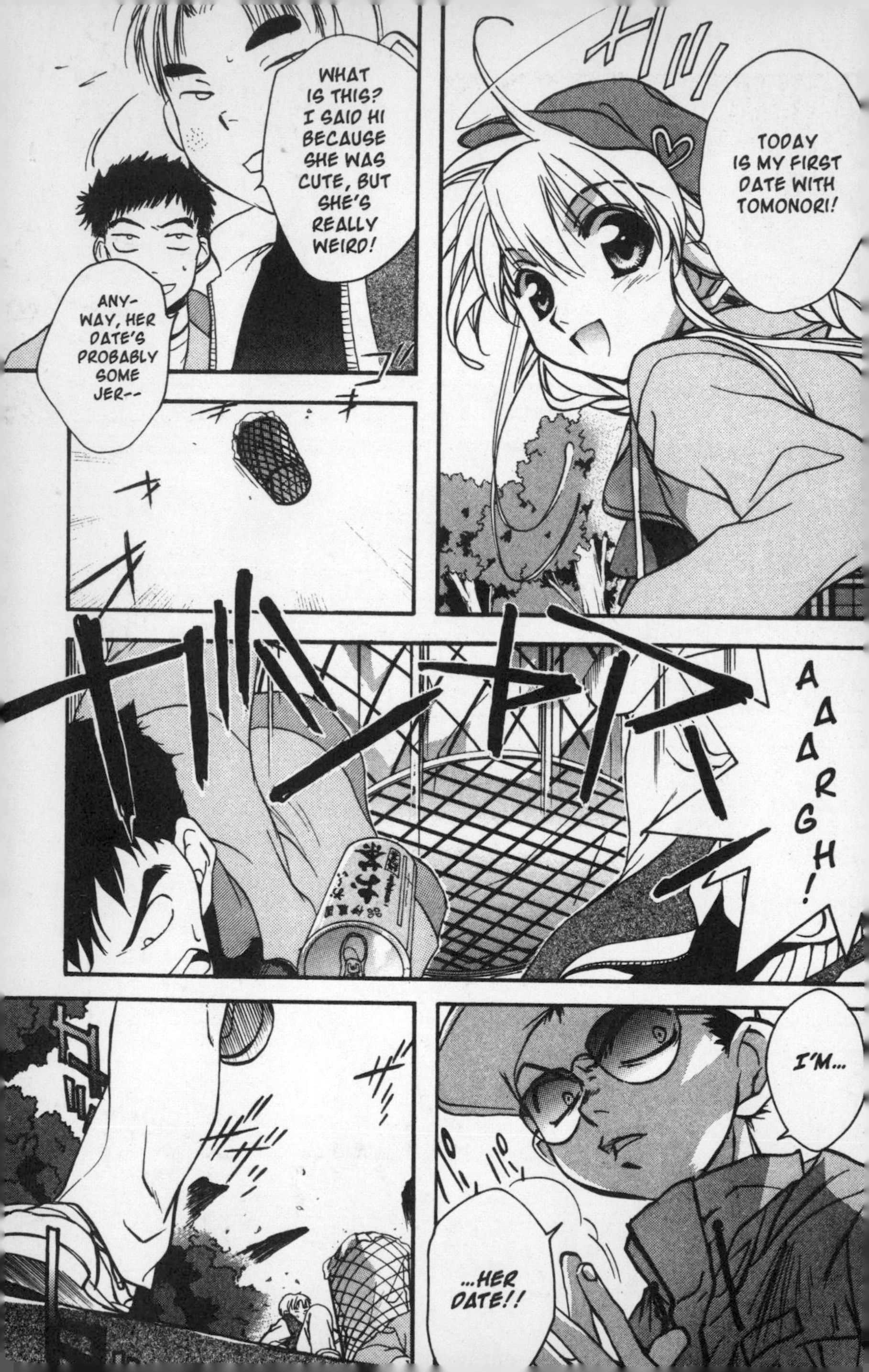
TODAY IS MY FIRST DATE WITH TOMONORI!
WHAT IS THIS? I SAID HI BECAUSE SHE WAS CUTE, BUT SHE'S REALLY WEIRD!
ANY-WAY, HER DATE'S PROBABLY SOME JER--
AAARGH!
I'M...
...HER DATE!!

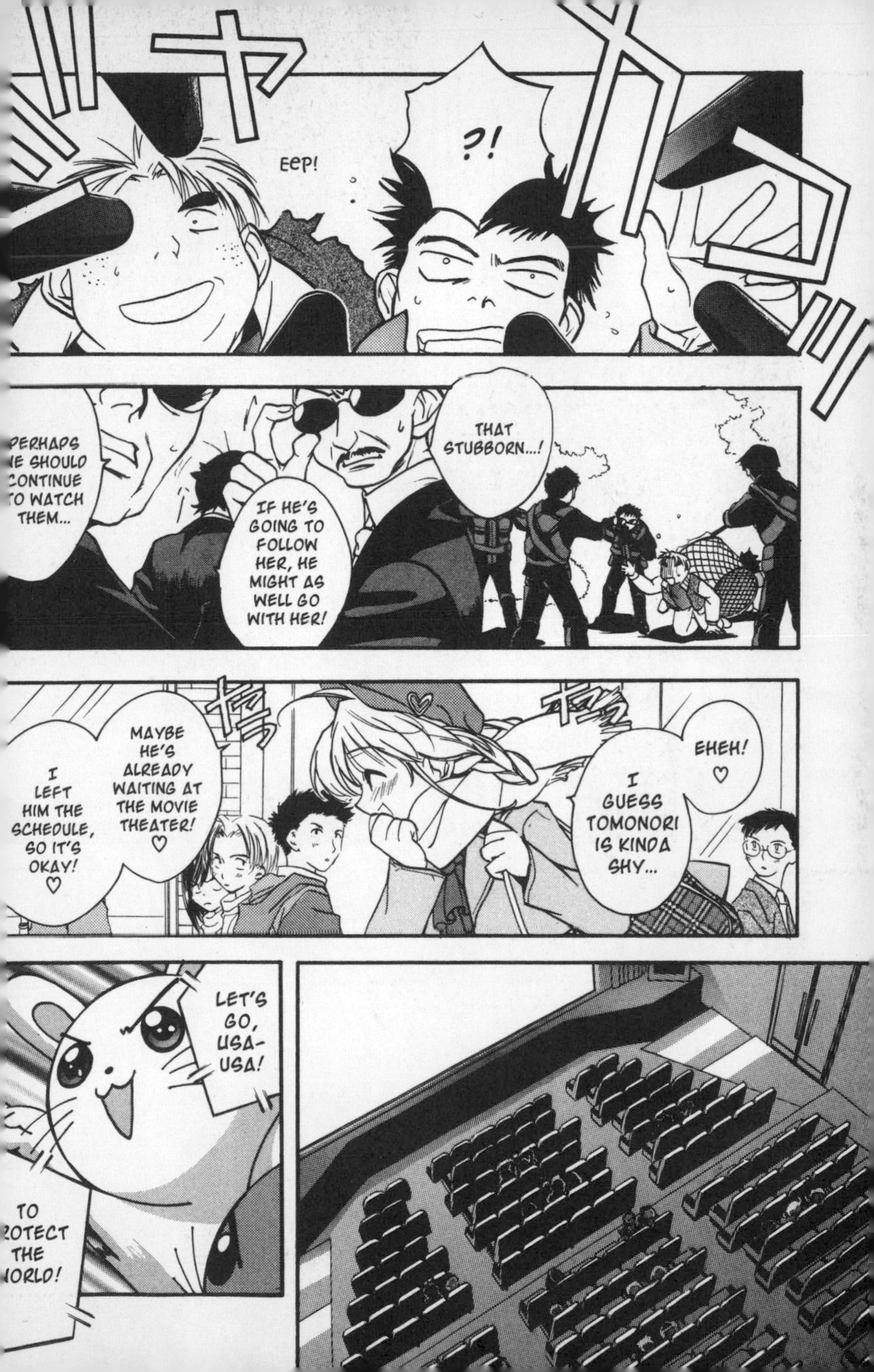
?!
EEP!
THAT STUBBORN...!
IF HE'S GOING TO FOLLOW HER, HE MIGHT AS WELL GO WITH HER!
PERHAPS E SHOULD CONTINUE O WATCH THEM...
EHEH! ♡
I GUESS TOMONORI IS KINDA SHY...
MAYBE HE'S ALREADY WAITING AT THE MOVIE THEATER! ♡
I LEFT HIM THE SCHEDULE, SO IT'S OKAY! ♡
LET'S GO, USA-USA!
TO ROTECT THE ORLD!

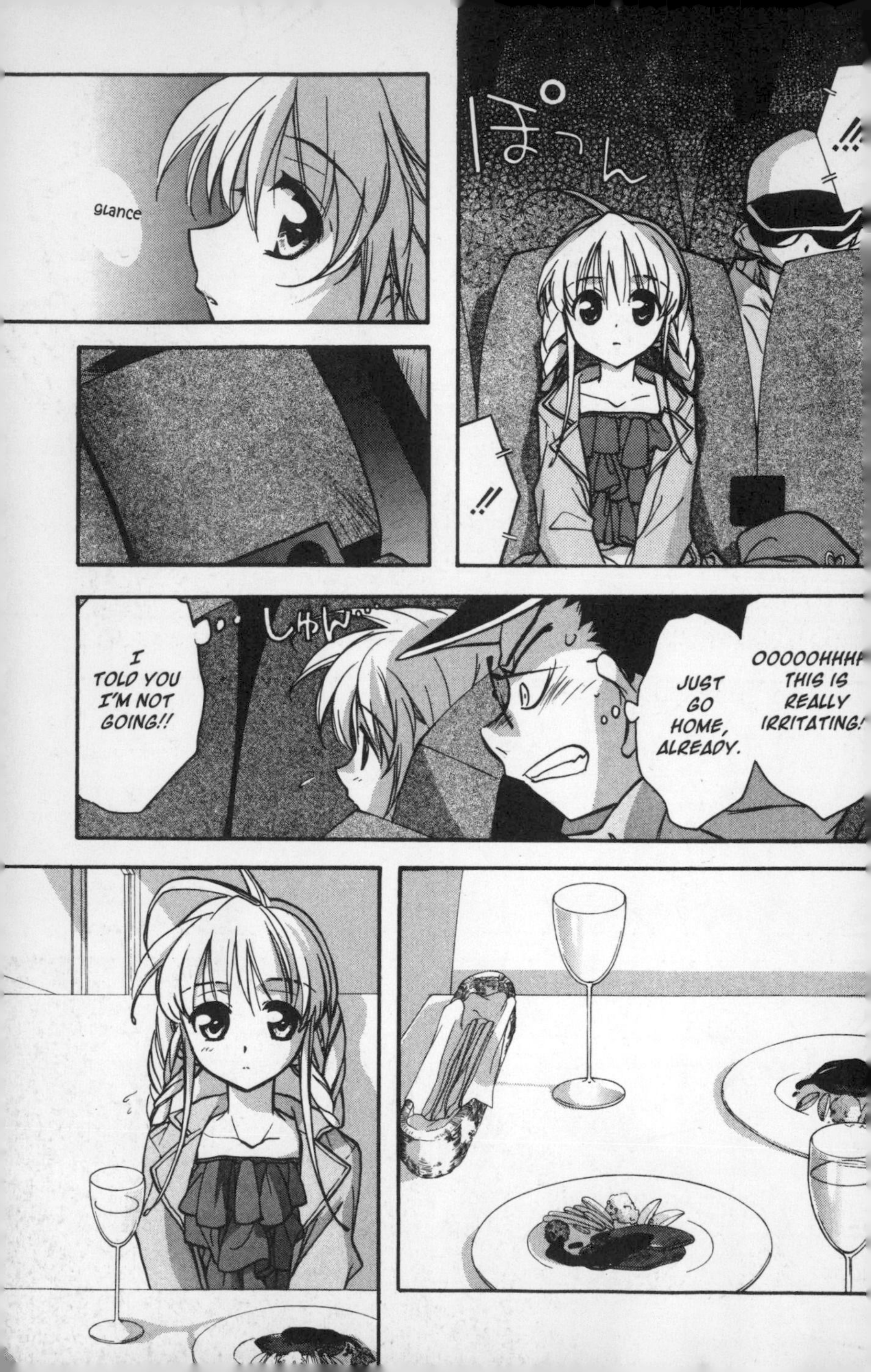
ぽっん
!!
!!
glance
OOOOOHHH THIS IS REALLY IRRITATING!
JUST GO HOME, ALREADY.
しゅん
I TOLD YOU I'M NOT GOING!!

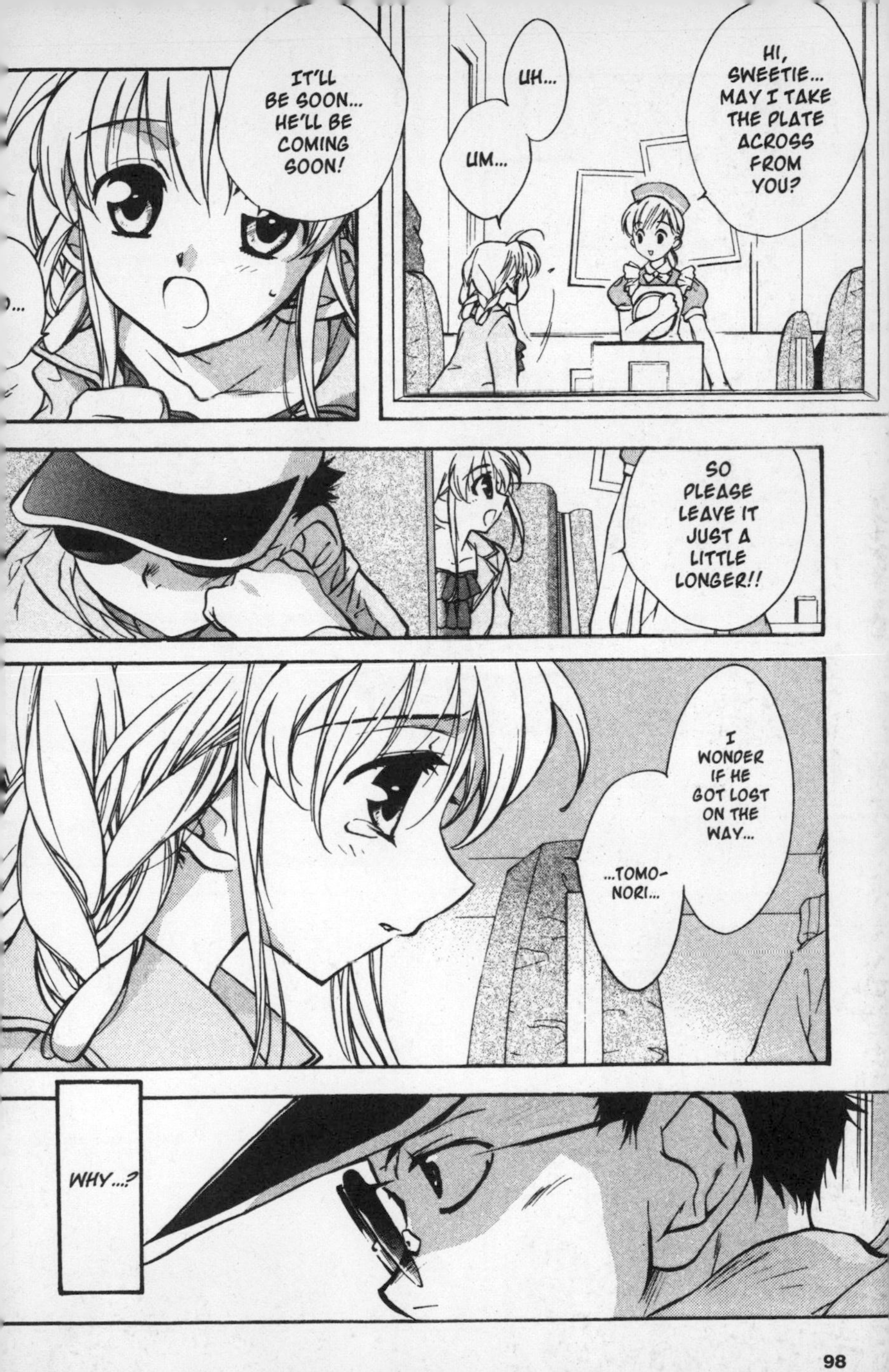
HI, SWEETIE... MAY I TAKE THE PLATE ACROSS FROM YOU?
UH...
UM...
IT'LL BE SOON... HE'LL BE COMING SOON!
SO PLEASE LEAVE IT JUST A LITTLE LONGER!!
I WONDER IF HE GOT LOST ON THE WAY...
...TOMO-NORI...
WHY...?

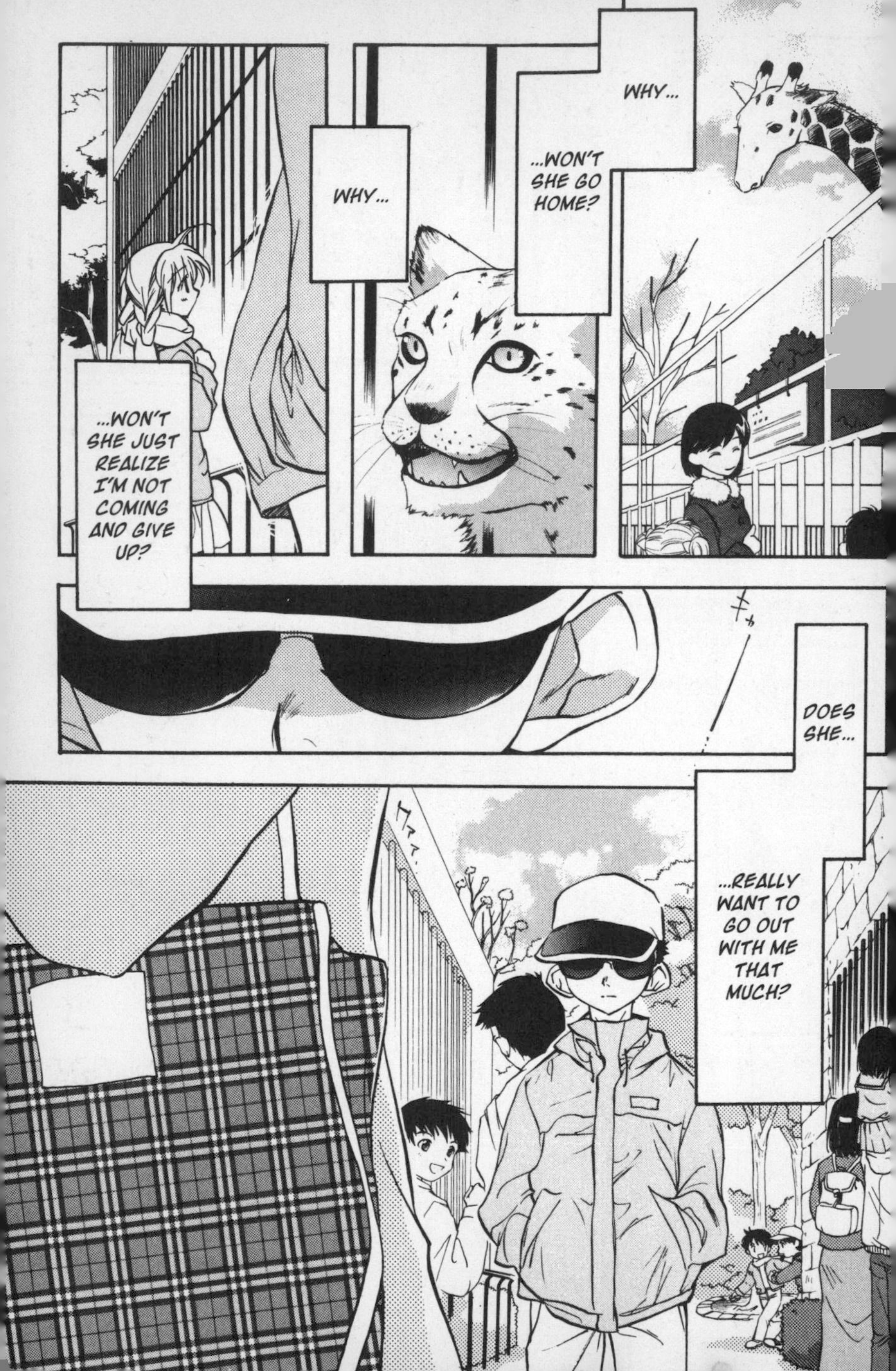
WHY...
...WON'T SHE GO HOME?
WHY...
...WON'T SHE JUST REALIZE I'M NOT COMING AND GIVE UP?
DOES SHE...
...REALLY WANT TO GO OUT WITH ME THAT MUCH?

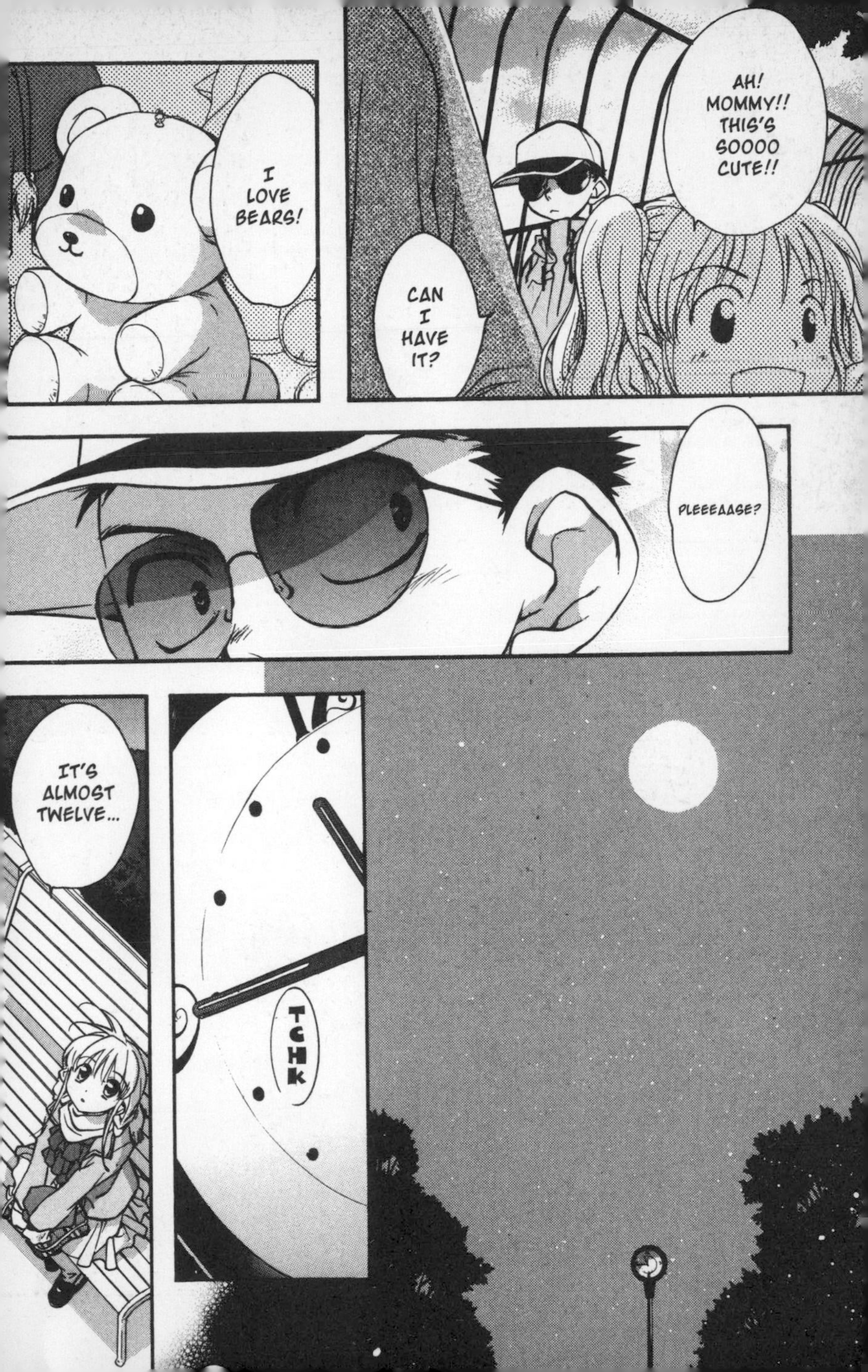
AH! MOMMY!! THIS'S SOOOO CUTE!!
CAN I HAVE IT?
I LOVE BEARS!
PLEEEAASE?
TCHK
IT'S ALMOST TWELVE...

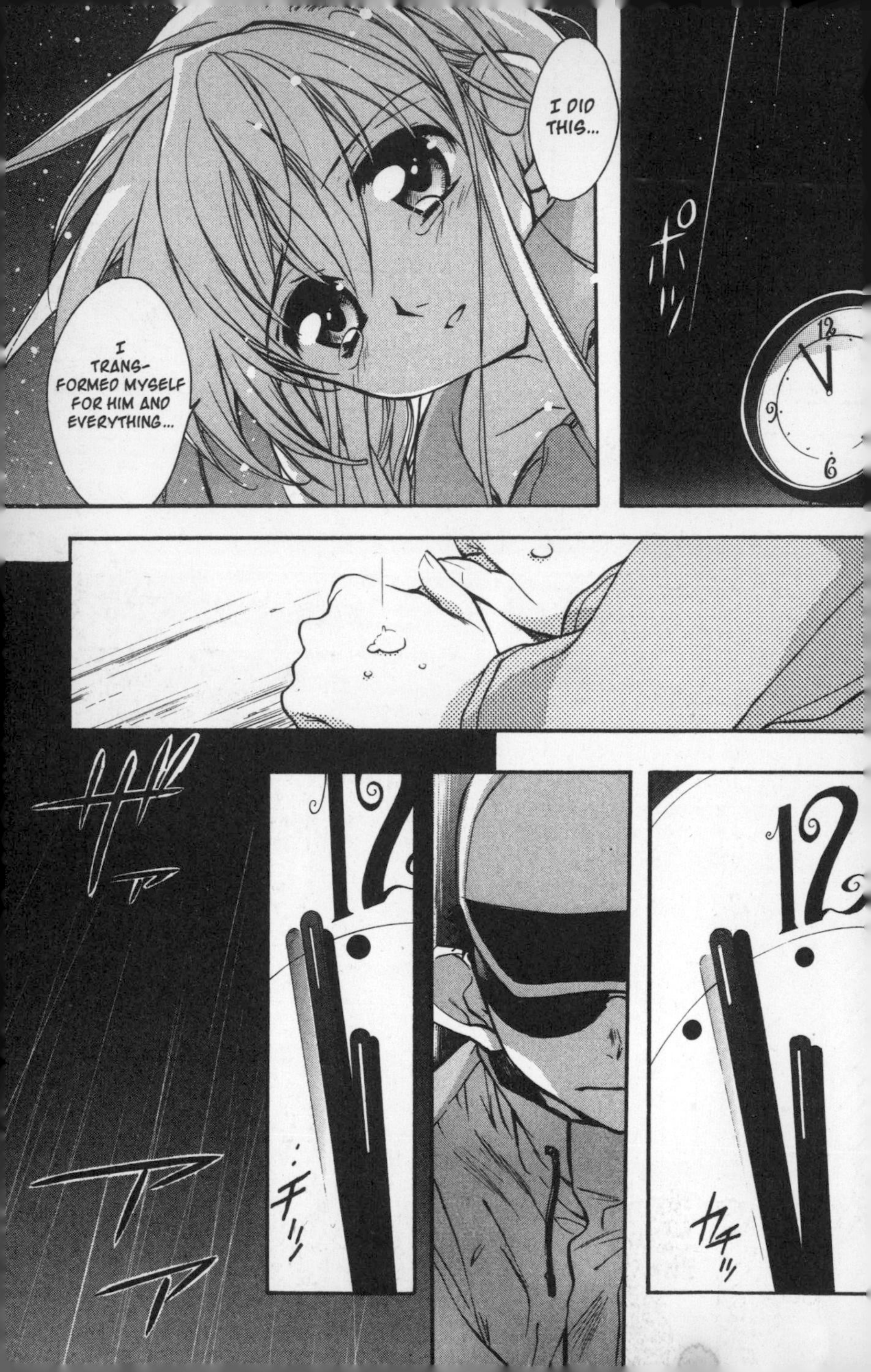
I DID THIS...
I TRANS- FORMED MYSELF FOR HIM AND EVERYTHING...

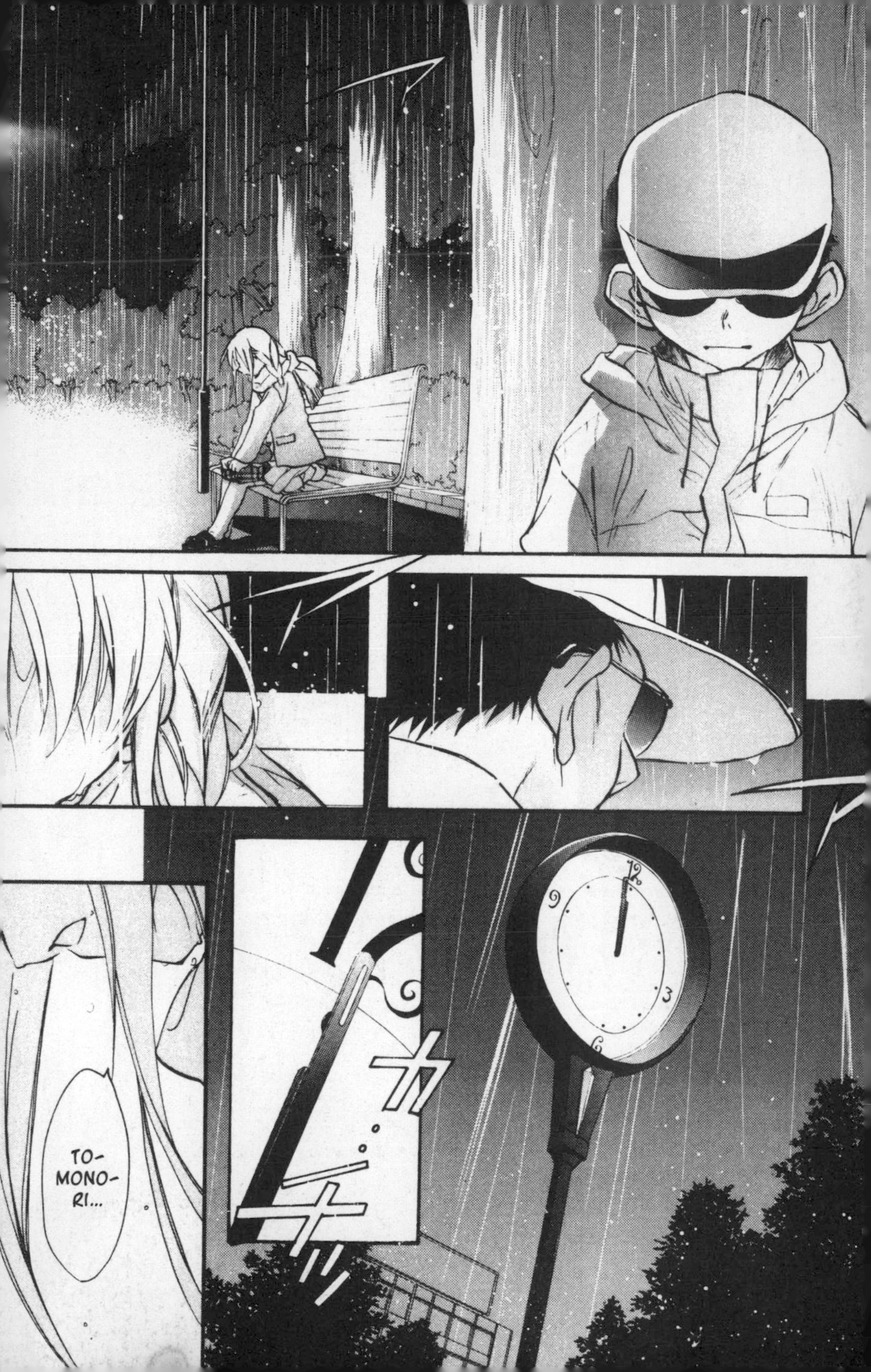
TO-MONO-RI...

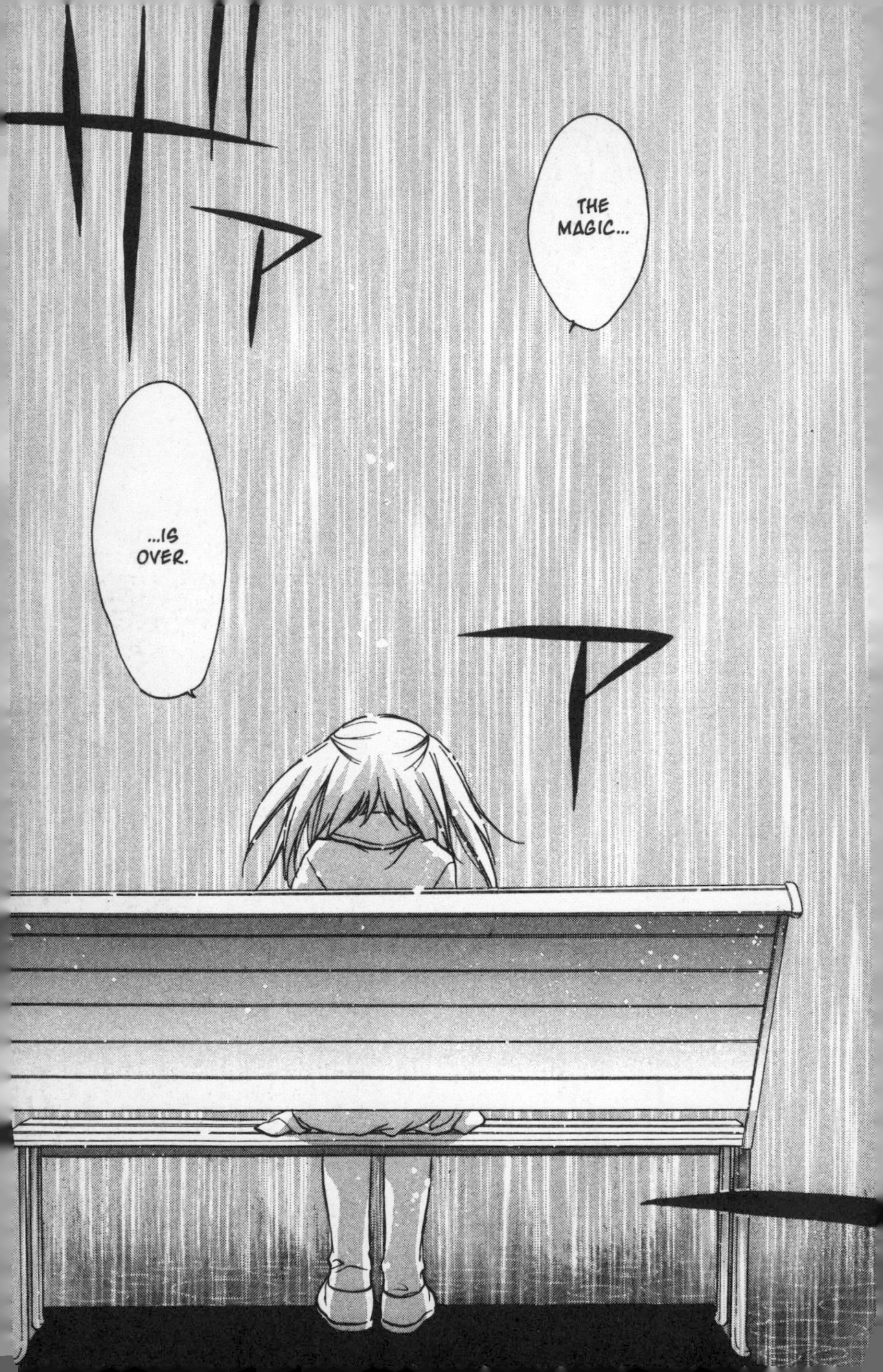
THE MAGIC...
...IS OVER.

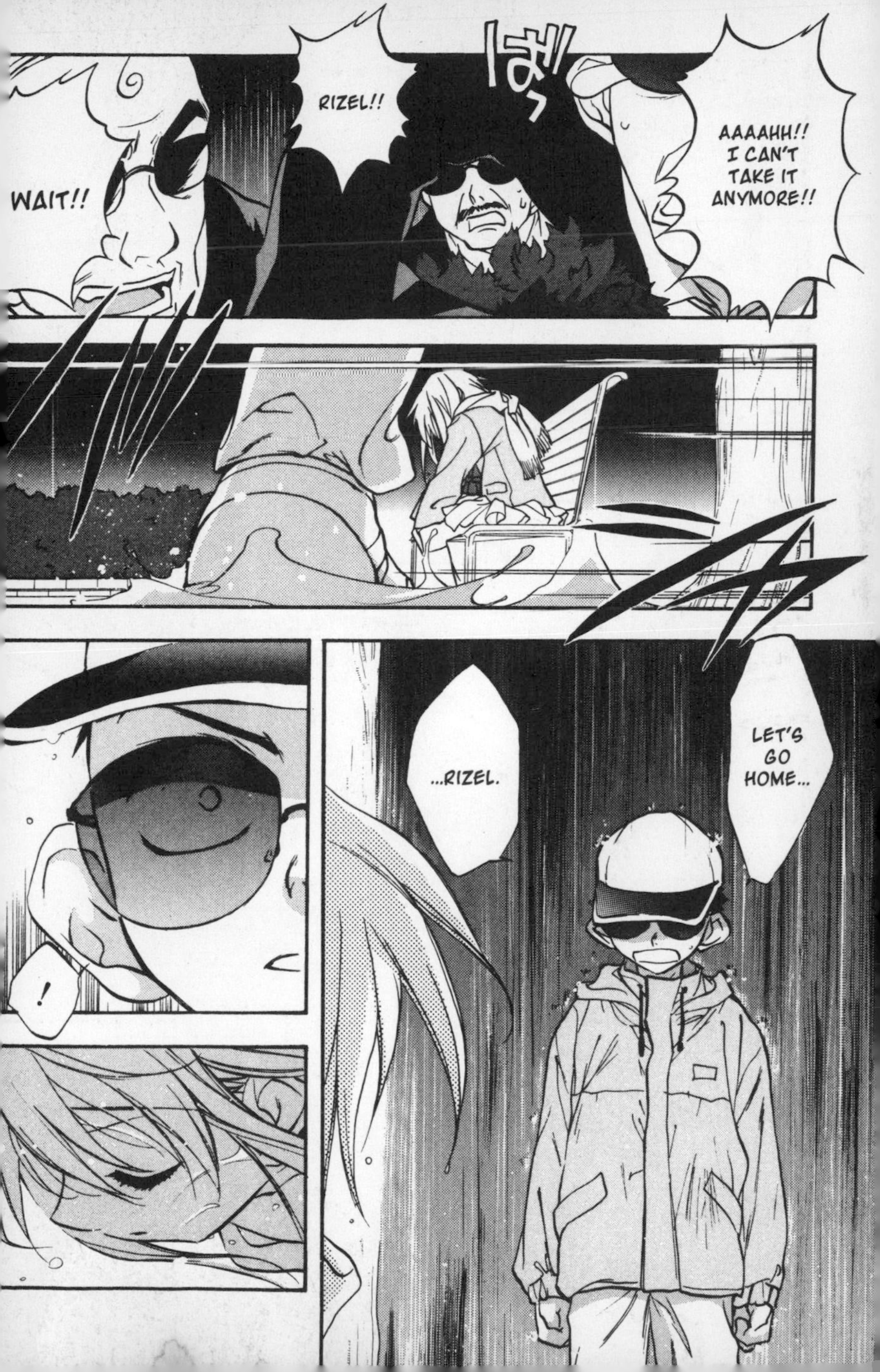
AAAAHH!! I CAN'T TAKE IT ANYMORE!!
ぱっ
RIZEL!!
WAIT!!
LET'S GO HOME...
...RIZEL.
!

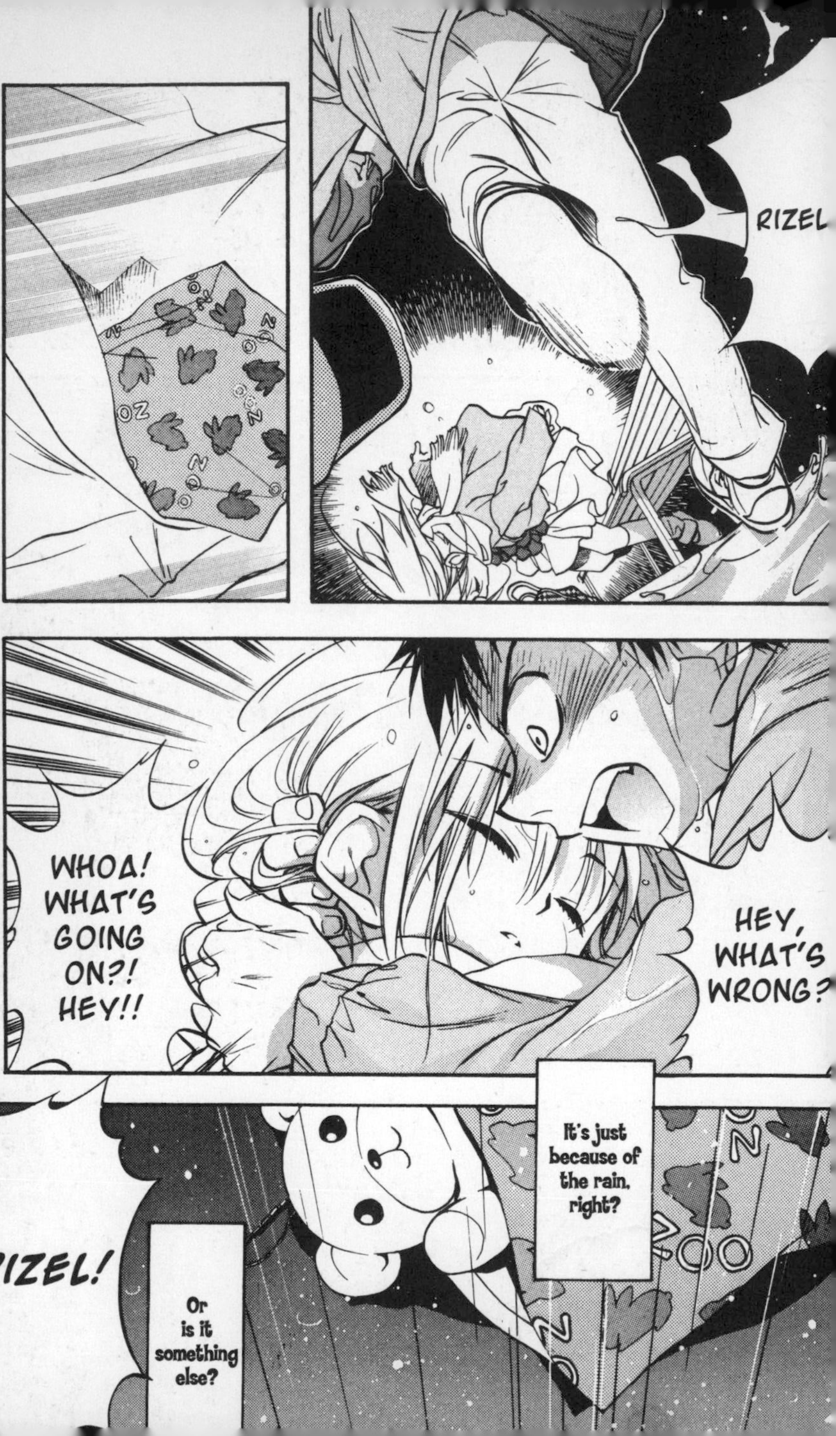
RIZEL
HEY, WHAT'S WRONG?
WHOA! WHAT'S GOING ON?! HEY!!
It's just because of the rain, right?
Or is it something else?
RIZEL!

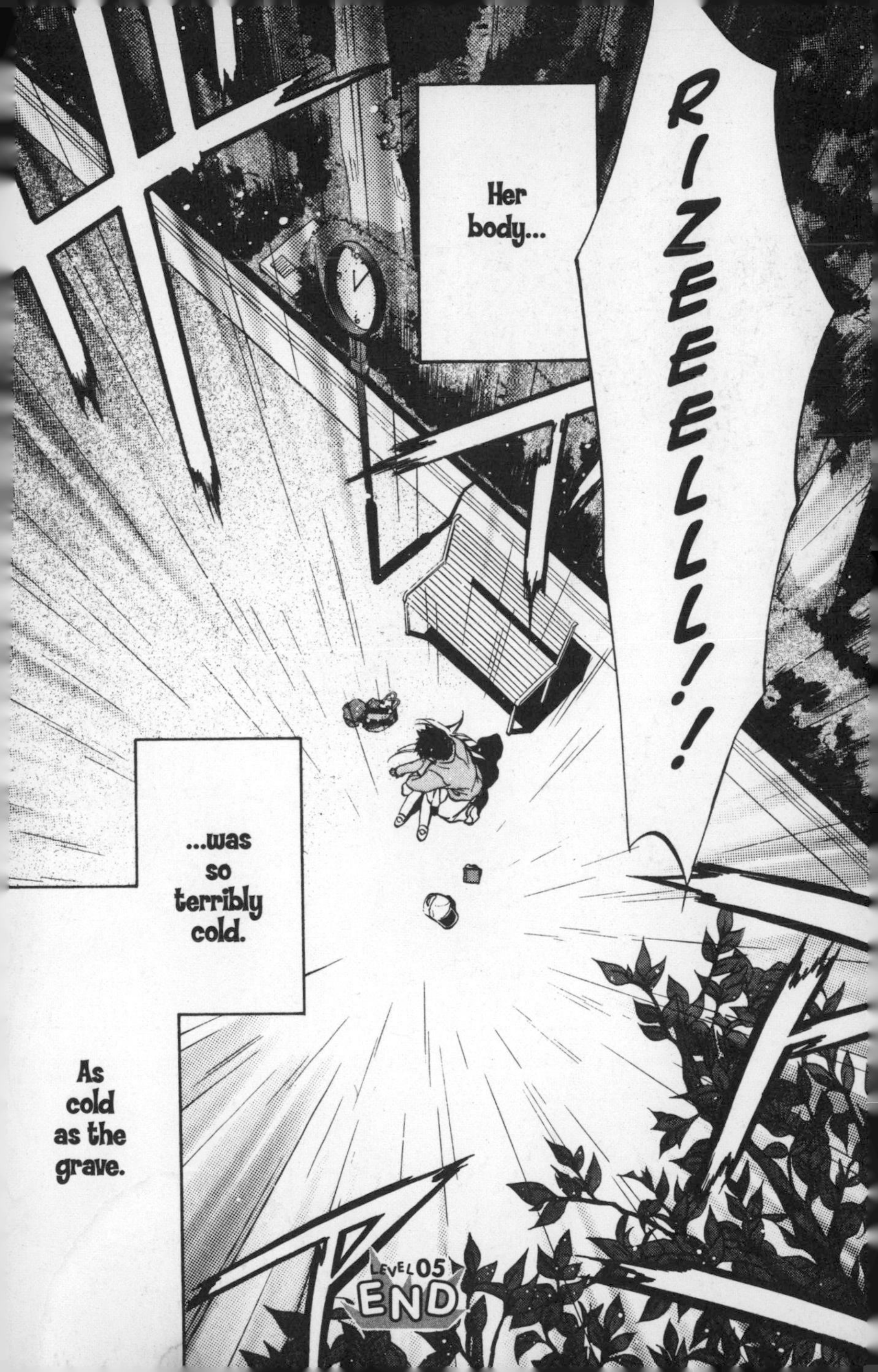
RIZEEELLL!!
Her body...
...was so terribly cold.
As cold as the grave.
LEVEL 05 END

MELT DOWN Love Comes with a First Encounter

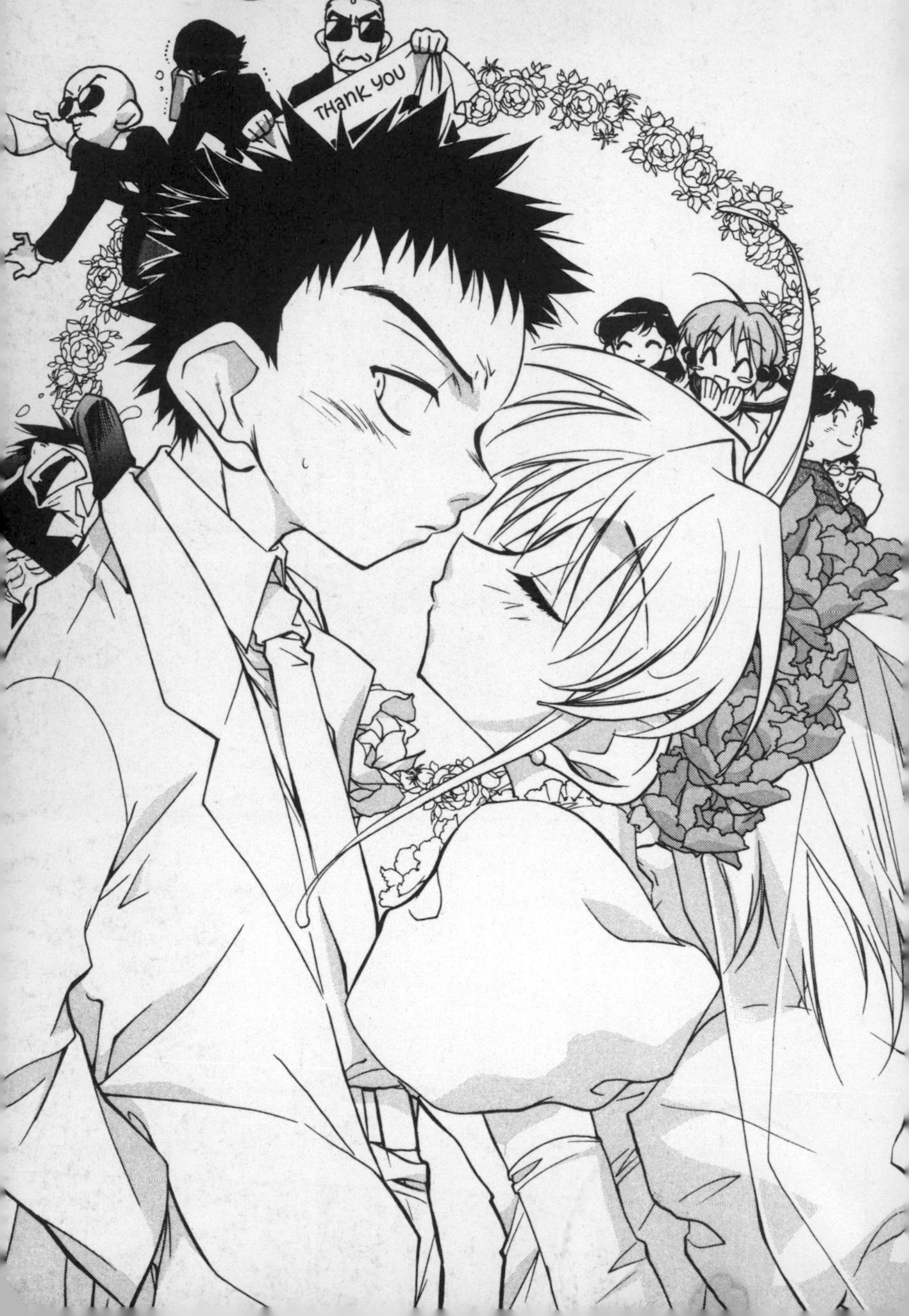
THANK YOU

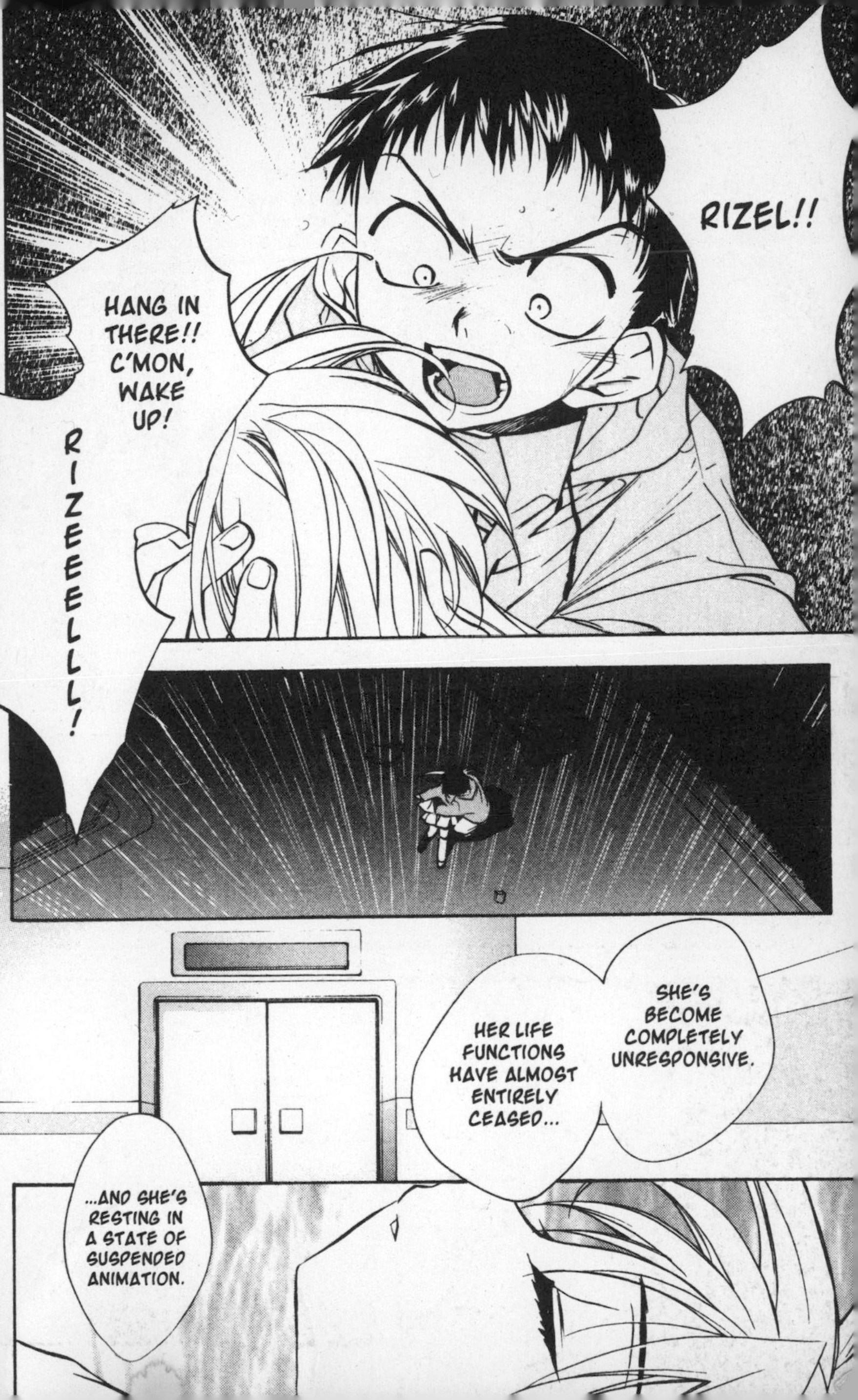
RIZEL!!
HANG IN THERE!! C'MON, WAKE UP!
RIZEEEELLLL!
SHE'S BECOME COMPLETELY UNRESPONSIVE.
HER LIFE FUNCTIONS HAVE ALMOST ENTIRELY CEASED...
...AND SHE'S RESTING IN A STATE OF SUSPENDED ANIMATION.

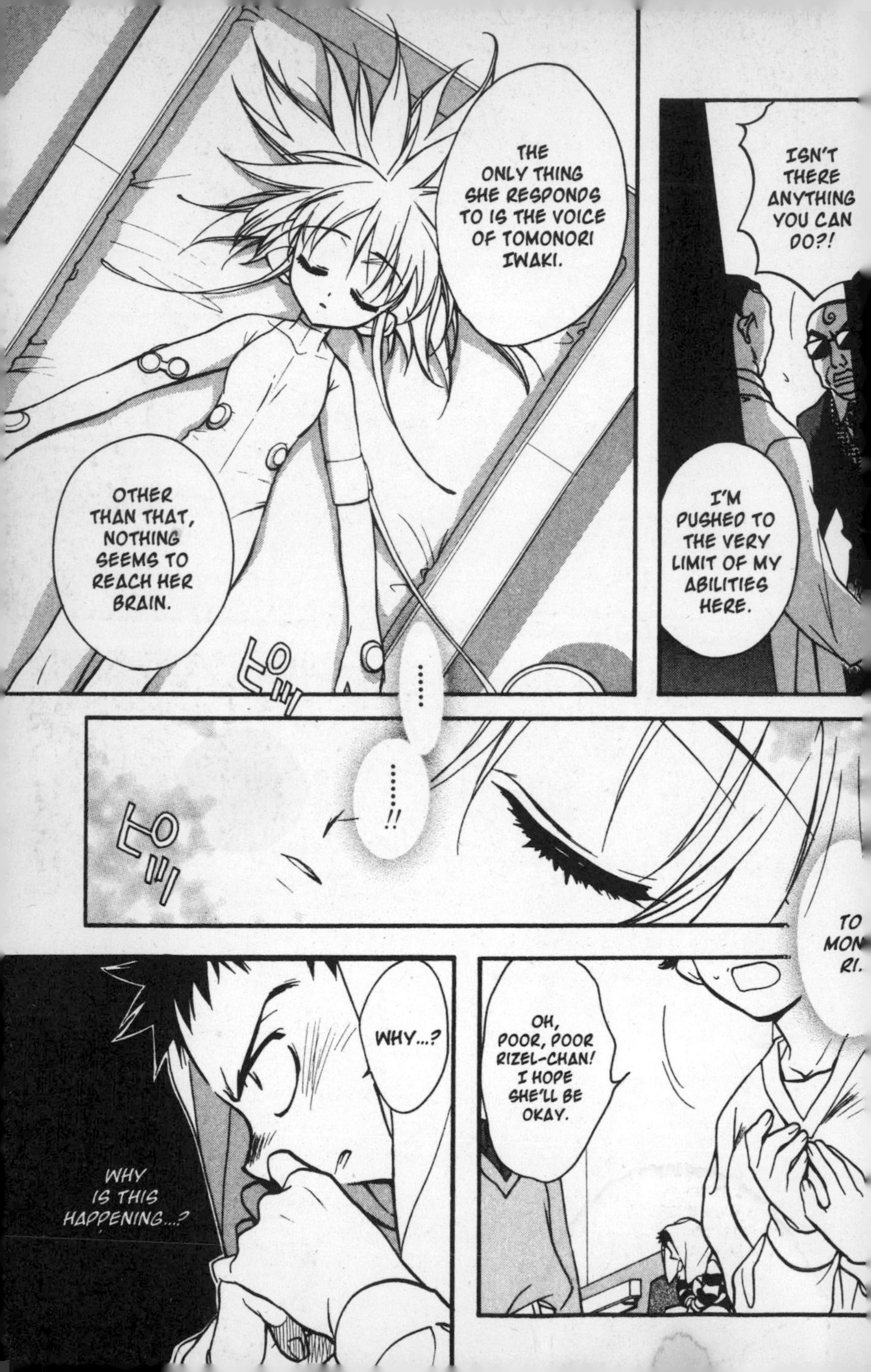
ISN'T THERE ANYTHING YOU CAN DO?!
I'M PUSHED TO THE VERY LIMIT OF MY ABILITIES HERE.
THE ONLY THING SHE RESPONDS TO IS THE VOICE OF TOMONORI IWAKI.
OTHER THAN THAT, NOTHING SEEMS TO REACH HER BRAIN.
......
......!!
TO MON RI.
OH, POOR, POOR RIZEL-CHAN! I HOPE SHE'LL BE OKAY.
WHY...?
WHY IS THIS HAPPENING...?

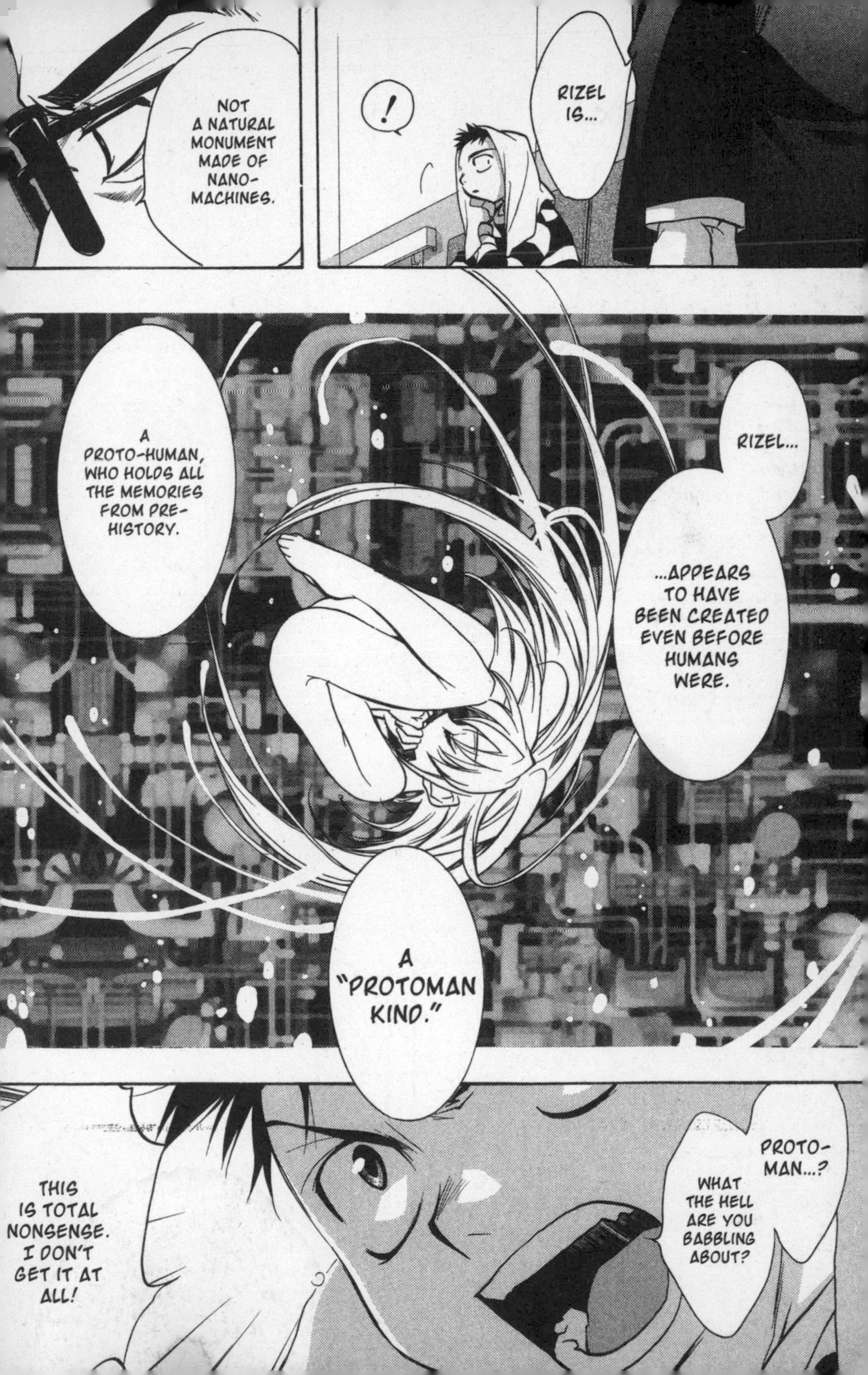
RIZEL IS...
!
NOT A NATURAL MONUMENT MADE OF NANO-MACHINES.
RIZEL...
...APPEARS TO HAVE BEEN CREATED EVEN BEFORE HUMANS WERE.
A PROTO-HUMAN, WHO HOLDS ALL THE MEMORIES FROM PRE-HISTORY.
A "PROTOMAN KIND."
PROTO-MAN...?
WHAT THE HELL ARE YOU BABBLING ABOUT?
THIS IS TOTAL NONSENSE. I DON'T GET IT AT ALL!

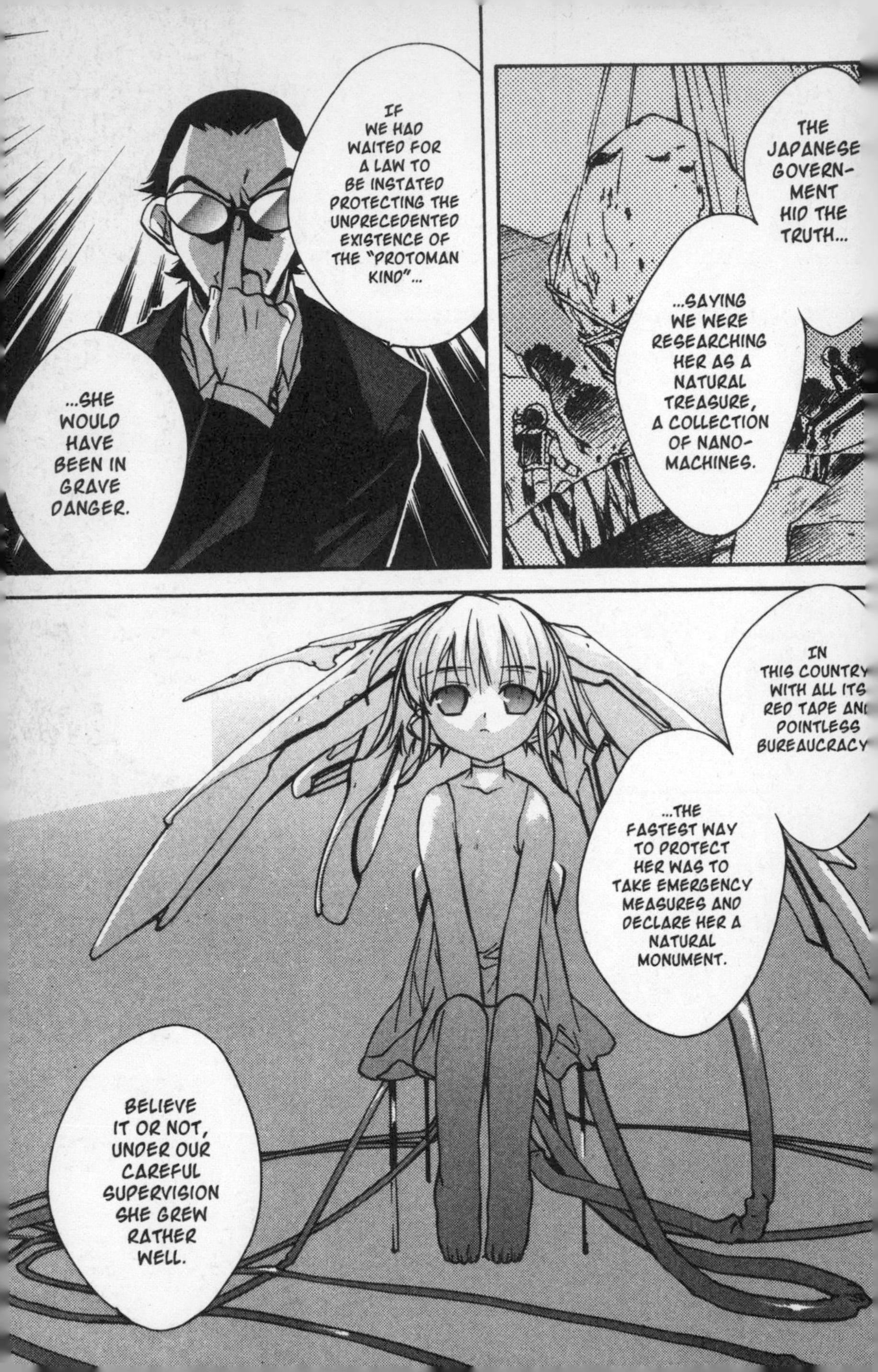
THE JAPANESE GOVERNMENT HID THE TRUTH...
...SAYING WE WERE RESEARCHING HER AS A NATURAL TREASURE, A COLLECTION OF NANO-MACHINES.
IF WE HAD WAITED FOR A LAW TO BE INSTATED PROTECTING THE UNPRECEDENTED EXISTENCE OF THE "PROTOMAN KIND"...
...SHE WOULD HAVE BEEN IN GRAVE DANGER.
IN THIS COUNTRY WITH ALL ITS RED TAPE AN POINTLESS BUREAUCRACY
...THE FASTEST WAY TO PROTECT HER WAS TO TAKE EMERGENCY MEASURES AND DECLARE HER A NATURAL MONUMENT.
BELIEVE IT OR NOT, UNDER OUR CAREFUL SUPERVISION SHE GREW RATHER WELL.

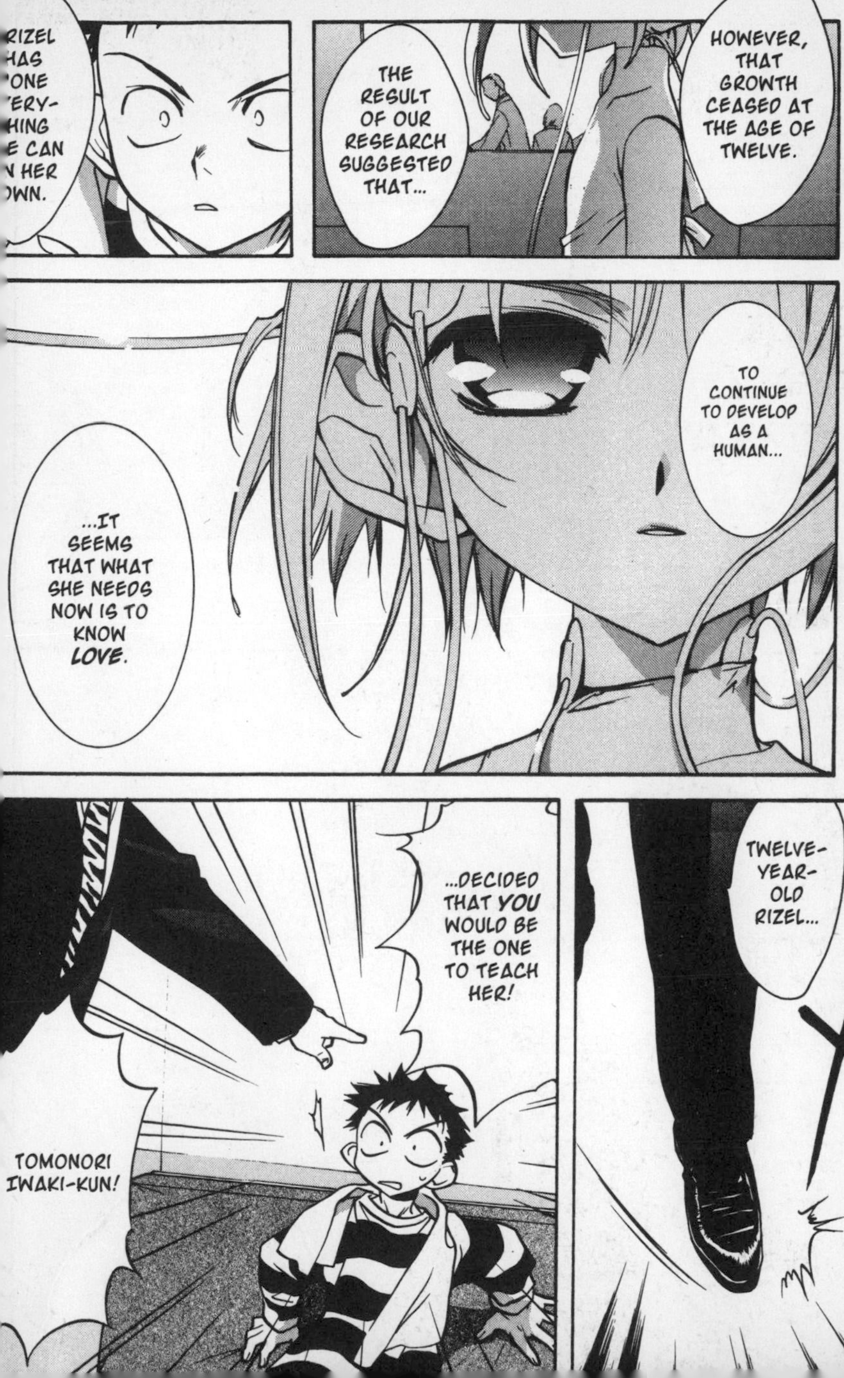
HOWEVER, THAT GROWTH CEASED AT THE AGE OF TWELVE.
THE RESULT OF OUR RESEARCH SUGGESTED THAT...
RIZEL HAS ONE ERY- HING E CAN N HER WN.
TO CONTINUE TO DEVELOP AS A HUMAN...
...IT SEEMS THAT WHAT SHE NEEDS NOW IS TO KNOW *LOVE*.
TWELVE-YEAR-OLD RIZEL...
...DECIDED THAT *YOU* WOULD BE THE ONE TO TEACH HER!
TOMONORI IWAKI-KUN!

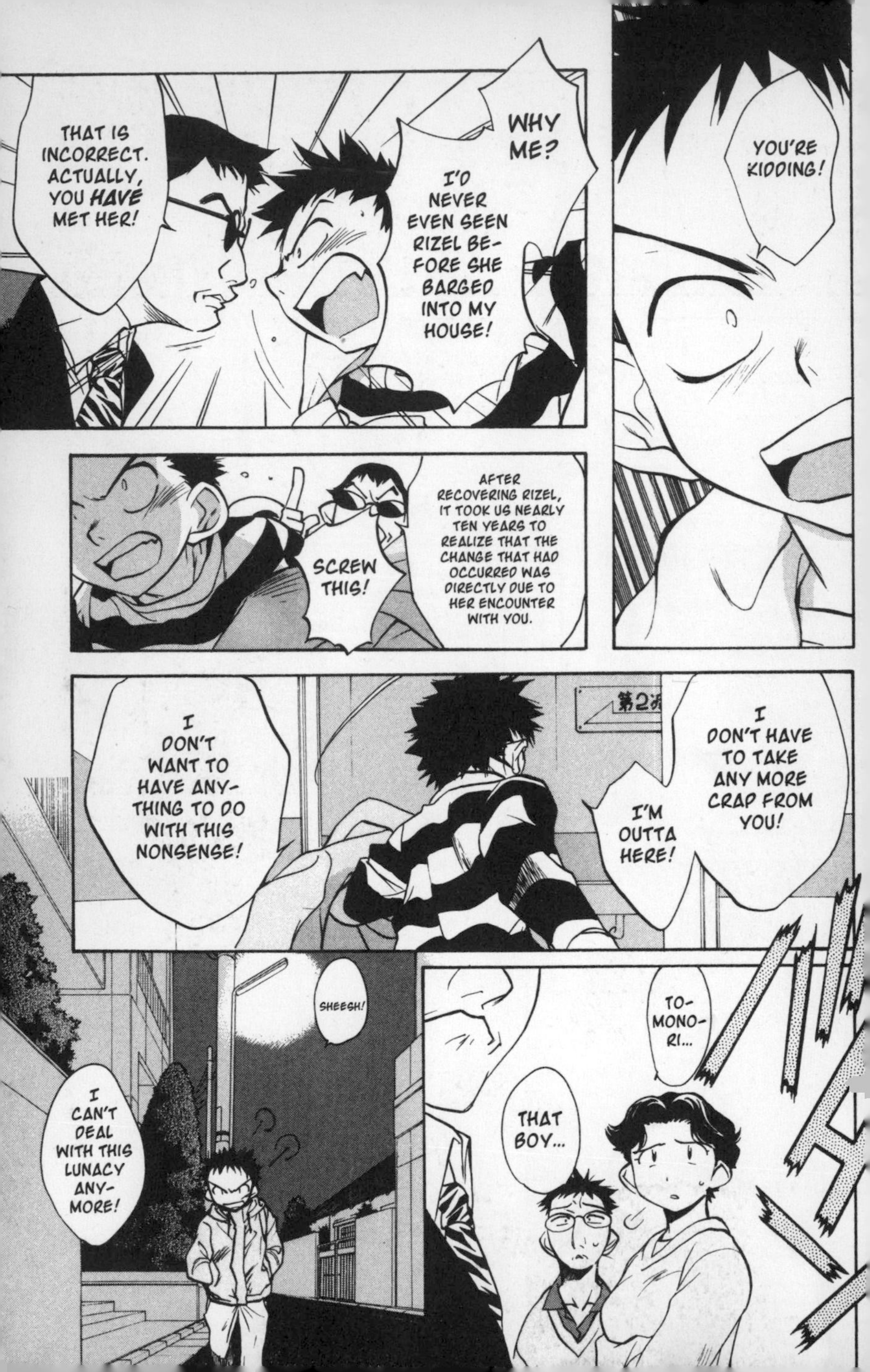
YOU'RE KIDDING!
WHY ME?
I'D NEVER EVEN SEEN RIZEL BEFORE SHE BARGED INTO MY HOUSE!
THAT IS INCORRECT. ACTUALLY, YOU *HAVE* MET HER!
AFTER RECOVERING RIZEL, IT TOOK US NEARLY TEN YEARS TO REALIZE THAT THE CHANGE THAT HAD OCCURRED WAS DIRECTLY DUE TO HER ENCOUNTER WITH YOU.
SCREW THIS!
I DON'T HAVE TO TAKE ANY MORE CRAP FROM YOU!
I'M OUTTA HERE!
I DON'T WANT TO HAVE ANYTHING TO DO WITH THIS NONSENSE!
TOMONORI...
THAT BOY...
SHEESH!
I CAN'T DEAL WITH THIS LUNACY ANYMORE!

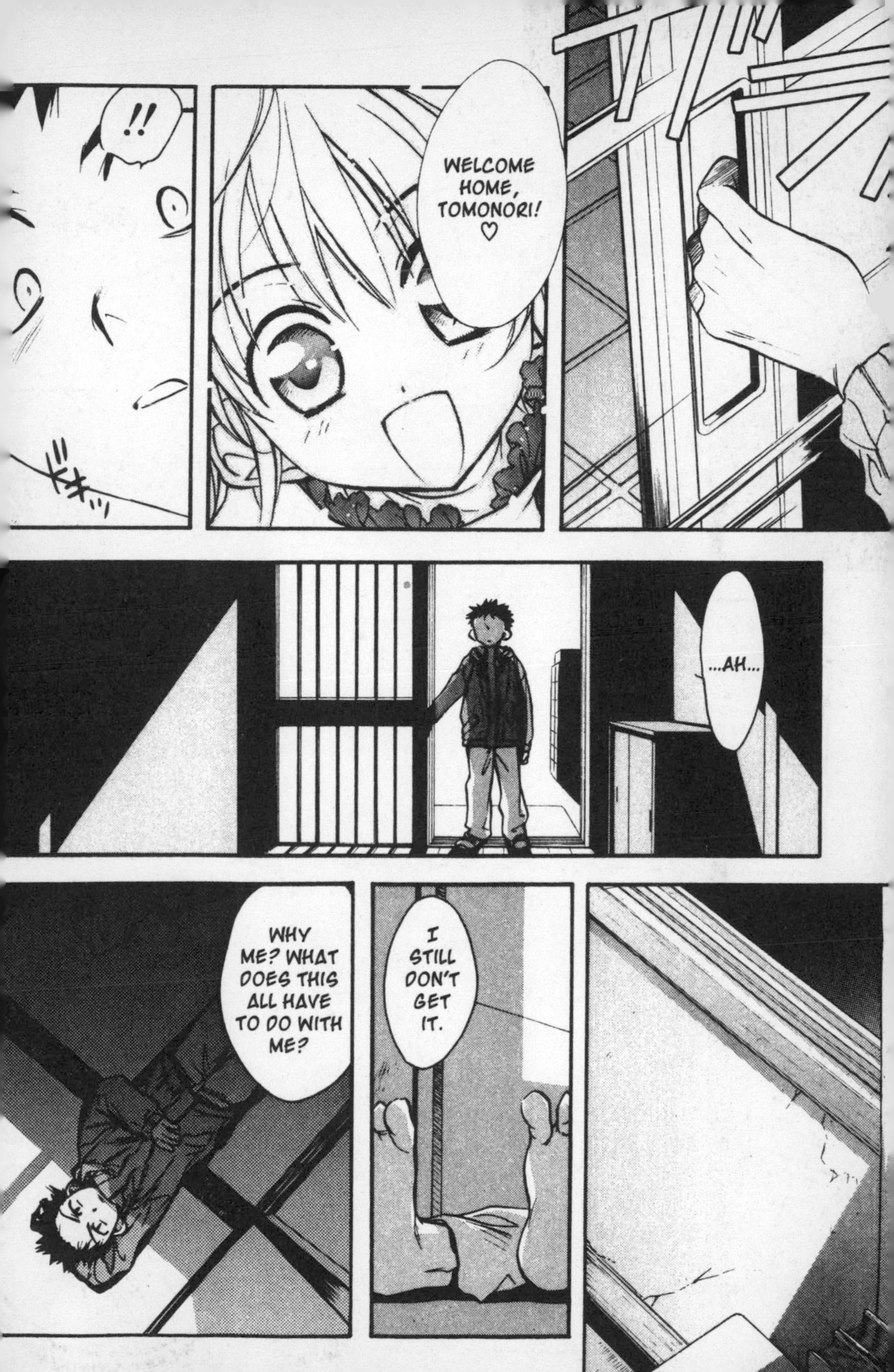
WELCOME HOME, TOMONORI! ♡
!!
...AH...
I STILL DON'T GET IT.
WHY ME? WHAT DOES THIS ALL HAVE TO DO WITH ME?

date schedule ♥♥♥

10:00	meet up with each other
11:00	movie
13:30	dinner
14:00	
15:00	zoo
16:00	
18:00	park
19:00	

OH, THIS...

!

CRUNCH

THAT MAY HAVE BEEN THE TRIGGER FOR HER CURRENT CONDITION...

RIZEL SAID SHE NEEDED TO TRANSFORM FOR MORE THAN THREE MINUTES...

...AND TOOK A DRUG THAT WOULD CAUSE THE TRANSFORMATION TO LAST LONGER.

TOMONORI...

TOMONORI.

TO-MONO-RI!

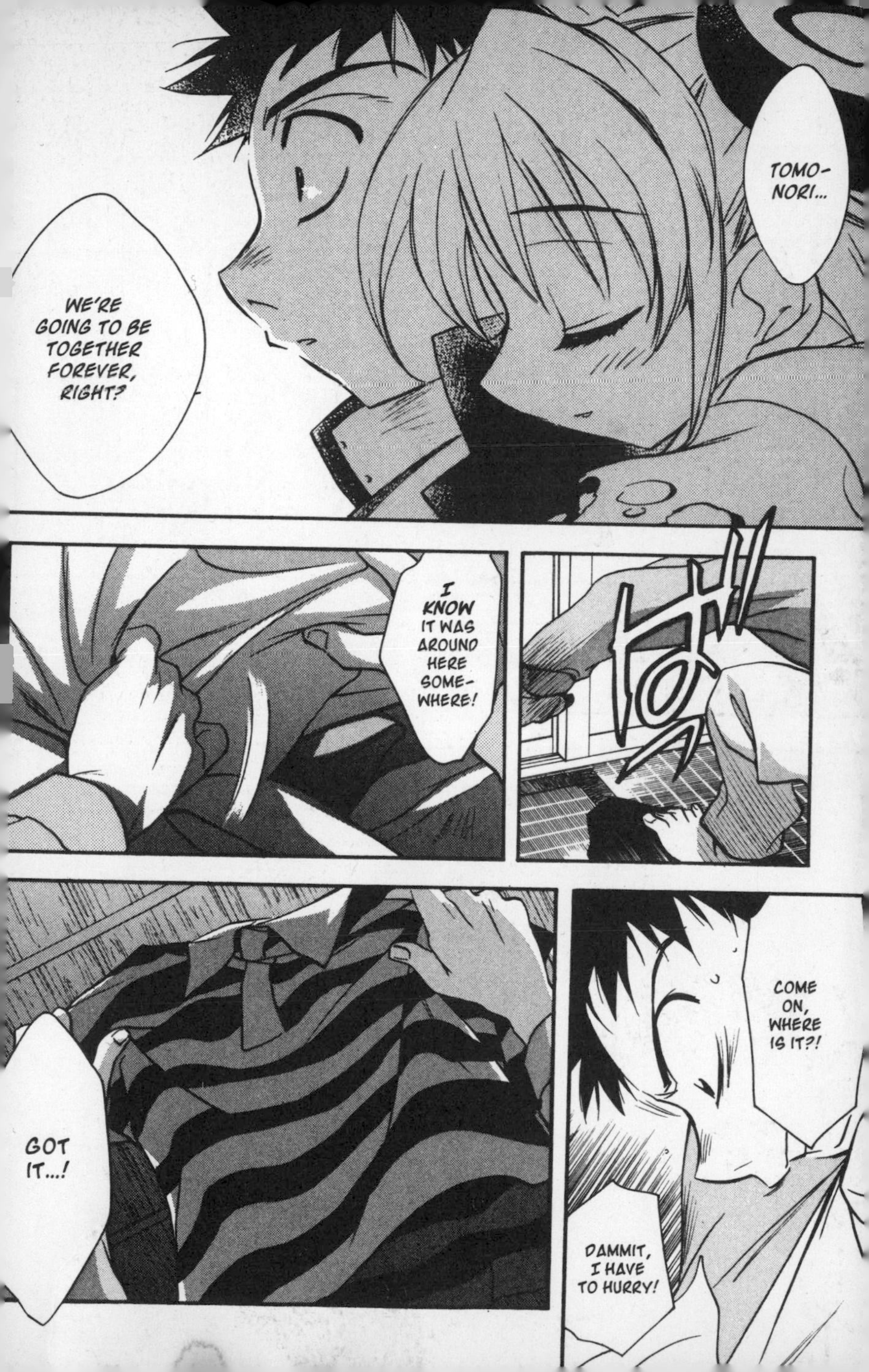
TOMO-NORI...
WE'RE GOING TO BE TOGETHER FOREVER, RIGHT?
I KNOW IT WAS AROUND HERE SOME-WHERE!
COME ON, WHERE IS IT?!
DAMMIT, I HAVE TO HURRY!
GOT IT...!

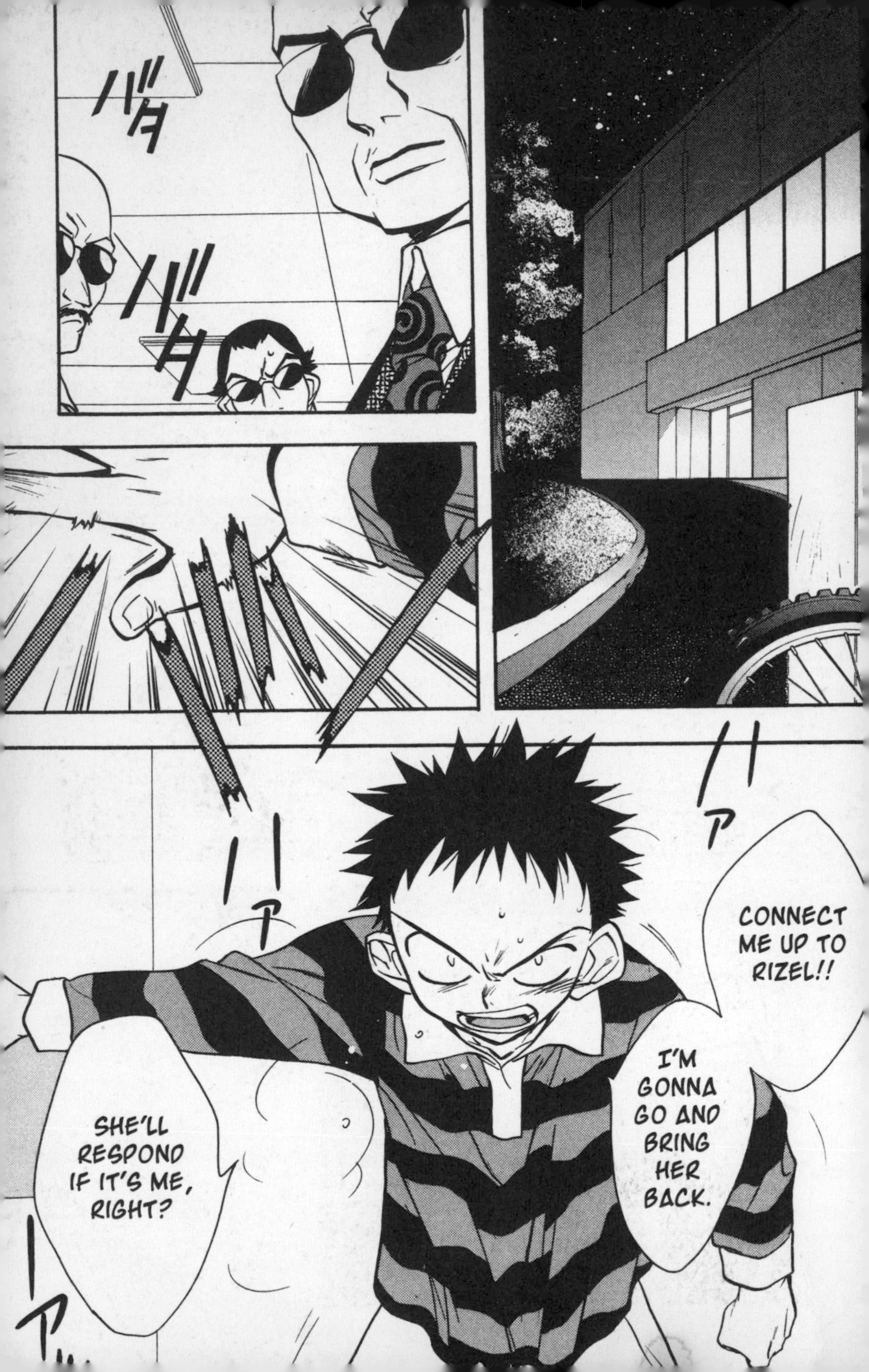
バタ
バタ
ハア
CONNECT ME UP TO RIZEL!!
I'M GONNA GO AND BRING HER BACK.
ハア
SHE'LL RESPOND IF IT'S ME, RIGHT?
ハア...

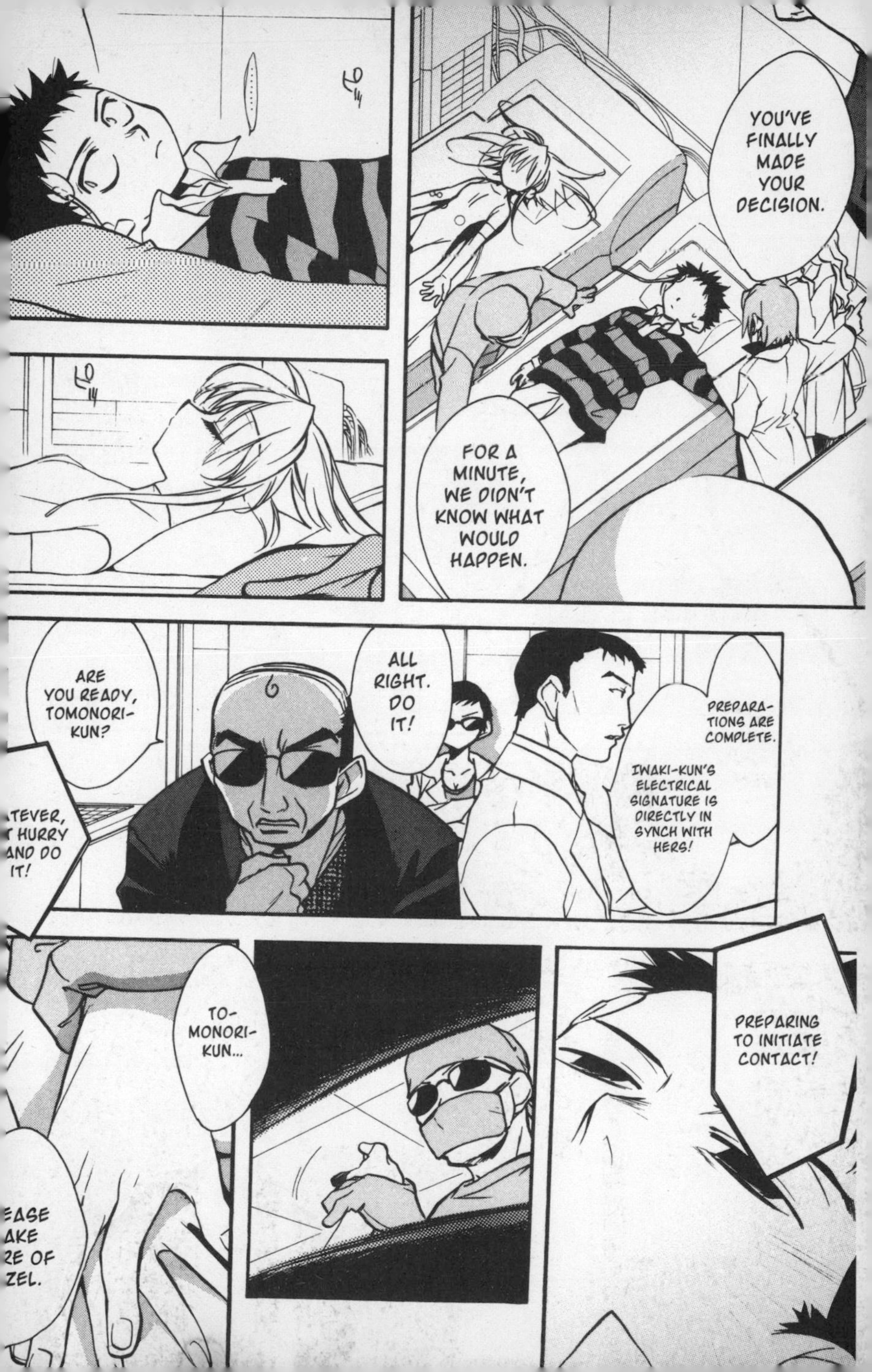
YOU'VE FINALLY MADE YOUR DECISION.
FOR A MINUTE, WE DIDN'T KNOW WHAT WOULD HAPPEN.
PREPARATIONS ARE COMPLETE.
IWAKI-KUN'S ELECTRICAL SIGNATURE IS DIRECTLY IN SYNCH WITH HERS!
ALL RIGHT. DO IT!
ARE YOU READY, TOMONORI-KUN?
ATEVER, T HURRY AND DO IT!
PREPARING TO INITIATE CONTACT!
TO-MONORI-KUN...
EASE AKE RE OF ZEL.

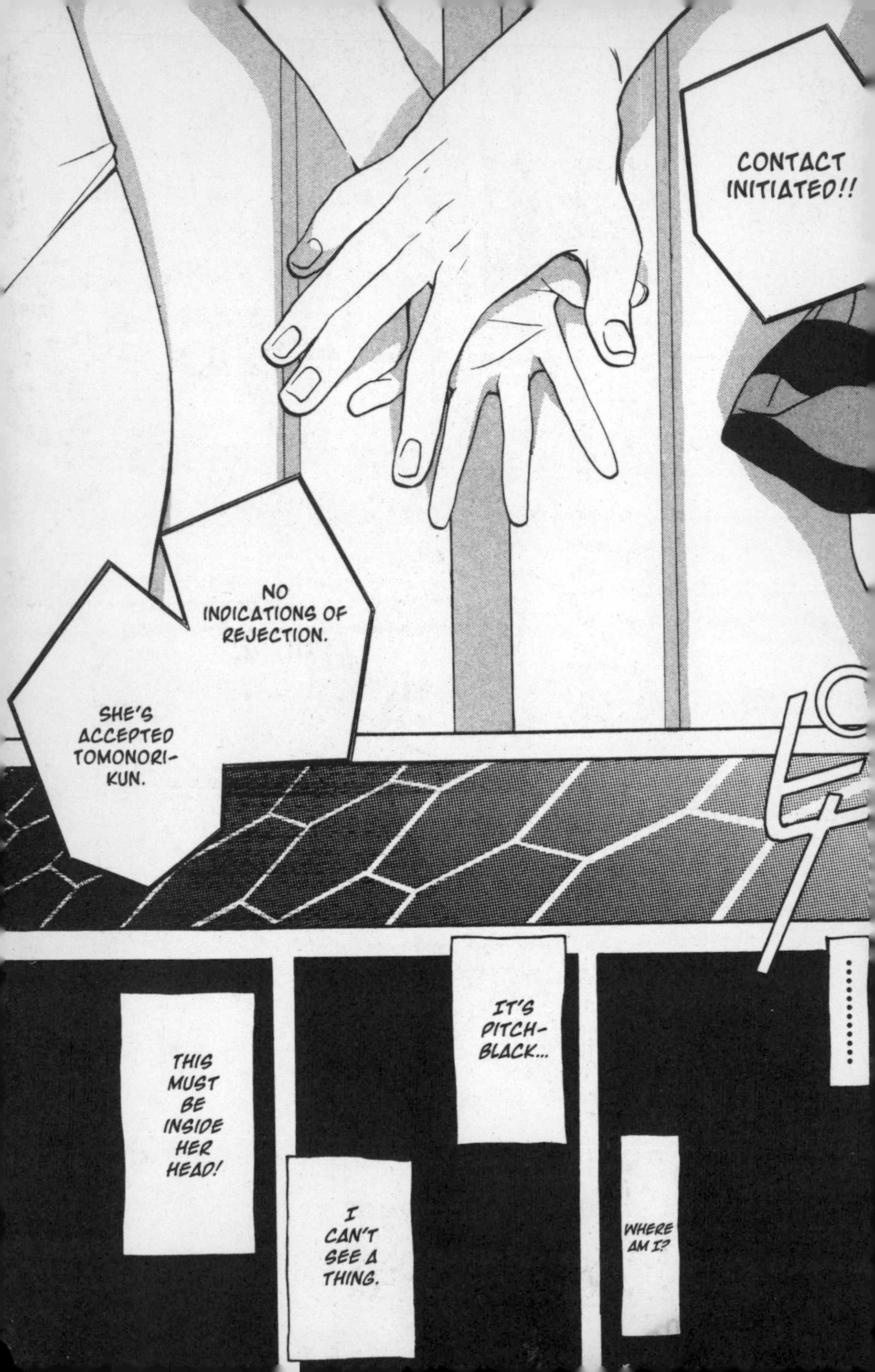
CONTACT INITIATED!!
NO INDICATIONS OF REJECTION.
SHE'S ACCEPTED TOMONORI-KUN.
....
WHERE AM I?
IT'S PITCH-BLACK...
I CAN'T SEE A THING.
THIS MUST BE INSIDE HER HEAD!

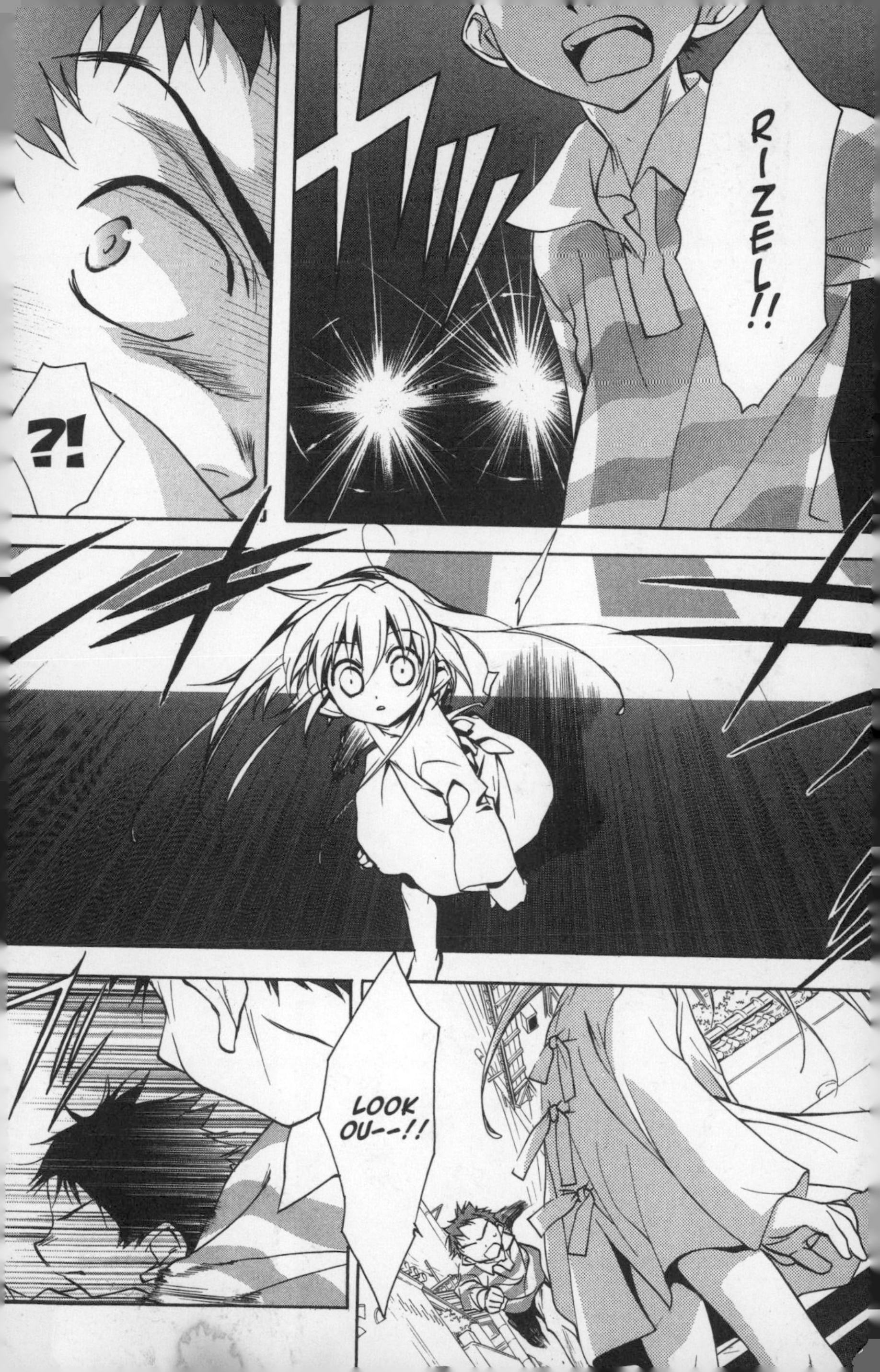
RIZEL!!
?!
LOOK OU--!!

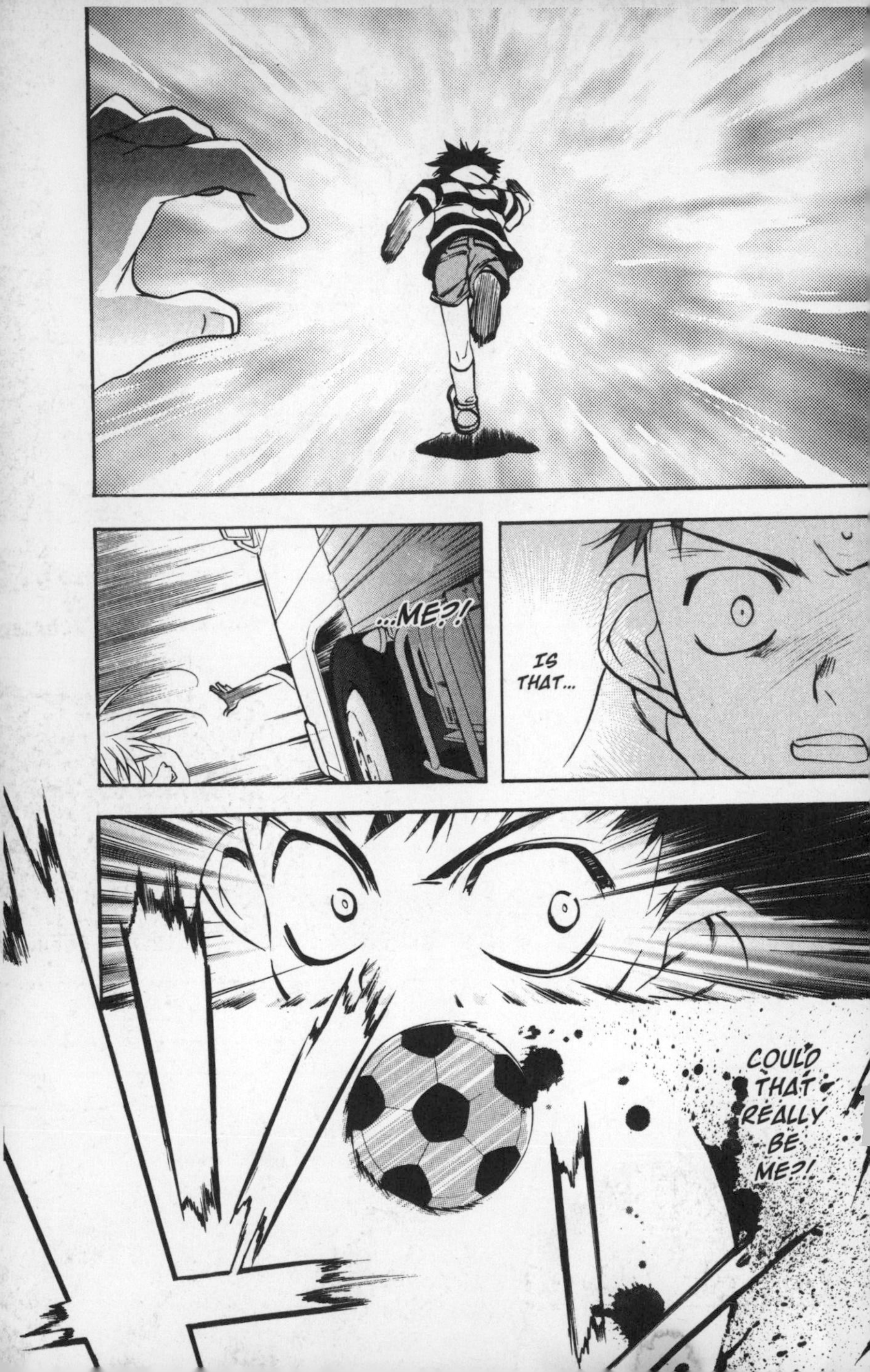
IS THAT...
...ME?!
COULD THAT REALLY BE ME?!

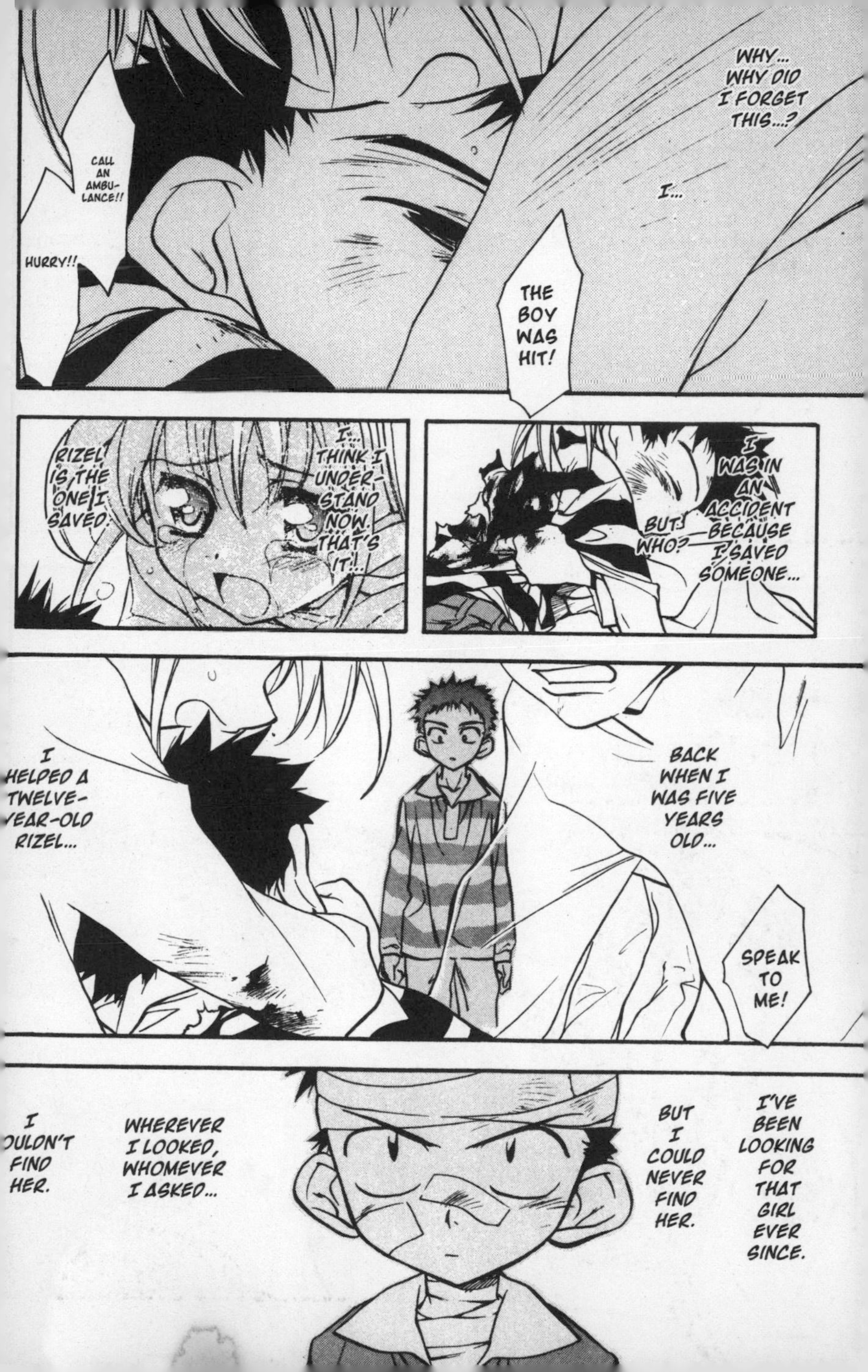
WHY... WHY DID I FORGET THIS...?
I...
THE BOY WAS HIT!
CALL AN AMBULANCE!!
HURRY!!
I WAS IN AN ACCIDENT BECAUSE I SAVED SOMEONE...
BUT WHO?
I... THINK I UNDERSTAND NOW. THAT'S IT!..
RIZEL IS THE ONE I SAVED.
BACK WHEN I WAS FIVE YEARS OLD...
SPEAK TO ME!
I HELPED A TWELVE-YEAR-OLD RIZEL...
I'VE BEEN LOOKING FOR THAT GIRL EVER SINCE.
BUT I COULD NEVER FIND HER.
WHEREVER I LOOKED, WHOMEVER I ASKED...
I OULDN'T FIND HER.

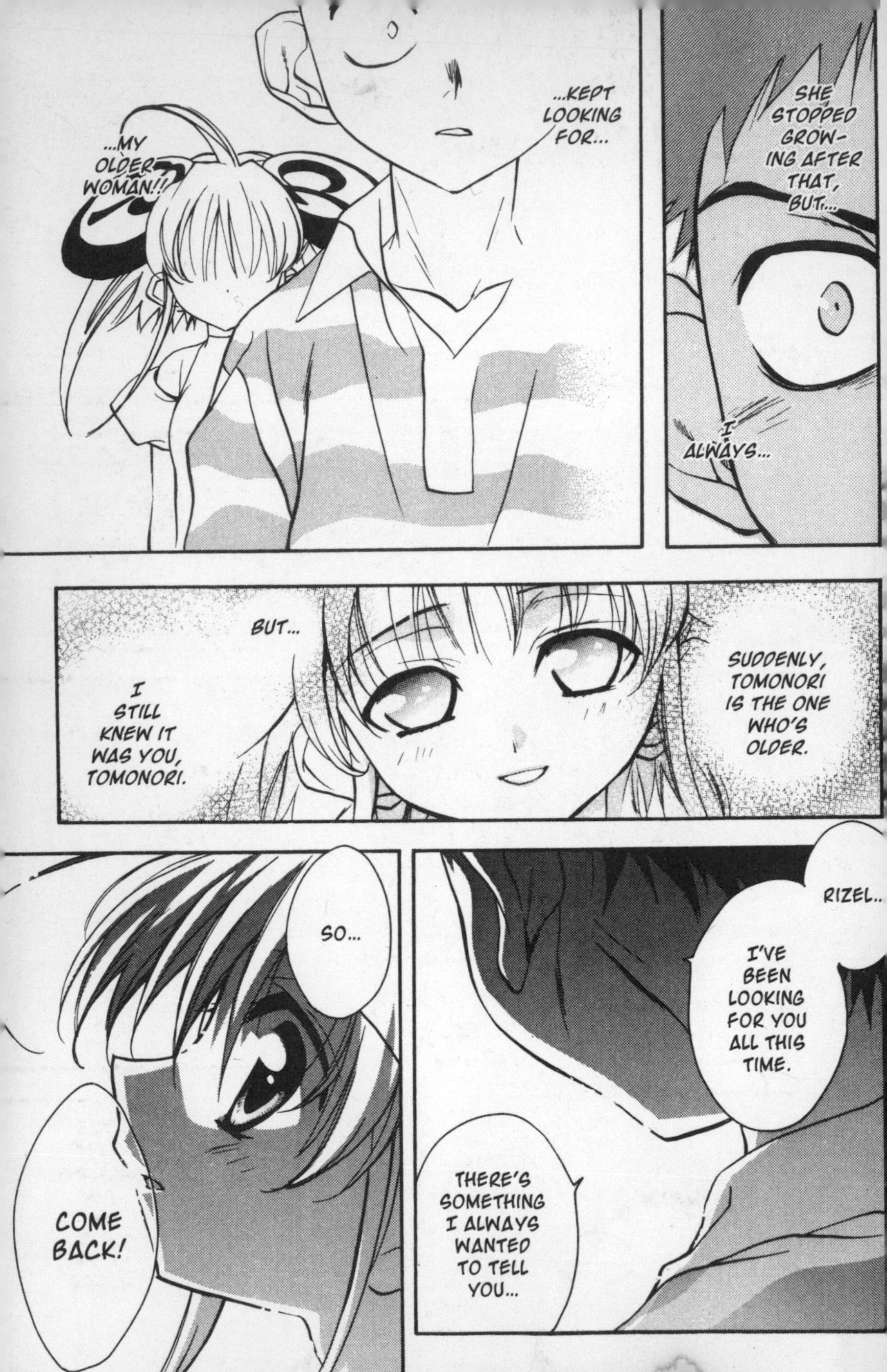
SHE STOPPED GROWING AFTER THAT, BUT...
I ALWAYS...
...KEPT LOOKING FOR...
...MY OLDER WOMAN!!
SUDDENLY, TOMONORI IS THE ONE WHO'S OLDER.
BUT...
I STILL KNEW IT WAS YOU, TOMONORI.
RIZEL...
I'VE BEEN LOOKING FOR YOU ALL THIS TIME.
THERE'S SOMETHING I ALWAYS WANTED TO TELL YOU...
SO...
COME BACK!

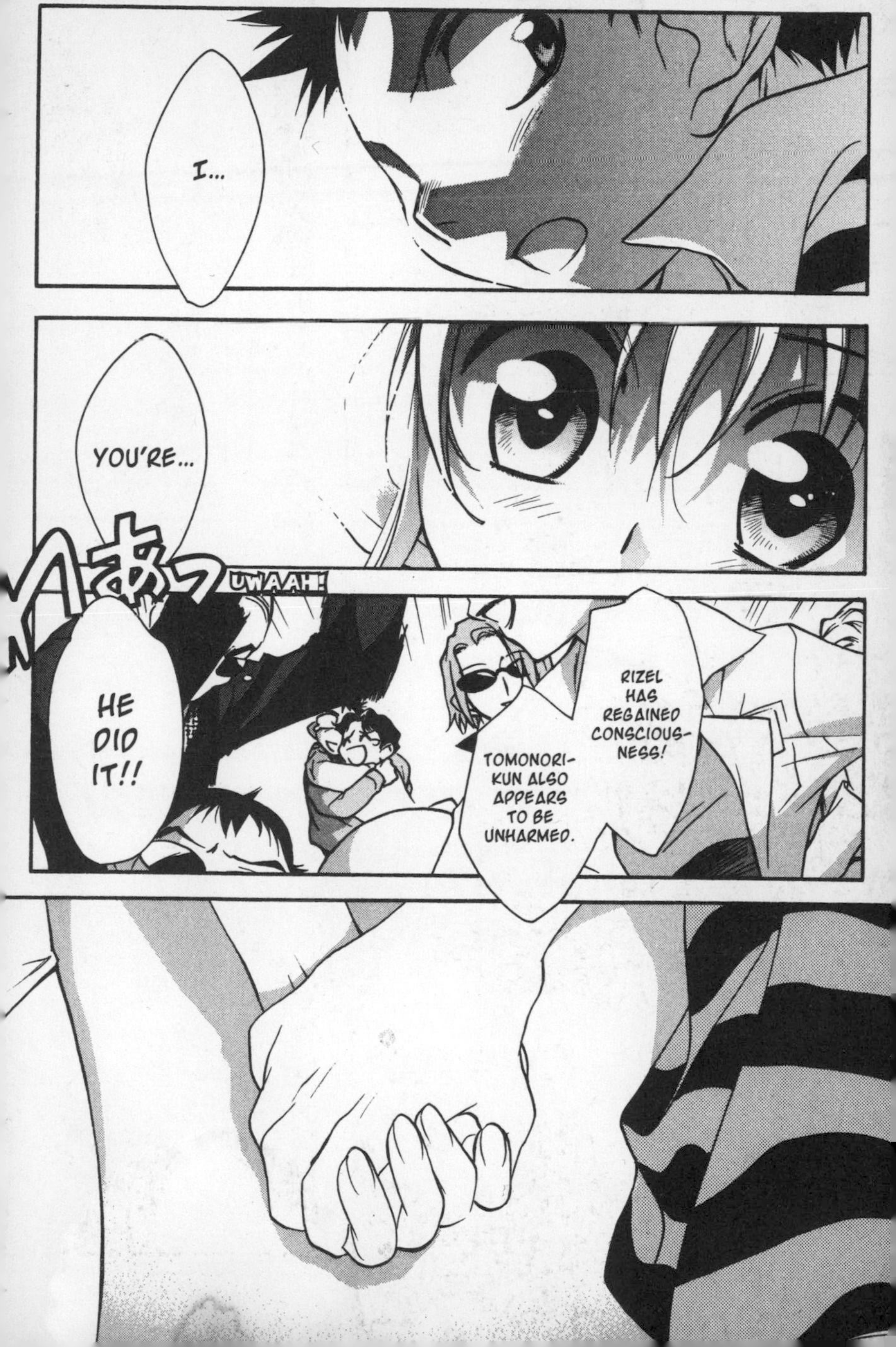
I...
YOU'RE...
RIZEL HAS REGAINED CONSCIOUSNESS!
TOMONORI-KUN ALSO APPEARS TO BE UNHARMED.
UWAAH!
HE DID IT!!

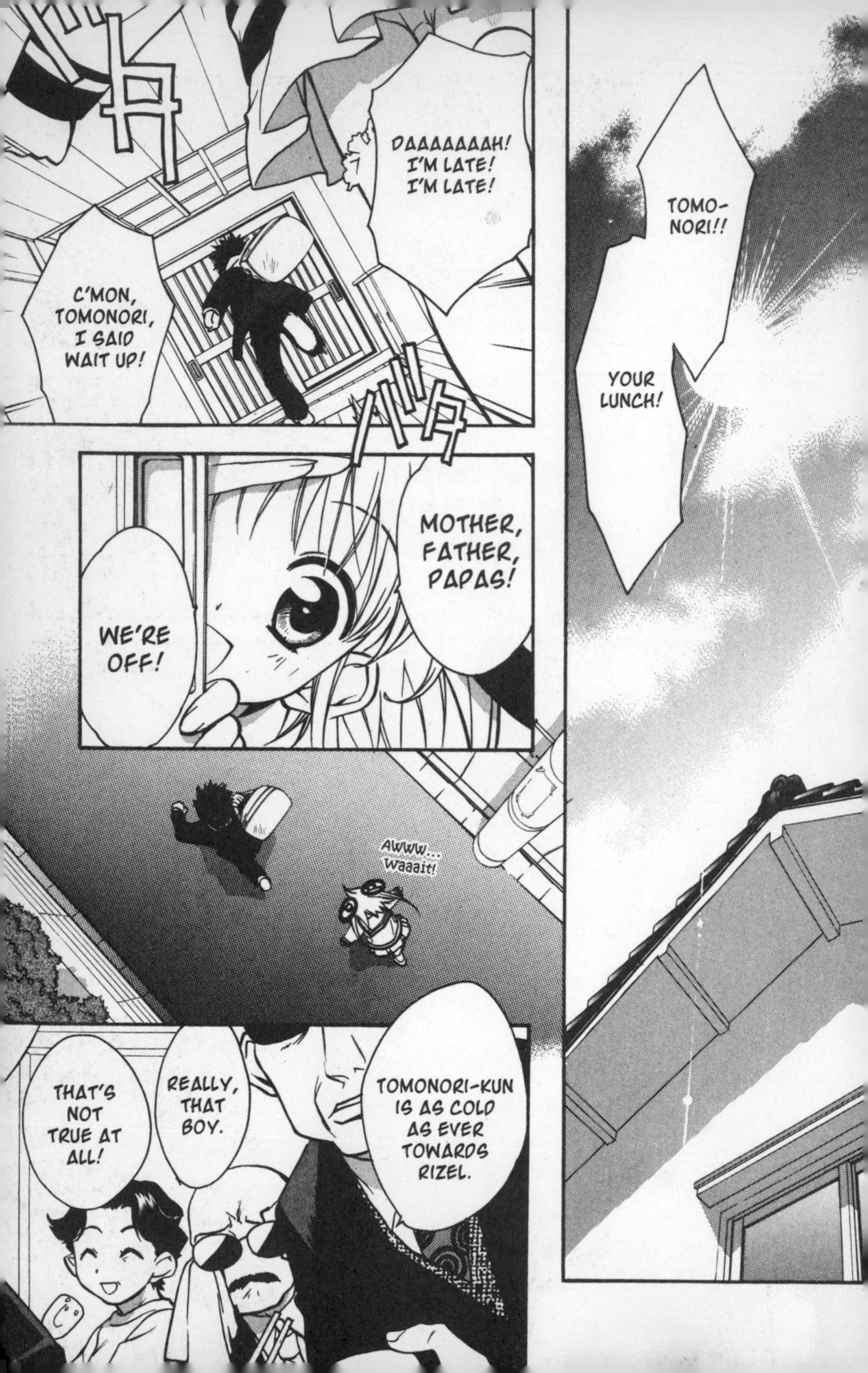
TOMO-NORI!!
YOUR LUNCH!
DAAAAAAAH! I'M LATE! I'M LATE!
C'MON, TOMONORI, I SAID WAIT UP!
MOTHER, FATHER, PAPAS!
WE'RE OFF!
AWWW... Waaait!
TOMONORI-KUN IS AS COLD AS EVER TOWARDS RIZEL.
REALLY, THAT BOY.
THAT'S NOT TRUE AT ALL!

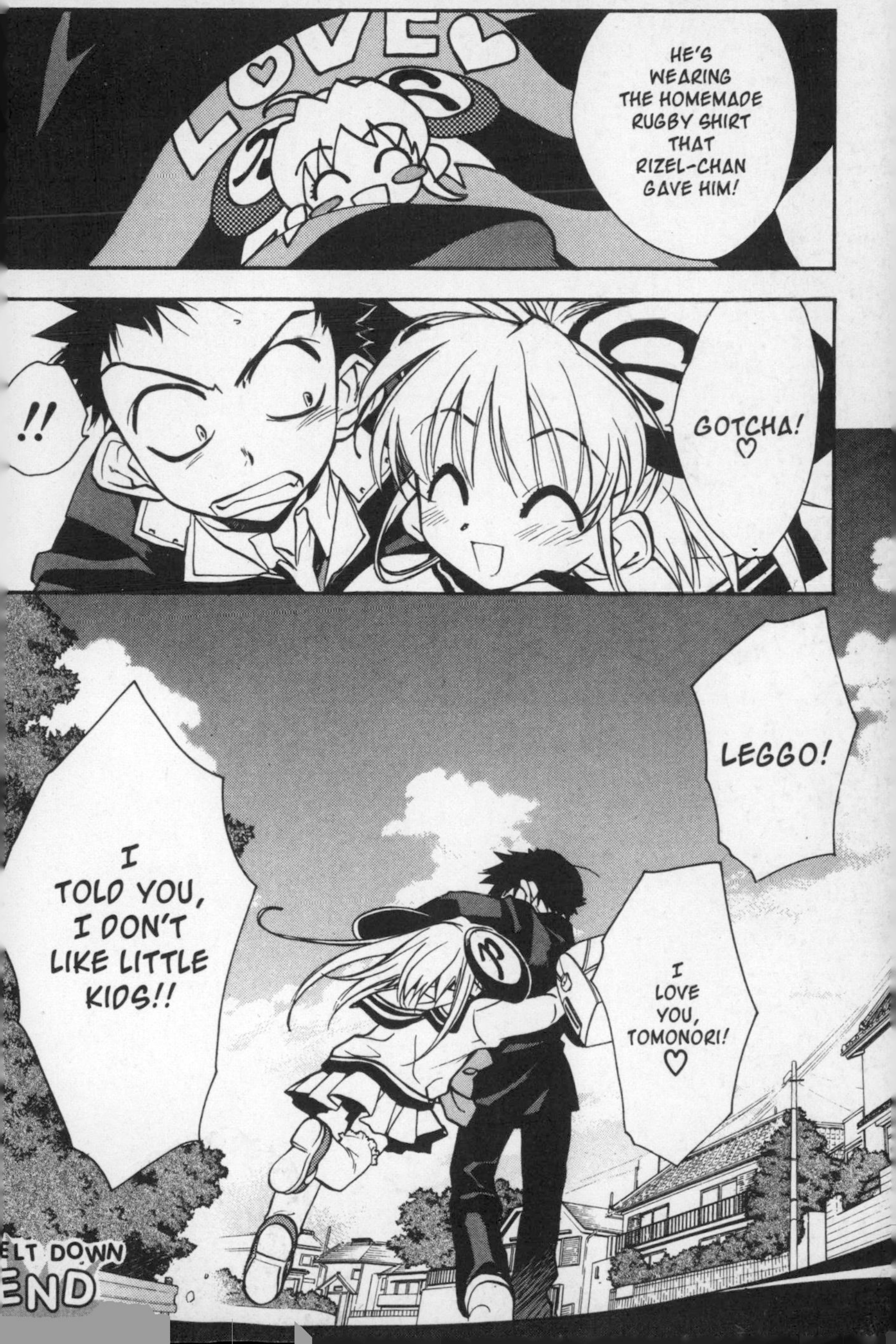
LOVE
HE'S WEARING THE HOMEMADE RUGBY SHIRT THAT RIZEL-CHAN GAVE HIM!
GOTCHA! ♡
!!
LEGGO!
I LOVE YOU, TOMONORI! ♡
I TOLD YOU, I DON'T LIKE LITTLE KIDS!!
LT DOWN
END

RIZELMINE

YUKIRU SUGISAKI

STAFF
MAMORU SUGISAKI
A.NAKAMURA
R.DOUDA
S.SHIMOZATO
Y.HONZAWA
J.OKU
R.IZUMI
M.NAKAMURA
Y.HISHINUMA

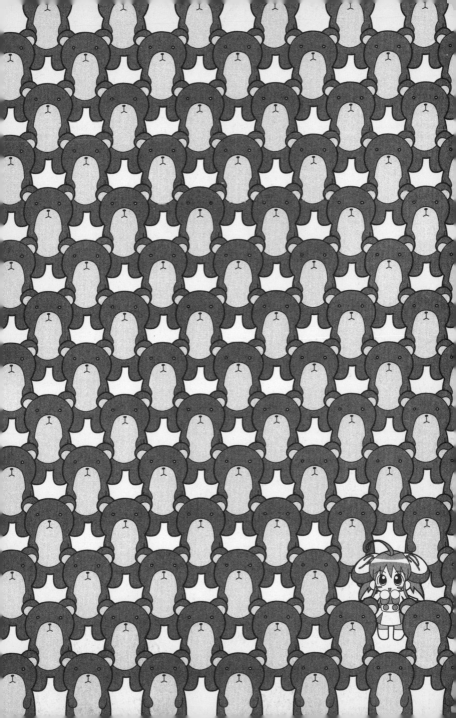

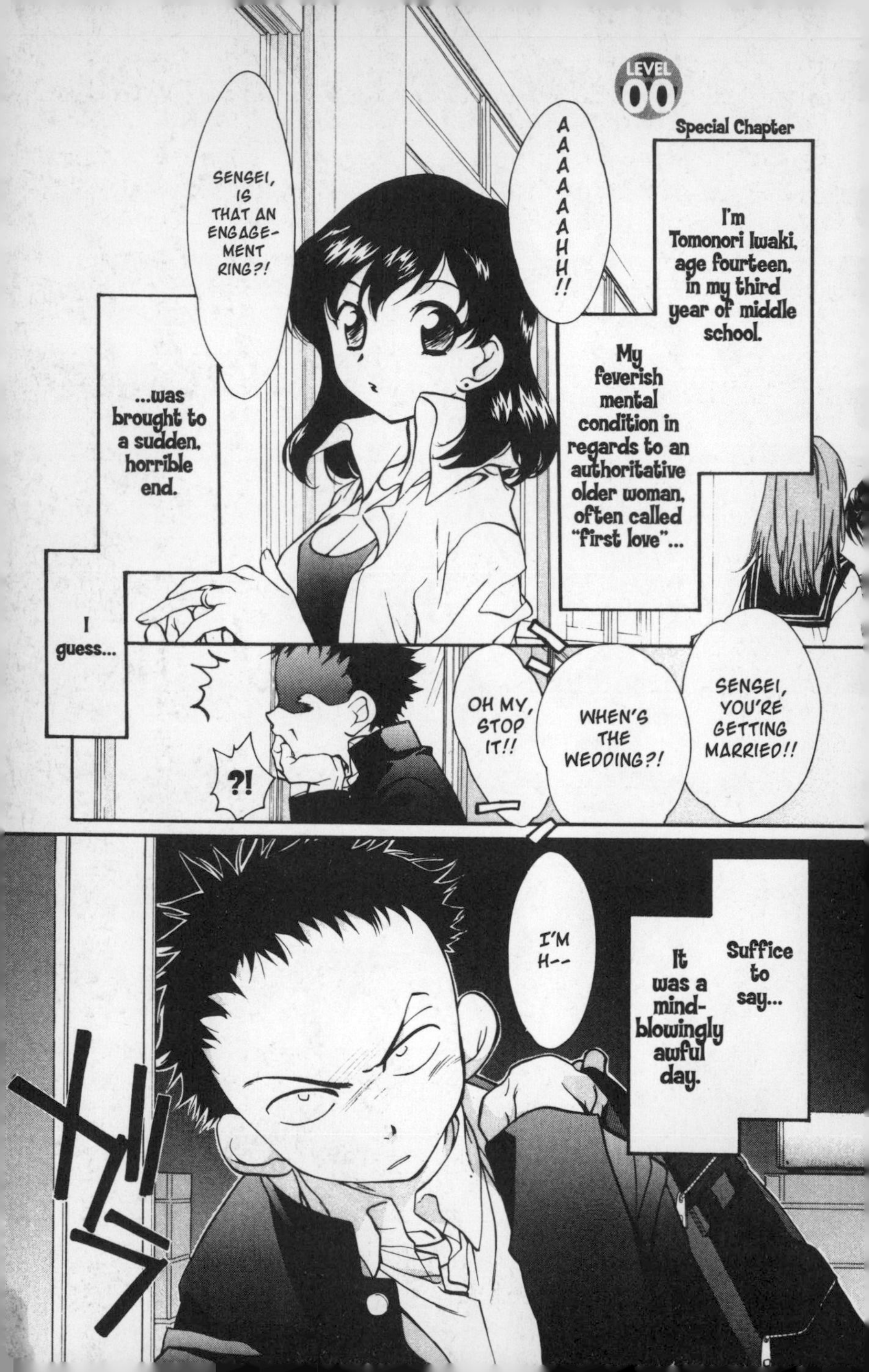
LEVEL 00
Special Chapter
I'm Tomonori Iwaki, age fourteen, in my third year of middle school.
AAAAAAAH!!
My feverish mental condition in regards to an authoritative older woman, often called "first love"...
SENSEI, IS THAT AN ENGAGEMENT RING?!
...was brought to a sudden, horrible end.
I guess...
SENSEI, YOU'RE GETTING MARRIED!!
WHEN'S THE WEDDING?!
OH MY, STOP IT!!
?!
Suffice to say...
It was a mind-blowingly awful day.
I'M H--

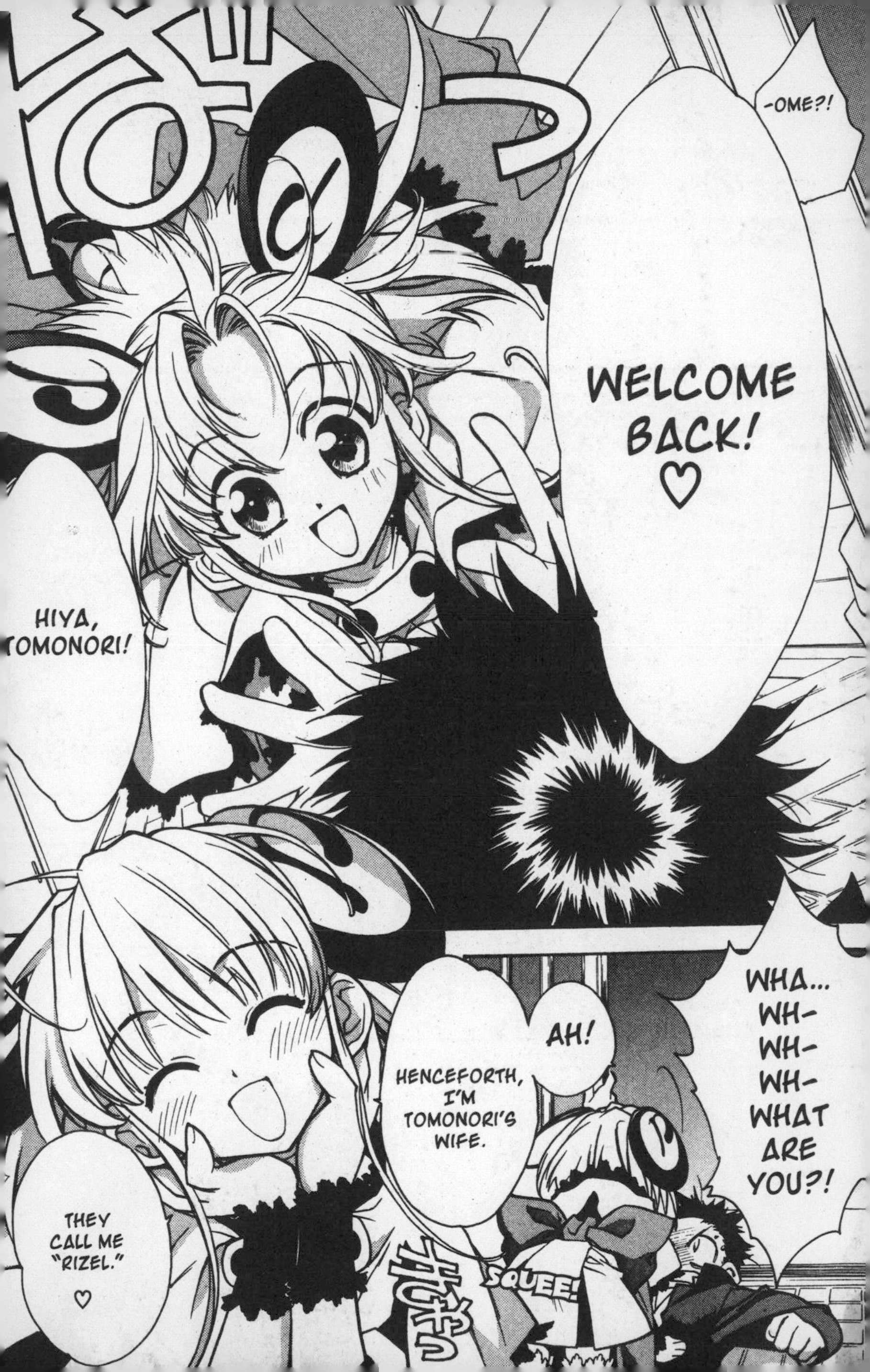
-OME?!
WELCOME BACK! ♡
HIYA, TOMONORI!
WHA... WH- WH- WH- WHAT ARE YOU?!
AH!
HENCEFORTH, I'M TOMONORI'S WIFE.
SQUEE!
THEY CALL ME "RIZEL." ♡

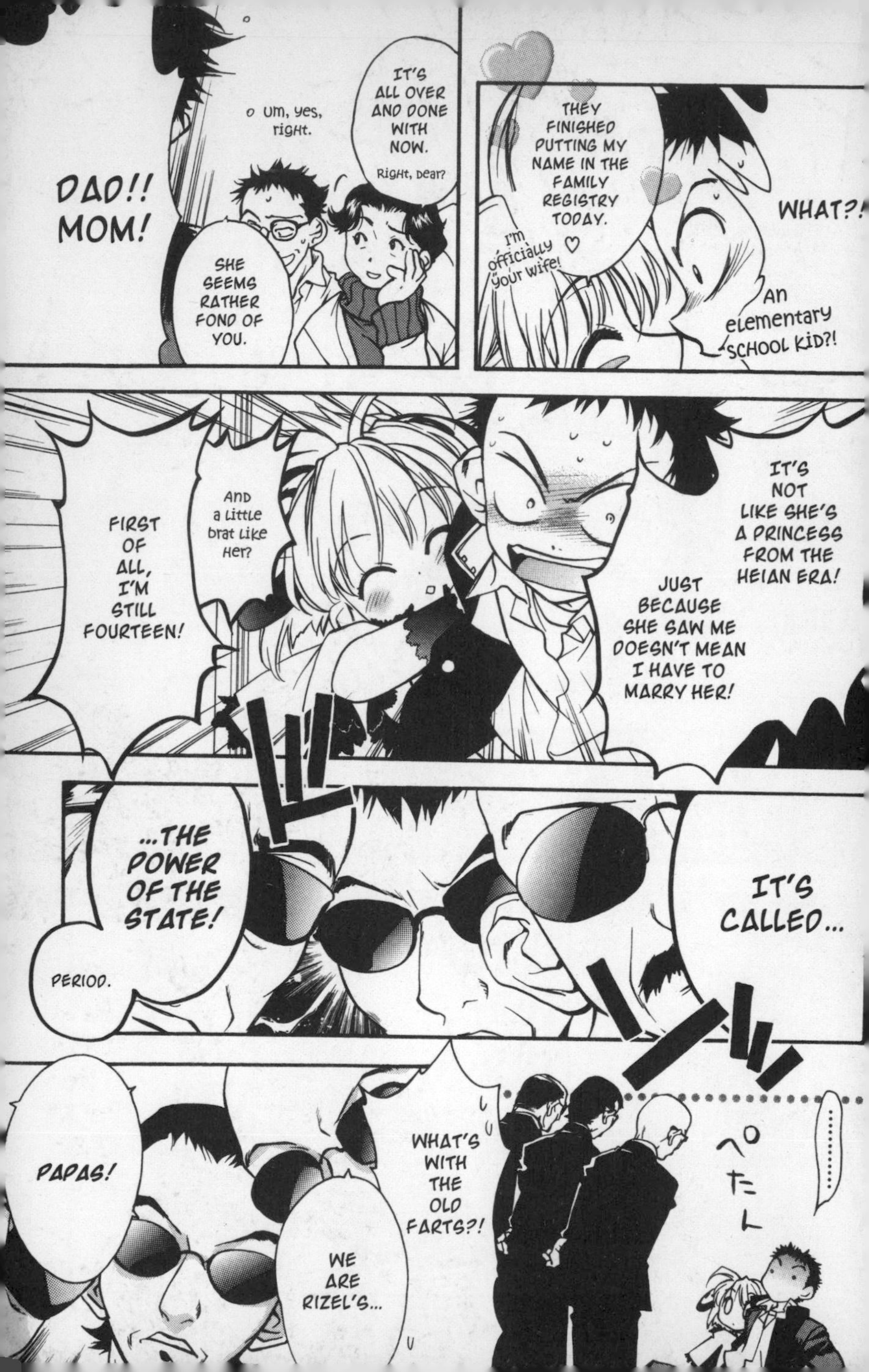
THEY FINISHED PUTTING MY NAME IN THE FAMILY REGISTRY TODAY.
I'm officially your wife! ♡
WHAT?!
An elementary school kid?!
IT'S ALL OVER AND DONE WITH NOW.
Right, dear?
Um, yes, right.
DAD!! MOM!
SHE SEEMS RATHER FOND OF YOU.
IT'S NOT LIKE SHE'S A PRINCESS FROM THE HEIAN ERA!
JUST BECAUSE SHE SAW ME DOESN'T MEAN I HAVE TO MARRY HER!
And a little brat like her?
FIRST OF ALL, I'M STILL FOURTEEN!
IT'S CALLED...
...THE POWER OF THE STATE!
PERIOD.
......
ぺたん
WHAT'S WITH THE OLD FARTS?!
WE ARE RIZEL'S...
PAPAS!

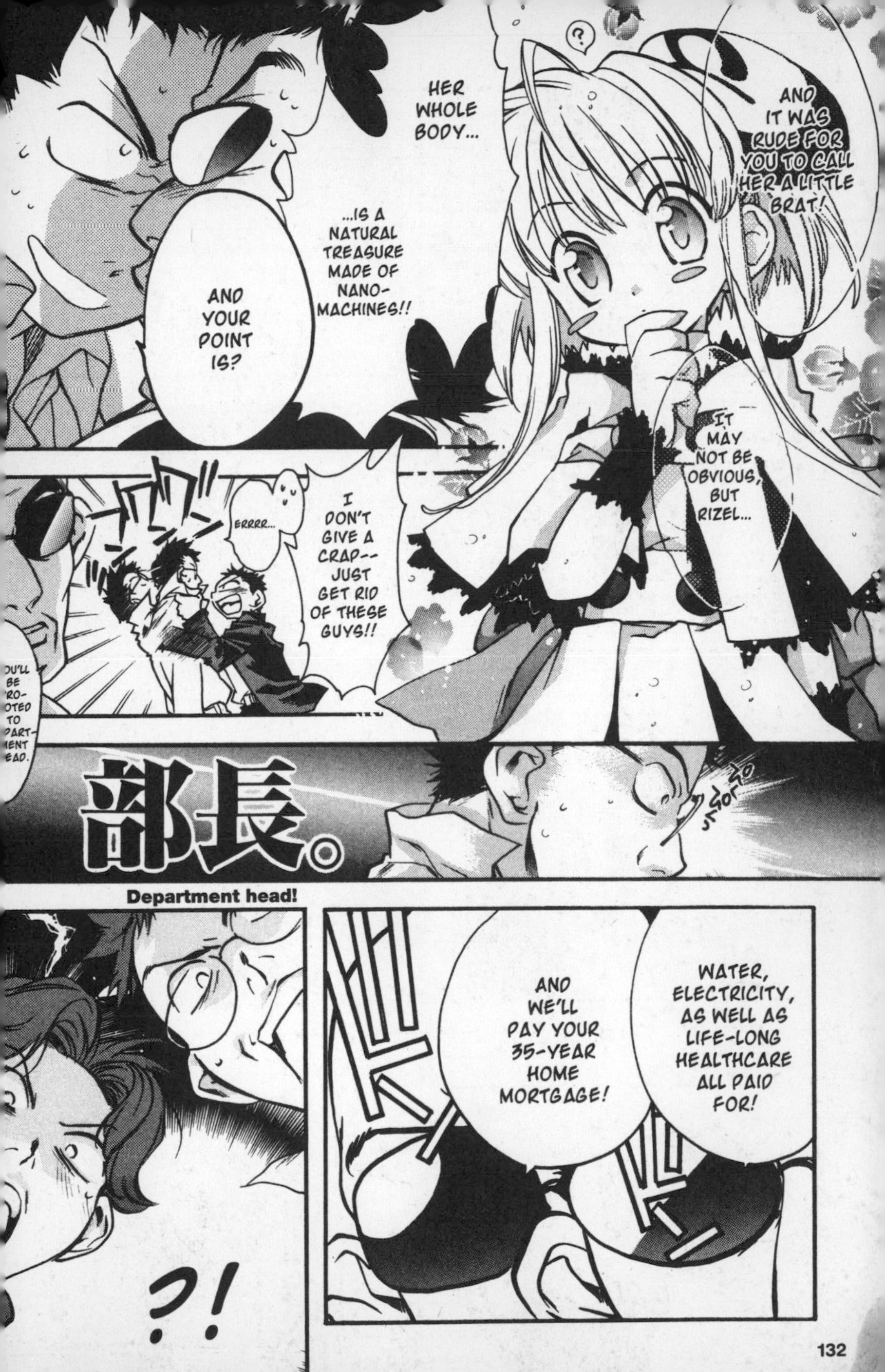
?
AND IT WAS RUDE FOR YOU TO CALL HER A LITTLE BRAT!
IT MAY NOT BE OBVIOUS, BUT RIZEL...
HER WHOLE BODY...
...IS A NATURAL TREASURE MADE OF NANO-MACHINES!!
AND YOUR POINT IS?
I DON'T GIVE A CRAP--JUST GET RID OF THESE GUYS!!
ERRRR...
OU'LL BE ROTED TO PART-MENT EAD.
部長。
Department head!
GORO GORO
WATER, ELECTRICITY, AS WELL AS LIFE-LONG HEALTHCARE ALL PAID FOR!
AND WE'LL PAY YOUR 35-YEAR HOME MORTGAGE!
?!

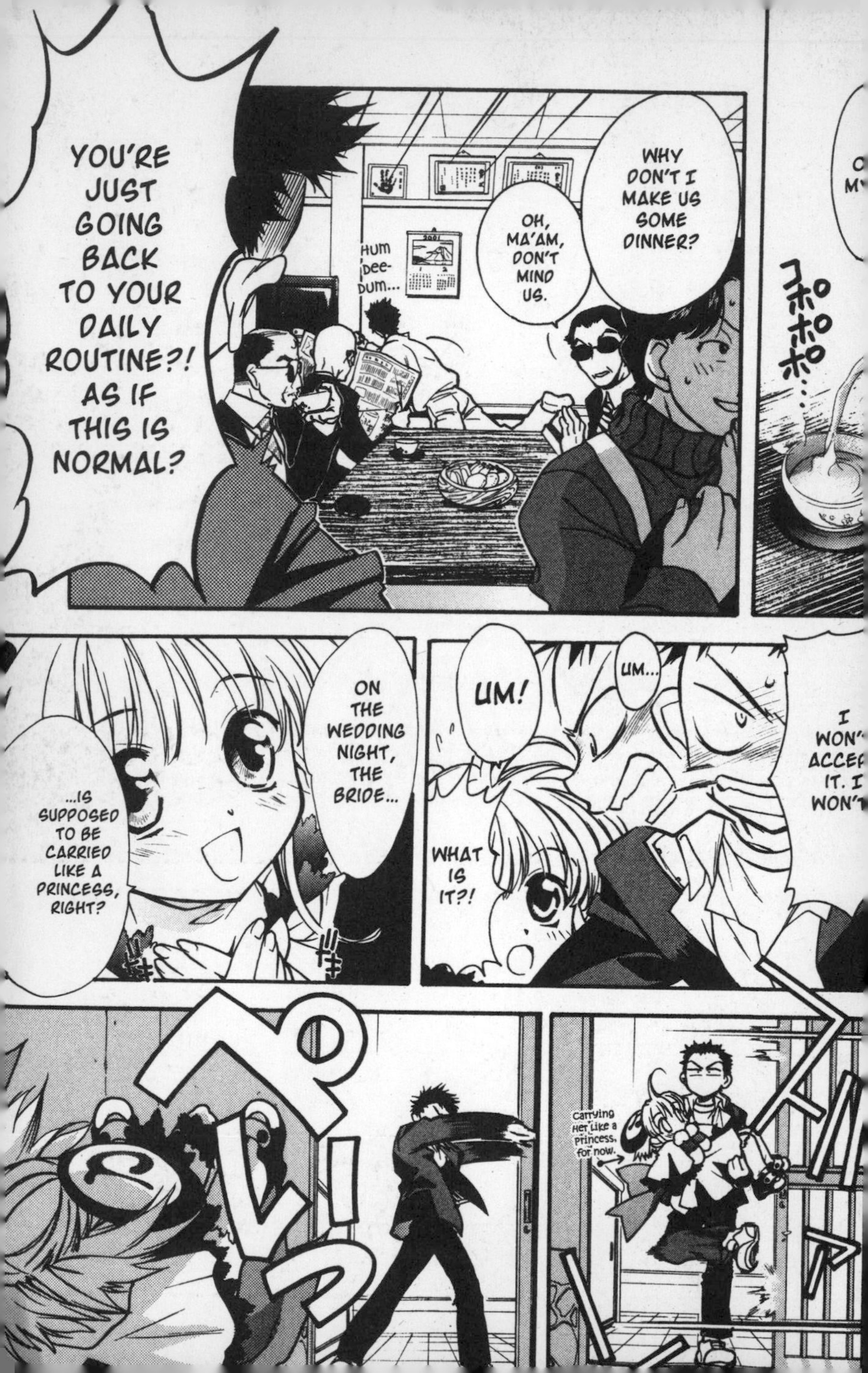
コポポポ…
WHY DON'T I MAKE US SOME DINNER?
OH, MA'AM, DON'T MIND US.
HUM DEE-DUM...
YOU'RE JUST GOING BACK TO YOUR DAILY ROUTINE?! AS IF THIS IS NORMAL?
UM...
UM!
WHAT IS IT?!
ON THE WEDDING NIGHT, THE BRIDE...
...IS SUPPOSED TO BE CARRIED LIKE A PRINCESS, RIGHT?
Carrying her like a princess, for now.

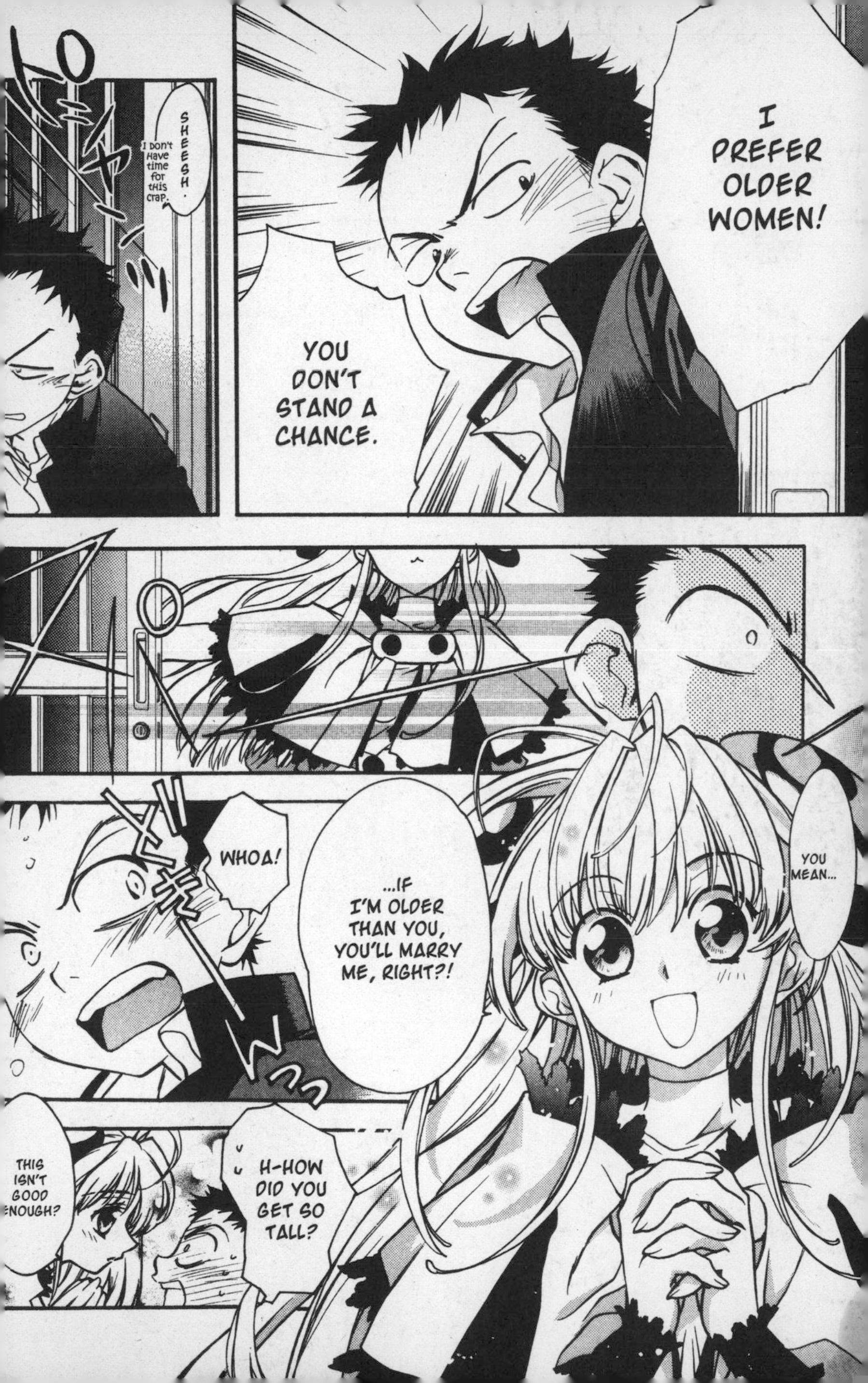
I PREFER OLDER WOMEN!
YOU DON'T STAND A CHANCE.
SHEESH.
I don't have time for this crap.
YOU MEAN...
...IF I'M OLDER THAN YOU, YOU'LL MARRY ME, RIGHT?!
WHOA!
H-HOW DID YOU GET SO TALL?
THIS ISN'T GOOD ENOUGH?

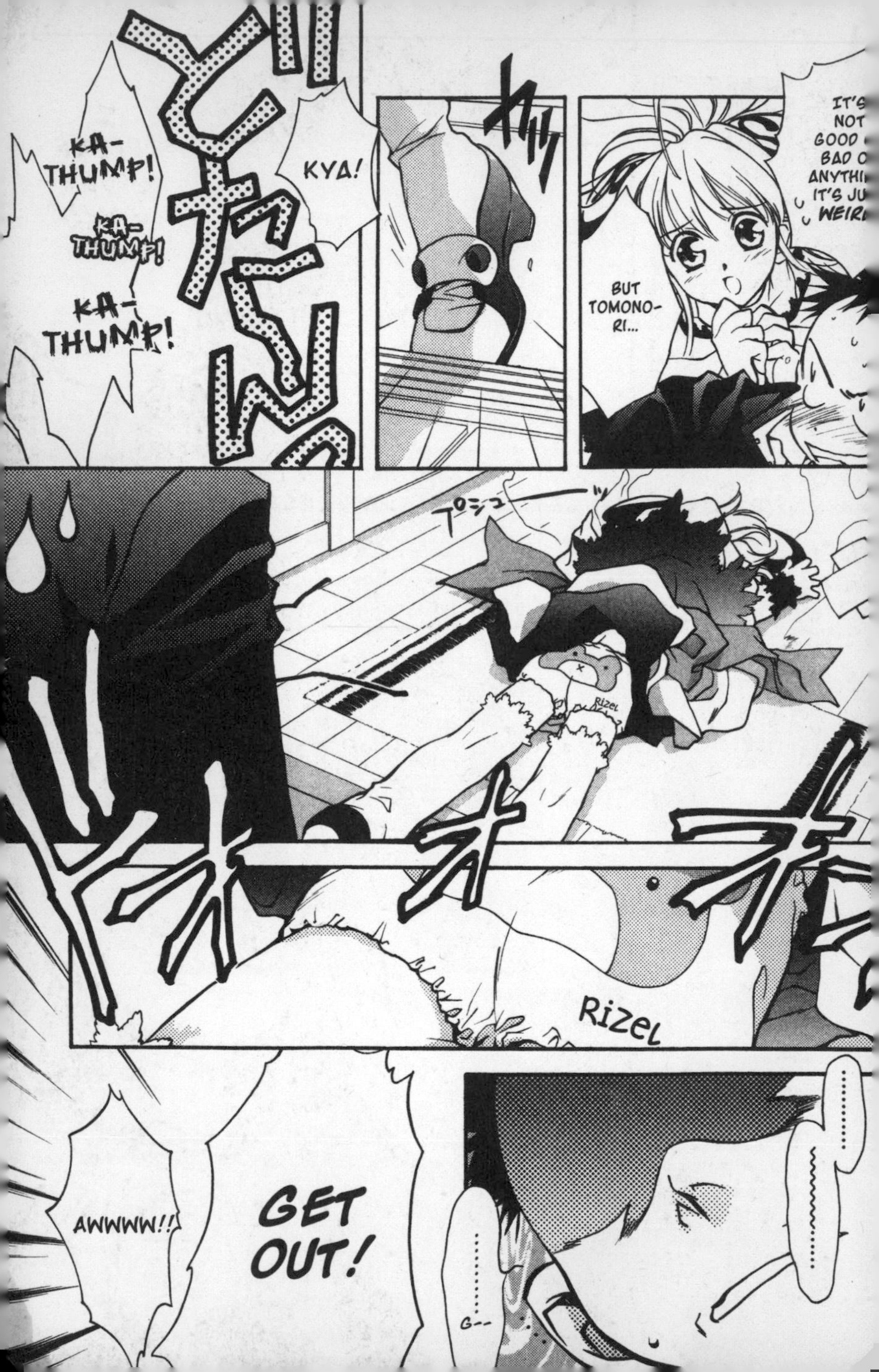

IT'S NOT GOOD BAD O ANYTHI IT'S JU WEIRD
BUT TOMONO-RI...
KYA!
KA-THUMP!
KA-THUMP!
KA-THUMP!
Rizel
RIZEL
......
......
G--
GET OUT!
AWWWW!!

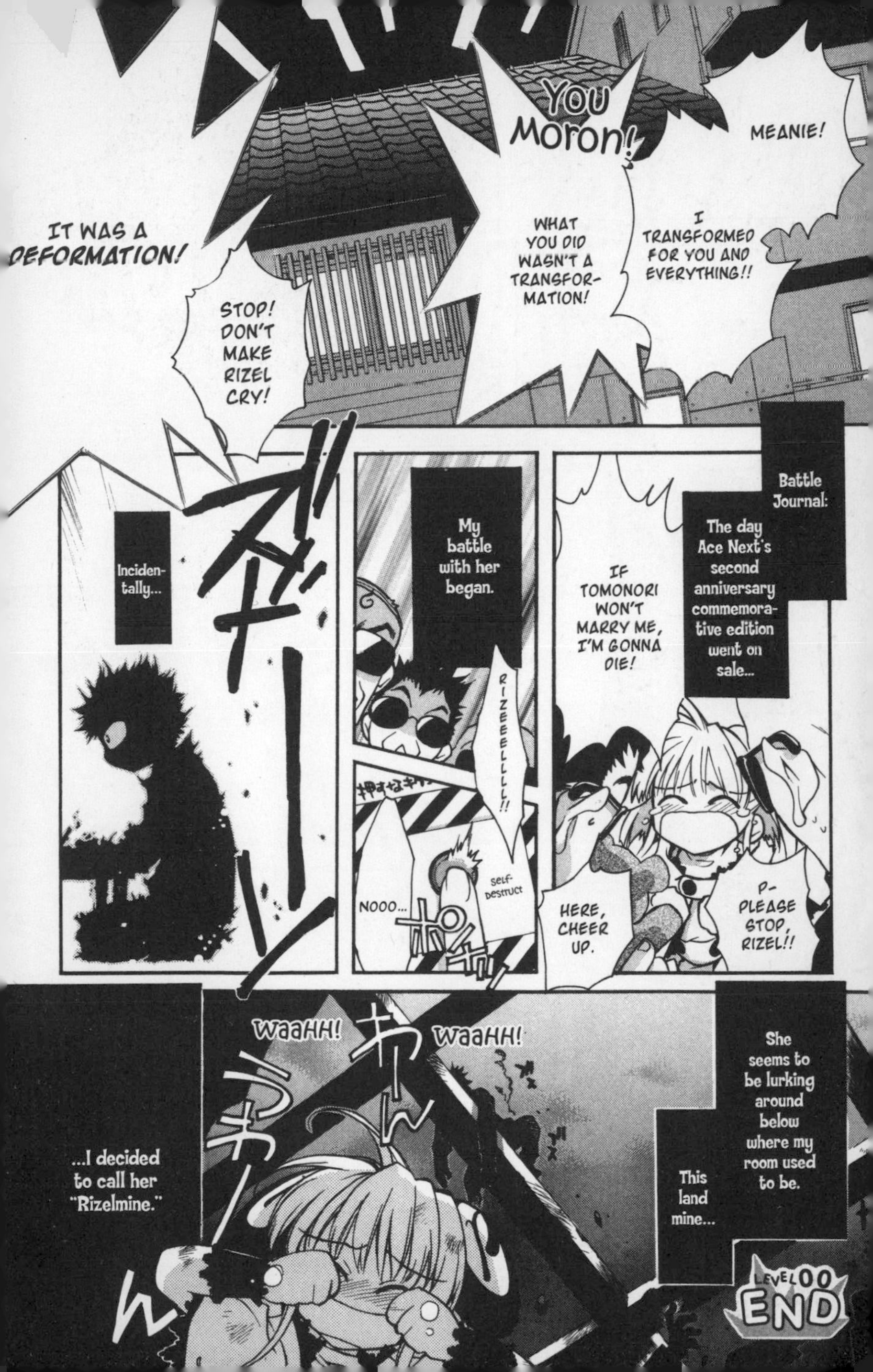
MEANIE!
I TRANSFORMED FOR YOU AND EVERYTHING!!
You Moron!
WHAT YOU DID WASN'T A TRANSFORMATION!
IT WAS A DEFORMATION!
STOP! DON'T MAKE RIZEL CRY!
Battle Journal:
The day Ace Next's second anniversary commemorative edition went on sale...
IF TOMONORI WON'T MARRY ME, I'M GONNA DIE!
P-PLEASE STOP, RIZEL!!
HERE, CHEER UP.
My battle with her began.
RIZEEEELLLLL!!
Self-destruct
NOOO...
Incidentally...
She seems to be lurking around below where my room used to be.
This land mine...
WAAHH!
WAAHH!
...I decided to call her "Rizelmine."
LEVEL 00 END

RIZELMINE CHARACTER ROUGH

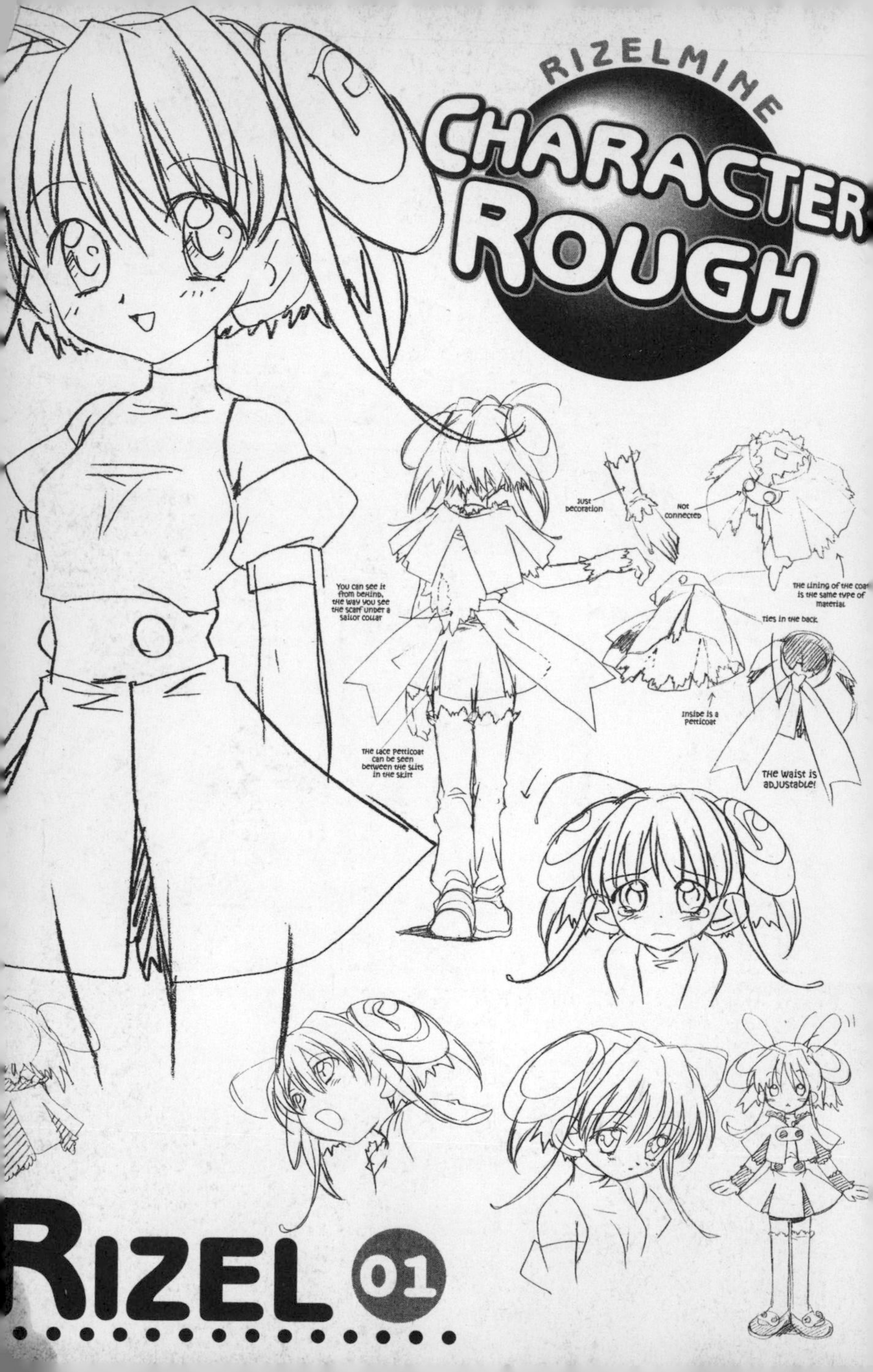
Just decoration
Not connected
You can see it from behind, the way you see the scarf under a sailor collar
The lining of the coat is the same type of material
Ties in the back
Inside is a petticoat
The lace petticoat can be seen between the slits in the skirt
The waist is adjustable!

RIZEL 01

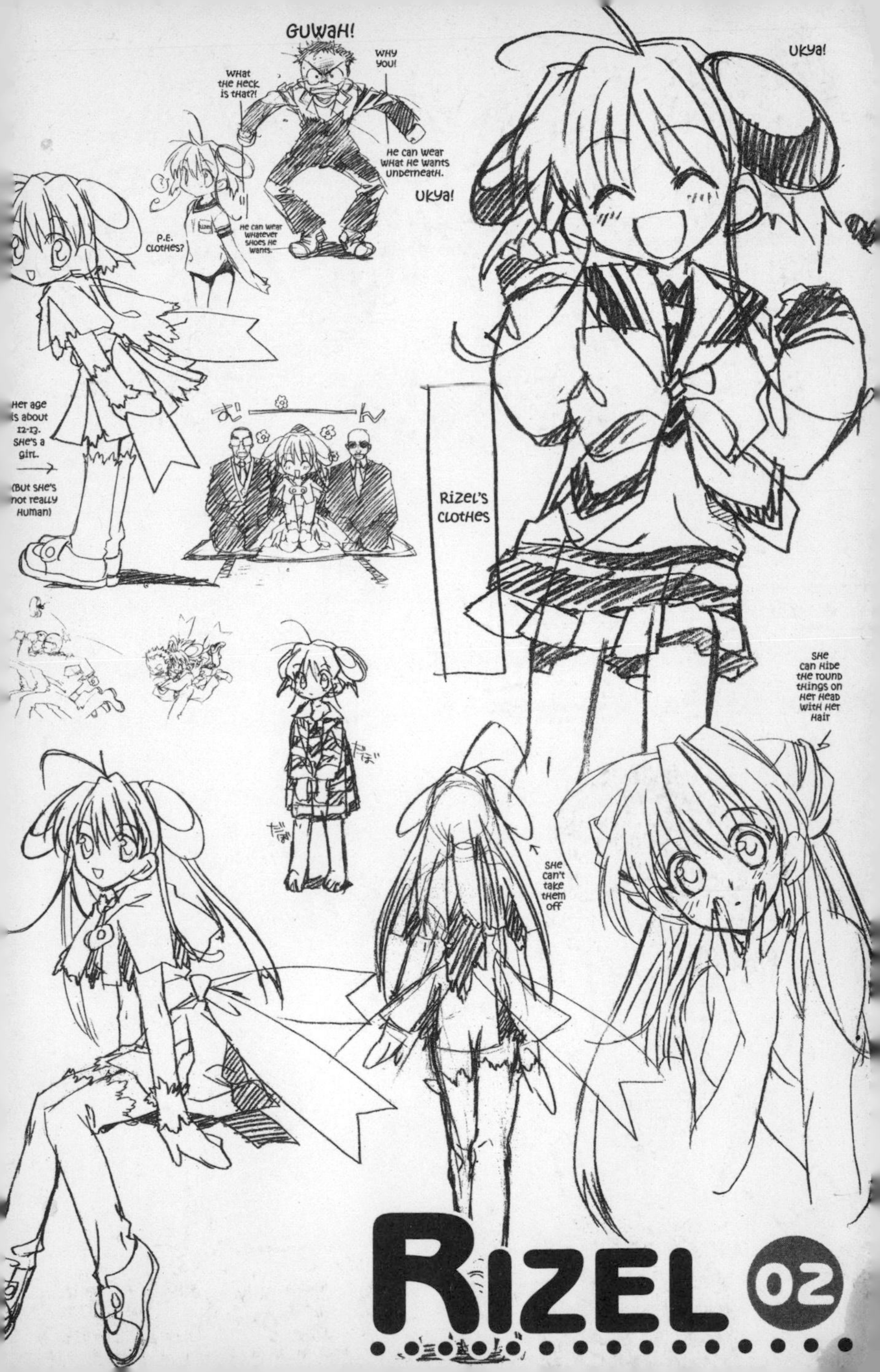
Ukya!
GUWAH!
Why you!
What the heck is that?!
He can wear what he wants underneath.
Ukya!
P.E. clothes?
He can wear whatever shoes he wants.
Her age is about 12-13. She's a girl.
(But she's not really human)
Rizel's clothes
She can hide the round things on her head with her hair
She can't take them off
RIZEL 02

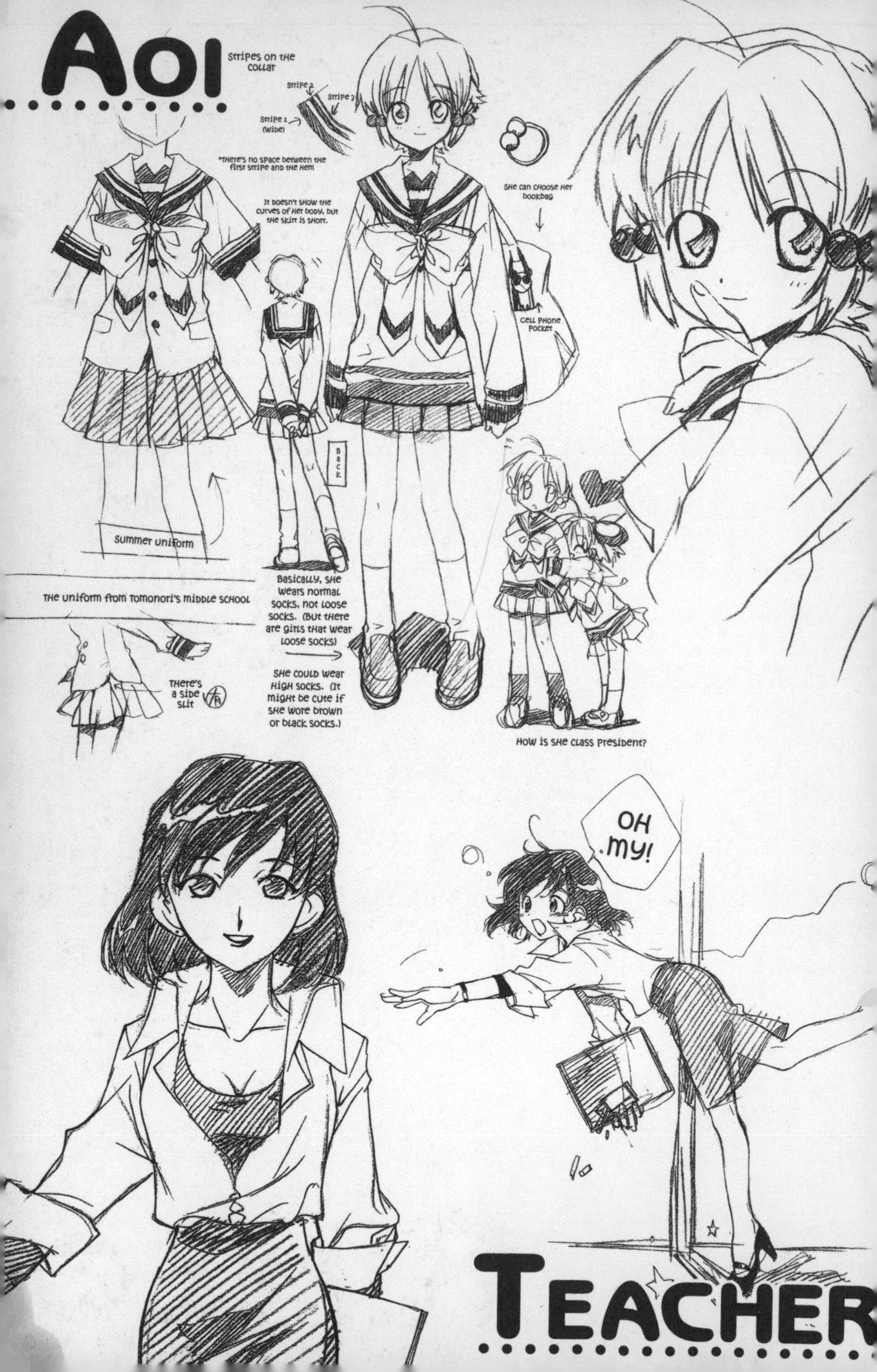
Aoi
Stripes on the collar
Stripe 2
Stripe 3
Stripe 1 (wide)
*There's no space between the first stripe and the hem
It doesn't show the curves of her body, but the skirt is short.
She can choose her bookbag
Cell phone pocket
Back
Summer uniform
The uniform from Tomonori's middle school
Basically, she wears normal socks, not loose socks. (But there are girls that wear loose socks)
There's a side slit
She could wear high socks. (It might be cute if she wore brown or black socks.)
How is she class president?
OH MY!
TEACHER

KYOKO

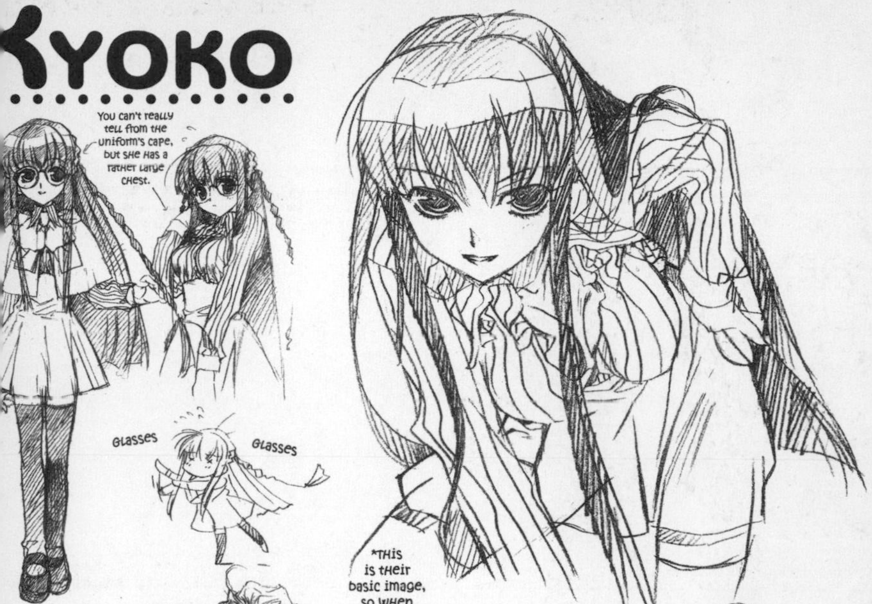

You can't really tell from the uniform's cape, but she has a rather large chest.
Glasses
Glasses

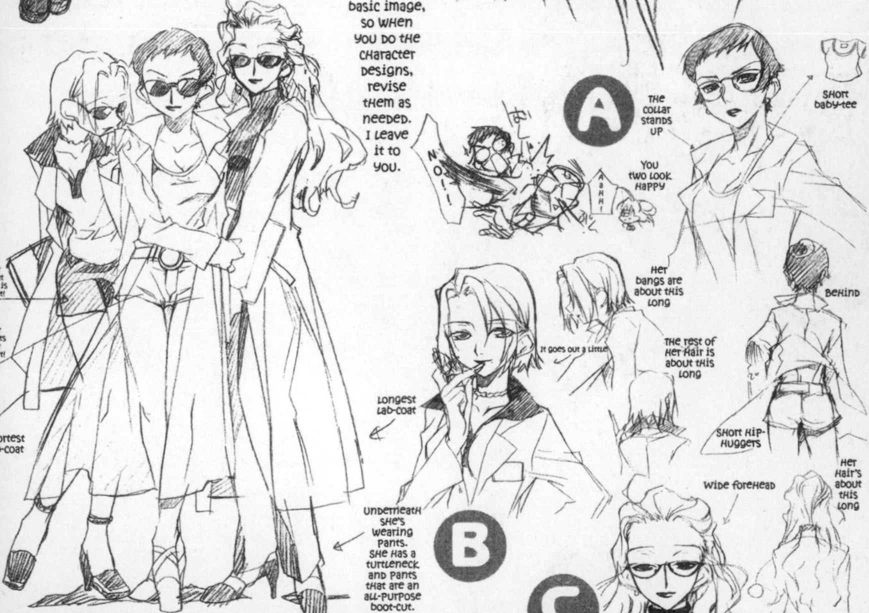

*This is their basic image, so when you do the character designs, revise them as needed. I leave it to you.
A
The collar stands up
Short baby-tee
NO!!
You two look happy
Her bangs are about this long
Behind
It goes out a little
The rest of her hair is about this long
Longest lab-coat
Short hip-huggers
Wide forehead
Her hair's about this long
Underneath she's wearing pants. She has a turtleneck and pants that are an all-purpose boot-cut.
B
C
Shortest → Middle → Tallest

RIZEL's MAMAs

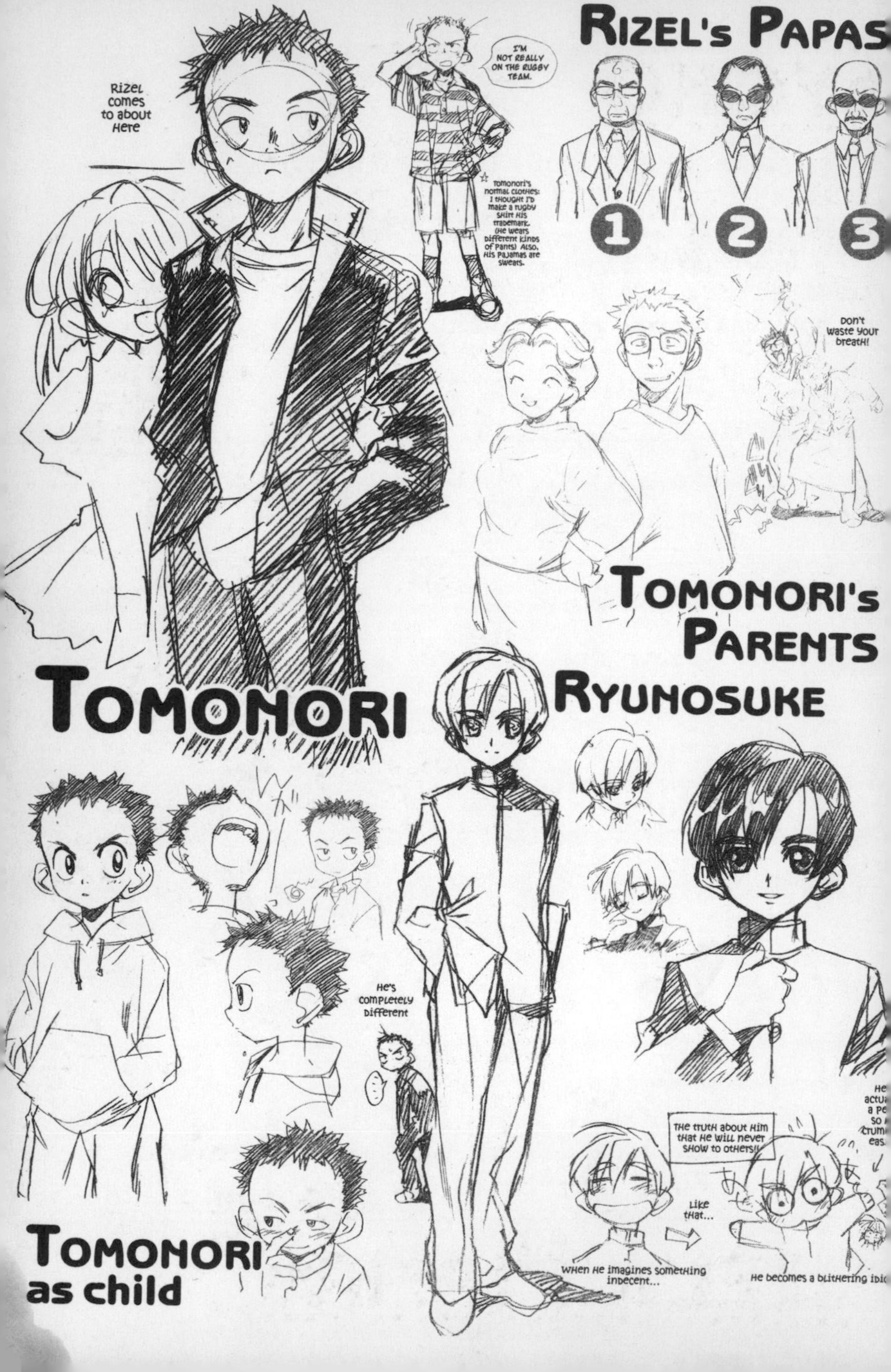
RIZEL's PAPAS
1
2
3
Don't waste your breath!
TOMONORI's PARENTS
I'M NOT REALLY ON THE RUGBY TEAM.
Tomonori's normal clothes: I thought I'd make a rugby shirt his trademark. (He wears different kinds of pants) Also, his pajamas are sweats.
Rizel comes to about here
TOMONORI
RYUNOSUKE
The truth about him that he will never show to others!!
When he imagines something indecent...
Like that...
He's completely different
TOMONORI as child

OT
OLDER TEEN
AGE 16+

In the deep South, an ancient voodoo curse unleashes the War on Flesh—a hellish plague of voracious Ew Chott hornets that raises an army of the walking dead. This undead army spreads the plague by ripping the hearts out of living creatures to make room for a Black Heart hive, all in preparation for the most awesome incarnation of evil ever imagined… An unlikely group of five mismatched individuals have to put their differences aside to try to destroy the onslaught of evil before it's too late.

VOODOO MAKES A MAN NASTY!

WAR ON FLESH

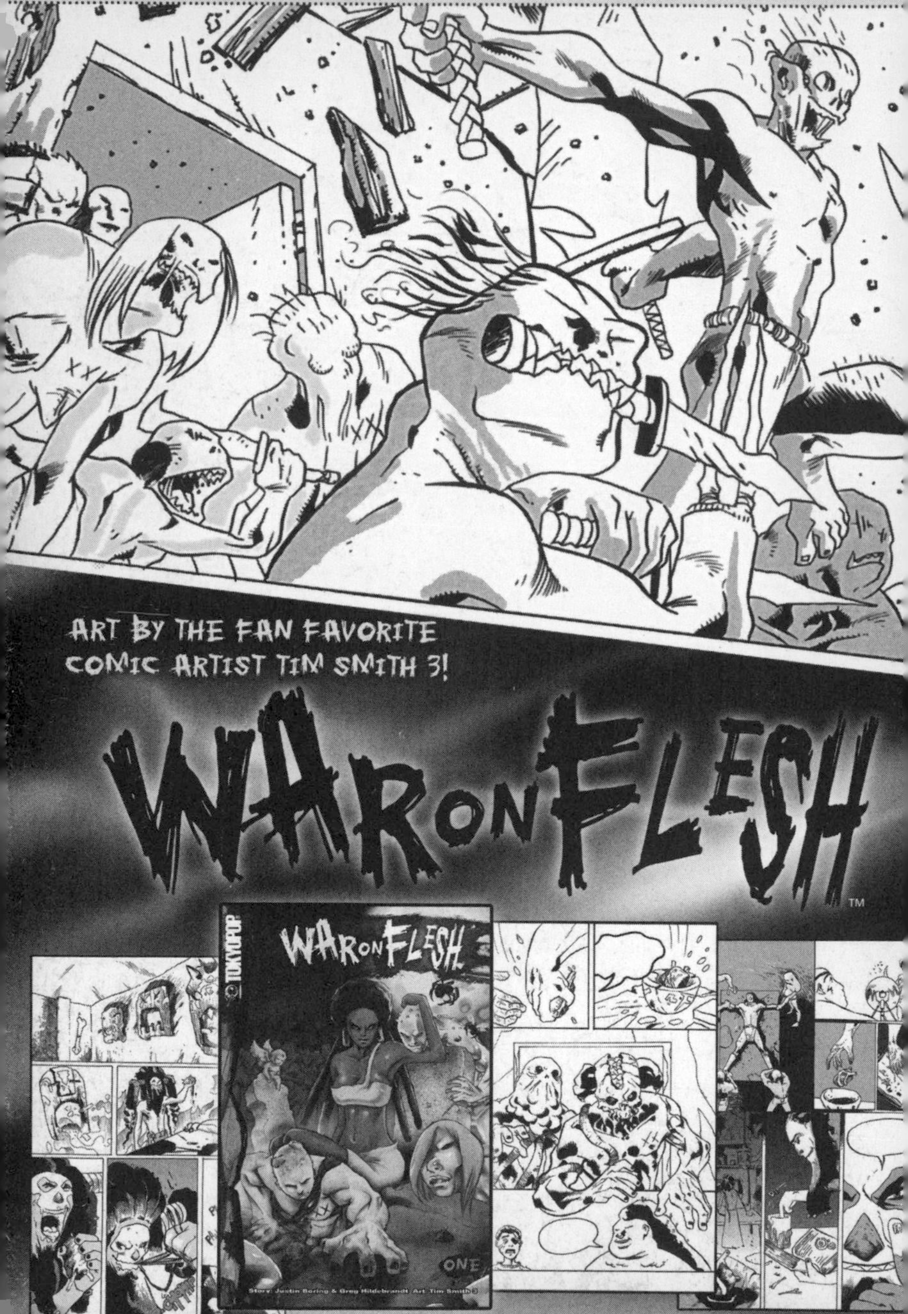

ART BY THE FAN FAVORITE
COMIC ARTIST TIM SMITH 3!
WAR ON FLESH™
WAR ON FLESH
TOKYOPOP
ONE
Story: Justin Boring & Greg Hildebrandt / Art: Tim Smith 3

SHOWCASE

RIZELMINE
BY YUKIRU SUGISAKI

Tomonori Iwaki is a hapless fifteen-year-old whose life is turned upside down when the government announces that he's a married man! His blushing bride is Rizel, apparently the adorable product of an experiment. She does her best to win her new man's heart in this wacky romantic comedy from the creator of *D•N•Angel*!

Inspiration for the hit anime!

© YUKIRU SUGISAKI / KADOKAWA SHOTEN.

HONEY MUSTARD
BY HO-KYUNG YEO

When Ara works up the nerve to ask out the guy she has a crush on, she ends up kissing the wrong boy! The juicy smooch is witnessed by the school's puritanical chaperone, who tells their strict families. With everyone in an uproar, the only way everyone will be appeased is if the two get married—and have kids!

© Ho-Kyung Yeo, HAKSAN PUBLISHING CO., LTD.

HEAT GUY J
BY CHIAKI OGISHIMA, KAZUKI AKANE, NOBUTERU YUKI & SATELIGHT

Daisuke Aurora and his android partner, Heat Guy J, work with a special division of peacekeepers to keep anything illegal off the streets. However, that doesn't sit too well with the new ruthless and well-armed mob leader. In the city that never sleeps, will Daisuke and Heat Guy J end up sleeping with the fishes?

The anime favorite as seen on MTV is now an action-packed manga!

© Satelight/Heatguy-J Project.

TOKYOPOP MANGA SUPPLEMENT

BLAME!

BY TSUTOMU NIHEI

WALK SOFTLY AND CARRY A BIG GUN!

CREATOR OF MARVEL'S *WOLVERINE: SNIKT!*

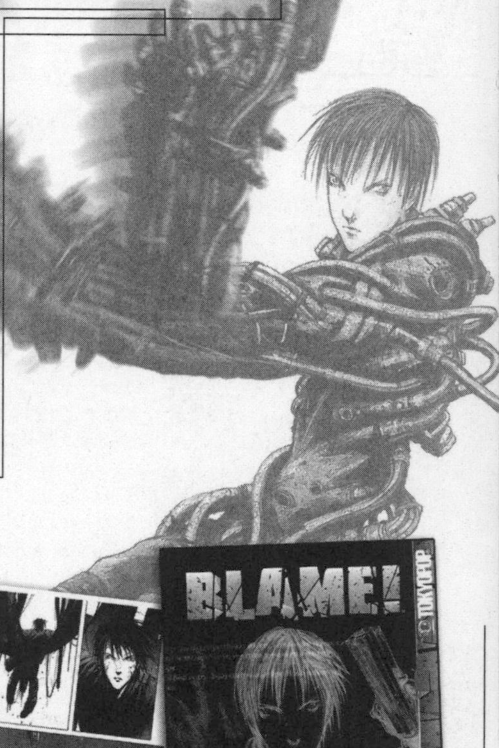

In a future rife with decay and destruction, Killy is a man of few words who packs one very powerful gun. He wanders an endless labyrinth of concrete and steel, fighting off cyborgs and other bizarre creatures. Everyone is searching for the "Net Terminal Genes," but no one is certain of the genes' function. The answer may lie hidden among the scattered human settlements of this vast and desolate world. Can Killy unlock the mystery of this nightmarish future and save the last remnants of humanity?

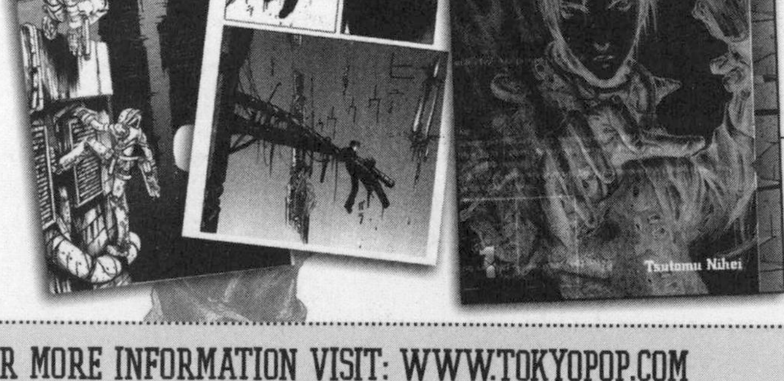
BLAME!
TOKYOPOP
1
Tsutomu Nihei

OT
OLDER TEEN
AGE 16+

FOR MORE INFORMATION VISIT: WWW.TOKYOPOP.COM

STOP!

This is the back of the book.
You wouldn't want to spoil a great ending!

This book is printed "manga-style," in the authentic Japanese right-to-left format. Since none of the artwork has been flipped or altered, readers get to experience the story just as the creator intended. You've been asking for it, so TOKYOPOP® delivered: authentic, hot-off-the-press, and far more fun!

DIRECTIONS

If this is your first time reading manga-style, here's a quick guide to help you understand how it works.

It's easy... just start in the top right panel and follow the numbers. Have fun, and look for more 100% authentic manga from TOKYOPOP®!